# THE DYNAMICS OF
# TRANSFORMATION

# THE DYNAMICS OF TRANSFORMATION

## TRACING AN EMERGING WORLD VIEW

Grant Maxwell

PERSISTENT PRESS

est. 2012

ISBN 978-0-692-81035-4 (paperback)

"Though there are many books on culture, history, and transitional processes of various kinds, this book is remarkable and nearly unique in its mastery and scope. There is a poetic sense behind the text that draws the reader along with pleasure. Maxwell has given us an insightful and wonderfully readable book exploring the many dimensions of transformation we see in our world today."

Allan Combs, Professor Emeritus at the University of North Carolina-Asheville and author of *Consciousness Explained Better* and *Synchronicity*

"*The Dynamics of Transformation* is an ambitious, insightful, and provocative book. It builds a complex argument integrating many important ideas and thinkers across multiple disciplines, moving steadily towards an articulation of an emerging philosophical cosmology for our time. It is an inspiring vision. Maxwell shows courage and confidence as he marshals his leading concepts and sends them forth into the paradigm wars that mark the frontiers of the contemporary academic world. We will no doubt be hearing more from this penetrating scholar with an eye for the big picture."

Richard Tarnas, Professor at the California Institute of Integral Studies and author of *The Passion of the Western Mind* and *Cosmos and Psyche*

"There is no shortage of books about the epochal transformations currently reshaping the planet, or about the shift in world views required to make sense of these transformations. Maxwell's *The Dynamics of Transformation*, however, is the first among the latter to present a compelling synthesis of leading-edge theories from across the disciplinary spectrum that not only identifies the deep structure of this shift, but invites the reader to participate creatively in its implementation. Through a masterful interweaving of core insights from process philosophy, archetypal psychology, integral theory, the natural sciences, and cultural studies, Maxwell sketches the outlines of an emerging participatory and (re)enchanted world view and an 'integrative method' for both perceiving and co-creating it. His treatment of the archetypal dynamics of process through the mutually implicative notions of formal and final causality, of fractality and discontinuity, of accelerating, intensified, and qualitative temporality, is remarkably clear and cogent. By the time one reaches the end of the argument, one has the sense of having undergone a kind of initiation into an ever-widening community of seekers for whom value and meaning, pattern and purpose are the real stuff of which worlds are made."

Sean Kelly, Professor at the California Institute of Integral Studies and author of *Coming Home: The Birth and Transformation of the Planetary Era*

"With an impressive command of a wide range of philosophical ideas and scientific theories applied across multiple dimensions of reality, Grant Maxwell skillfully elucidates the underlying principles and dynamics shaping the evolutionary emergence of an integral mode of consciousness and worldview. As we look beyond the strife and uncertainty of our moment in history, and beyond the deconstructive trends of much contemporary thought, Maxwell outlines the essential form that a new participatory worldview might take, making a persuasive case for the centrality of the emerging discipline of archetypal cosmology within this vision. *The Dynamics of Transformation* is an important and insightful contribution to understanding the creative transition into a new paradigm of intellectual thought."

Keiron Le Grice, Professor at Pacifica Graduate Institute and author of *The Archetypal Cosmos* and *Archetypal Reflections*

"Grant Maxwell explains that, ever since Hegel at the beginning of the nineteenth century, influential thinkers have been articulating aspects of the same basic idea that at each scale of the cosmos, from the atomic through the organic to the cultural, the same pattern of transformation unfolds. That fractal pattern indicates that nature is constantly pulled toward the future by some final goal of wholeness, defined roughly as a state of development in which previously incommensurable oppositions are reconciled. This reiterating process of transformation accelerates exponentially as it approaches a new synthesis of opposites at each scale, which is achieved relatively suddenly, in a kind of quantum leap after some tipping point has been reached. Maxwell suggests that we are rapidly approaching a cultural tipping point toward a new world view, consisting of a synthesis of the previously incommensurable philosophies of the premodern and modern eras. That emerging world view—similar in some ways to what Nietzsche imagined as the birth of the Ubermensch from the human-all-too-human—is rooted to the realization that each of us is one with the entire trajectory of cosmic history, in as much as each of us and all of nature are being constantly transformed by the same archetype of wholeness. Combining insights from the canon of thinkers who have dedicated themselves to this quest toward wholeness, Maxwell traces out twelve basic parameters of the emerging world view. Nietzsche's Zarathustra said 'I would only believe in a god who knows how to dance'; Maxwell traces out those dance steps, which he calls the dynamics of transformation."

Timothy Desmond, author of *Psyche and Singularity: Jungian Psychology and Holographic String Theory*

TO MOM AND DAD

.

# CONTENTS

# INTRODUCTION
## "THAT SLIGHTEST CHANGE OF TONE WHICH YET MAKES ALL THE DIFFERENCE"

It has been suggested that postmodernity is an interregnum between world views, a clearing away and deconstruction of modern assumptions that have rendered modernity, once the vanguard of the evolution of consciousness, now a dead end.[1] As is usually the case, the mode of thought that was once so liberating and revolutionary has eventually settled into a static, constraining orthodoxy in the apparently inevitable onward march of successive cultural transformations. In the following pages, I will propose that a novel world view has been emerging with increasing insistence over the last few centuries that seeks to move beyond a mere rejection of the modern in favor of a more participatory, vital, and integrative mode of cognizance. In seeking a coherent explanation for the way processes change over time, perhaps the most general possible description for many areas of human inquiry, this perspective emphasizes the reconciliation of seemingly incommensurable oppositions for the production of emergent wholes.

My contention is that G.W.F. Hegel's idealism, William James' pragmatism, C.G. Jung's analytical psychology, Alfred North Whitehead's process philosophy, and numerous other theoretical approaches promulgated by their contemporaries and successors are all confluent streams that have gradually been converging into an increasingly potent conceptual flood, which appears primed for a dramatic entrance into the preeminent currents of academic and intellectual culture. These thinkers have all articulated certain essential aspects of the theoretical orientation presented here, and many of them have suggested in various inflections that the last few centuries have witnessed the incipient emergence of a mode of thought indicative of something like a new world view after the modern.

In fact, it appears that this novel perspective seeks to integrate modes characteristic of the premodern, the modern, and the postmodern in a dialectical synthesis. This integration can be thought of as something like deconstruction turned on its head (or "on its feet" as Marx said of Hegel), as both modes recognize the radically constructed quality of reality, produced through complexly interpenetrating modes of discourse and material relation. However, whereas the deconstructive mode generally infers from this insight that the world is an ultimately purposeless play of surfaces, the emerging mode appears to infer that the human mind participates in the production of the world's meaning, an instance of what Whitehead refers to as "that slightest change of tone which yet makes all the difference."[2] While the effects of these two modes are dramatically and pervasively different, even opposed, the logical structure of the basic insight—that reality is to a great extent constructed—is essentially the same in both world views, roughly the postmodern and the emerging, whatever it comes to be called. But the unprovable, subjective meaning attributed, whether consciously or unconsciously, to that neutral insight can elicit from the world either an empty, meaningless void or an infinitely rich pleroma filled with meaning and purpose. In this shift of perspective, the exterior, quantitative aspect of reality remains initially unaltered, but the interior, qualitative aspect is fundamentally transformed, which ultimately feeds back in a recursive loop to transform the material aspects of the world.

Despite many significant differences among the thinkers on whom I have relied, I have extrapolated twelve concepts that seem to trace the contours of an emerging world view from numerous texts characteristic of this novel orientation. Most of the theorists from whom I have drawn articulate at least several of these concepts, usually in deeply interconnected ways, and often directly influencing one another. I will inevitably have neglected certain facets of the novel mode in favor of others, as my inclination, my "individual way of just seeing and feeling the total push and pressure of the cosmos,"[3] to quote William James, has led me toward certain theorists over others, and toward certain aspects of their work over others. But I submit that these concepts from these representative thinkers provide the outline of a relatively straightforward framework for the integration of diverse and immensely complex ideas articulated by these individuals who, to my mind, have formed the vanguard of philosophical thought in late modernity. I have chosen not to include concepts from a number of areas of study that I see as vitally important elements of the emerging mode, but which seem to me concrete applications of the more general and abstract concepts presented here, including those more particular subjects having to do with ecology, health, art, morality, religion, politics, and economics to name a few.[4]

The main difficulty I have faced in writing this book has not been so much in defining the concepts, but in separating these concepts into distinct chapters and placing them in a sequential order, as these insights are deeply intertwined with one another, a semiotic network perhaps more conducive to expression through a hyperlinked website than in the inherently linear form of a book. However, as I write in an era when books remain the predominant format for the expression of philosophical thought, I have done my best to render relatively discrete and linear a diverse and multiform tendency that seems to be in the process of being born from the crucible of modernity's slow demise.

The primary organizing principle I have adopted to determine the order of the chapters that follow is to begin with those concepts about which there is general consensus in at least some of the main streams of academia, and to move toward those concepts which are more speculative, though I hope to show that these more unconventional ideas follow logically from the somewhat more established ideas. Within this trajectory however, it is unclear where some of the intermediate concepts should be placed in this rough progression from near the centers of academic and intellectual power toward the liminal margins, which are almost always the loci for the inception of profound novelty, so I have acted on the subordinate organizing principle of grouping together concepts that seem especially connected with one another.

Within the chapters themselves, my primary organizing principle has been to explicate sequentially how that particular chapter's concept implies the other concepts. I have chosen to take this approach rather than showing how the other concepts imply each insight within its own chapter, despite strong arguments for the latter approach, because it seems to me that the former relational trajectory is more characteristic of the emerging mode, so that each concept is primarily defined in its own home, so to speak, by how it serves and supports the other concepts, rather than by the service it receives from them. Finally, the Epilogue presents the method of archetypal cosmology, demonstrating how each of the concepts discussed in each of the chapters implies that method, as well as reciprocally demonstrating how that method supports the other concepts.

My intention in writing this study has not primarily been to produce a justification for these concepts, which have been argued for brilliantly and copiously over the last few centuries by numerous venerable theorists in various forms. Rather, I have sought to provide a relatively systematic and coherent descriptive account of the mode that these concepts collectively constellate. Each of us can and must determine for ourselves the value of this mode of thought.

The first chapter, **"World Views Create Worlds": The Participatory Quality of Process**, demonstrates that the fundamental premises we hold about the nature of reality deeply condition the kinds of meaning we can elicit from immediate experience and, thus, that by acting on our beliefs, whatever they may be, we participate in the creation of the world's significance.

The second chapter, **"The Circle of the Given": Novelty and the Will to Believe**, suggests that we tend to become fixed in our way of seeing the world, that modes of thought tend to settle into conventional orthodoxies, so in order to produce genuine novelty, we must actively decide to give credence to new premises, which is the only way that unconventional ideas can viably be explored and elaborated into a developed conceptual system.

The third chapter, appropriately titled **"The Reconciling Third": An Integrative Method**, presents the idea that polarized, seemingly incommensurable modes of thought can almost always be reconciled by working through apparent paradox to a deeper domain of coherence. In this method, the positive content of each perspective can be seen as complementary, while the negative content, constituted in the denial of the opposing counterpart's positive assertions, can often be set aside as an anachronistic historical necessity for forging these opposed concepts through the tension of difference, which ultimately prepares the seemingly irreconcilable ideas for synthesis.

4

The fourth chapter, **"Jumps of All Sorts": The Discontinuity of Process**, explicates the recognition that discontinuous leaps occur in many domains, including atomic electron transitions in physics (the "quantum leap"), changes of state in chemistry, punctuated mutations in biology, the birth process, religious conversions, psychological breakthroughs, political, cultural, and scientific revolutions, and the relatively abrupt transitions between historical eras.

The fifth chapter, **"A Series of Stages": Development through Emergent Phases**, elucidates the tendency of being to evolve through distinct, emergent stages on different orders of complexity, in both the individual and the collective, each one subsuming the previous stages as implicit but integral parts of its more encompassing embrace.

The sixth chapter, **"An Extraordinary Threshold": The Emergence of a New World View**, offers that the developmental process of history has been marked by the successive emergence of distinct world views, and that we now seem to be engaged in the decades-long climax, which we have called postmodernity, of the transition from the modern era to a qualitatively new epoch of human development.

The seventh chapter, **"Symmetry across Scale": The Fractal Quality of Process**, delineates the insight that the same patterns or structures of organization are repeated self-similarly on many orders of magnitude, from the microscopic to the macroscopic, and from the simplest systems of inanimate matter to the most complex systems of life, consciousness, and culture.

The eighth chapter, **"A Potentiality for Actual Entities": Forms, Archetypes, and Eternal Objects**, shows that there are implicit potentialities for becoming endemic to process that manifest in many different instances through countless complex actualities.

The ninth chapter, **"A Falling Together in Time": Qualitative Temporality and Formal Causation**, examines the idea that duration, the lived experience of time, is qualitative, that each moment has a quality particular to it, and that the events that occur in these moments synchronically participate in the character of each instance, even when those events are materially unconnected.[5]

The tenth chapter, **"The Teleological Introduction of Novelty": Final Causation**, submits that there is an intrinsic tendency in the nature of reality toward the production of novelty, as well as the intimately related qualities of consciousness and order. This trajectory can be conceived as a complementary force of nature to the four forces of physical science and, especially, to entropic disorder.

The eleventh chapter, **"An Exponentially Accelerating Process":** **The Increasing Ingression of Novelty**, posits that the occurrence of novelty over time in the trajectory that manifests through the human appears to be accelerating at an exponential rate, so that if we trace the expansion of novelty's material, quantitative substrates, we find that life emerged billions of years ago, hominids emerged millions of years ago, humans emerged hundreds of thousands of years ago, civilization emerged thousands of years ago, modern science and technology emerged hundreds of years ago, computers and the internet emerged decades ago, and each emergence appears to have marked a qualitatively new stage of novelty's ingression into actuality, its coming into concrete being. Each new substrate has built upon the previous platforms to make possible the qualitative, relational modes that accompany each quantitative emergence. And if one can judge by what has occurred thus far in the process of cosmic evolution, one suspects that this accelerating trajectory may continue.[6]

The twelfth chapter, **"The Concretion of Time": Progressive** **Degrees of Spatio-Temporal Freedom**, advances the hypothesis that life has been a process of ascending through increasing orders of dimensionality, so that the simplest organisms, as the vanguard of life in their epoch, were able to perceive and move toward or away from sustenance in an essentially one-dimensional existence. Subsequently, plants and animals of increasing complexity were able to perceive and move in two and eventually three spatial dimensions. Finally, the mathematical description of time in general relativity as a fourth dimension suggests that the more complex animals who perceive temporality, particularly humans, are perhaps in the process of emerging into the consciousness of a more expansive manifold describable in dimensional terms. However, the fact that we generally appear to move through time in a static, linear progression (not a result of the current laws of physics but solely of their probabilistic interpretation), rather than possessing the full degree of freedom that we possess in the other three dimensions, may suggest that what we call time is actually a fraction of a dimension (i.e. a fractal dimension) and that the complete emergence of a new world view will consist in the coming to awareness of the fourth, temporal dimension as a full integer.

The Epilogue, **"A Third Copernican Revolution": Archetypal Cosmology**, recommends a method for discerning correlations between the external, physical cosmos and the internal, subjective psyche, which serve to complicate that binary distinction. This method relies upon the other twelve concepts to produce a cosmological mode of thought that integrates subject and object in the perception of, and participatory engagement with, matter moving through time, archetypally discerning the qualitative contours of the temporal dimension in relation to quantitative motion in the three spatial dimensions.

# THE CONCEPTS

## 1. The Participatory Quality of Process

Each of us holds assumptions about the nature of reality. Whether one is a member of a tribe living in the depths of the Amazon uncontacted by outsiders who believes that the world is flat and full of spirits, or a postmodern academic living in the depths of New York City who believes in reductionist materialism and the socially constructed quality of reality, we all must necessarily hold beliefs about the world. To act is to act on premises, often unconscious, but premises nonetheless. As William James particularly understood, this pragmatic insight is an ancient one expressed in different inflections by Socrates, Plato, and Aristotle, and by Locke, Berkeley, and Hume. But as James also understood, this mode of thought did not come to consciousness in the main streams of philosophical discourse until the decades surrounding the beginning of the twentieth century, largely through the work of James and his intellectual forebears, followers, and associates. Put simply, the premises we bring to bear in our interpretation of reality deeply condition the kinds of meaning that can be produced from the immediate experience of that reality.[7]

## 2. Novelty and the Will to Believe

It may not be too much to claim that every revolution that has occurred in the history of thought has met with great resistance from the current established orthodoxy. The old order has always had decades, if not centuries, to elaborate its point of view, to fill volumes with justification and explanation, to critique modes of thought that seem contrary to its premises, to develop forms of language to express its deepest beliefs. Consequently, it seems likely that every revolution in thought that has occurred in the history of the world, whether on individual or collective scales, has required an act of will, a leap of faith outside the established modes into unmapped realms of cognizance. In fact, these leaps of belief are often accompanied by the venturing of cultures that undergo such transformations into new realms of spatial exploration. For instance, the voyages of Columbus, Magellan, and Vasco da Gama disclosed the unity of the round Earth by traversing it during the same decades that Copernicus was attempting to prove that our planet revolves around the Sun, which is perhaps the single most significant discovery that impelled the subsequent trajectory of modernity. Similarly, the initiation of space exploration in the twentieth century, an entrance into a new orthogonal dimension, seems to have accompanied the multigenerational emergence of a novel mode of thought. The perspective from outside the planet afforded by the "Earthrise" photograph taken in 1968, which shows the Earth rising majestically over the Moon, appears to have symbolized and impelled the incipient integration of terrestrial world views.

Each revolution required transgressive acts by a few individuals, Luther posting his ninety-five theses on the door of the Wittenburg church near the dawn of modernity as much as Nietzsche declaring the "death of God" near its twilight, these acts rippling through networks of discourse and relation to transform those cultural streams. And these transformative individuals and groups are often derided, trivialized, or condemned, as they are attempting to articulate a mode of thought that has never been successfully expressed in a way that can be understood and participated in by the collective. New modes of thought almost always contradict orthodox presuppositions, so a great deal of controversy and debate must be undertaken in order to develop the novel perspective into a viable point of view. And in order for the new mode eventually to emerge triumphant in the cultural psyche, the majority of individuals who constitute the collective must decide, sooner or later, provisionally to adopt the new premises that form the core of the novel world view, to live and act as if they were true, which is the only way to prove the new conceptual system's validity and value.

## 3. An Integrative Method

By their very nature, revolutions in thought define themselves against the mode that precedes them. On a large scale, the privileging of rationality in modernity defined itself in relation to the comparatively naïve lack of differentiation between intellect and affect in premodernity. Similarly, whereas teleological thought was a dominant mode in premodernity, modernity has often defined itself by a rejection of teleology. The emerging mode does appear to define itself in relation to the mode that precedes it, the postmodern, which is founded upon the most fundamental premises of modernity taken to their logical conclusion. However, to a greater degree than the previously dominant modes of thought, the novel mode appears to subsume the previous world views in an emergent synthesis that transcends and includes all of these antecedent modes. This incipient world view shares with the postmodern a recognition of the radically constructed quality of lived reality, and even acknowledges the limited validity of the predominant postmodern interpretation of this insight as indicating that, if there is no fixed, transcendent truth, then the world is void of intrinsic meaning.

However, in a paradoxical operation characteristic of the emerging mode's recursive complexity, this deconstructive interpretation of the world is simultaneously recognized as pragmatically plausible but contradicted by the integrative world view's affective attitude, which affirms the partial validity of all points of view, and only denies the validity of those elements of developmentally previous world views which in their turn deny the positive beliefs affirmed by other modes of consciousness. Thus, the emerging mode appears to affirm the conditional validity of all positive beliefs, defined as those beliefs that do not explicitly or implicitly contradict another mode's positive premises. This mode even affirms the temporary, historical necessity of the negative denial of positive beliefs for the forging of novelty. However, the emerging mode ultimately reconciles seemingly irreconcilable world views by discovering the inevitably partial truths in each side of any controversy. By refusing to succumb to the seductive ease of defining oneself in relation to what one is against, including the paradoxical act of defining oneself against being against anything at all, this mode of thought holds the tension between apparently incommensurable oppositions to allow a novel entity, "the reconciling third" as Jung puts it, to emerge from discord. Ultimately, one is not faced with a genuine controversy unless both parties to the disagreement have legitimate claims to some aspect of a larger reality, a multivalence revealed through the confrontation and reconciliation of the opposed perspectives.

## 4. The Discontinuity of Process

The discovery of the quantum theory in the early twentieth century was, to some degree, a mathematical formalization of intuitive insights that have been expressed in many domains over the course of human history, both before and after the quantum revolution of the nineteen-twenties. In particular, the premodern ideas of inspiration, epiphany, apotheosis, conversion, revelation, transfiguration, and alchemical transmutation are all recognitions that change occasionally occurs in sudden leaps that reconfigure the entire meaning of a process. In modernity, this discrete quality of reality was variously recognized in chemistry as the change of state, in the mutation theory of Hugo de Vries, in the processes of mitosis, meiosis, and binary fission in cell biology, in punctuated equilibrium in evolution, and in the very structure of scientific revolutions, which disrupt and reconfigure the processes of normal science. This discontinuous quality of being can equally be seen in the changing of the seasons, the start of a rainstorm, a sunset, and the budding of a flower, or in the conception, birth, and pubescence of an animal. However, what quantum theory suggests, and what Erwin Schrödinger and others have made explicit in varying inflections, is that all of these discrete phenomena are related to the discontinuous nature of the atomic electron transition described in physics, sometimes through direct efficient causation, but always through the fractal reiteration characteristic of formal causation.

## 5. Development through Emergent Phases

The evolution of process in various domains appears to occur through a series of relatively discrete stages, which finds one of its most basic forms in the three-stage schema of premodern, modern, and an apparently emerging mode after the postmodern. G.W.F. Hegel, William James, C.G. Jung, Henri Bergson, Alfred North Whitehead, Pierre Teilhard de Chardin, and many others have generally employed this three-stage schema, whether explicitly or implicitly, and I will often refer to these broad stages extrapolated from these various conceptual systems. However, some theorists have subdivided these overarching divisions in finer detail. For instance, Jean Gebser traces a five-stage schema—archaic, magic, mythical, mental, and integral—further subdividing each stage into "efficient" and "deficient" phases. I will generally employ Gebser's five-stage schema when a finer-grained approach is wanted, as I have found his terminology and his description of these stages to be the clearest and most useful articulation of the more specific phases of ingression.

These five stages appear to manifest fractally in various progressions at different scales: from nonlife to prokaryotic life to animality to hominidity to human consciousness on the scale of evolution; from unfertilized egg to infant to child to adolescent to adult in individual human development; and from archaic to magic to mythical to mental and, perhaps, on to a novel mode in the collective development of human consciousness. These phases of process are rarely completely distinct from one another, as each stage generally contains the earlier stages within it as the very constitution of its emergence, and there are many compromise formations, regressions, and side roads that complicate the discernment of these stages of development. Furthermore, in contradistinction to premodern and modern hierarchical modes, the emergent view of developmental stages generally asserts that no stage is qualitatively superior to any other stage. So the adult is not superior to the child, who possesses profound imaginal capacities that are inevitably diluted by passage into the more complex later stages. Similarly, earlier cultures possess forms of knowledge and activity that developmentally subsequent stages have generally forgotten, or which have become diminished from neglect. However, while an earlier stage may be viewed as a "golden age" by some, the emerging mode does not usually deem these originary phases of process as qualitatively superior to later stages.[8]

At our historical moment in the early twenty-first century, we live in a world in which cultures at all stages of development coexist, starting with a very few scattered instances of archaic humans, such as those rare children raised by animals, for example, abiding in an undifferentiated, dreamlike, preverbal consciousness nearly indistinguishable from the modes of relation experienced by the most conscious animals such as dogs, cats, and nonhuman primates. However, we have all experienced this mode of consciousness in ourselves and in others as infancy, a stage of development when there is essentially no awareness of self. It seems that this stage of consciousness in humans is only separable from a similar mode in nonhuman primates by the intuitively felt capacity to go beyond this phase facilitated through the enlarged neocortex of the human brain. At this archaic stage, one is essentially an animal, only transcending animality in the completely unarticulated bodily sense that one is destined for something more. But this is not a judgment of value, as the archaic stage is Adam and Eve in the Garden, a pure and undifferentiated innocence and embeddedness to be cherished, and to which we should all perhaps occasionally return. In fact, we do seem to return to something like the archaic stage of awareness every night in dreams.

A significantly larger group of people apparently abide in uncontacted or isolated tribes that primarily inhabit the magic stage of consciousness, though this group still appears to be a small percentage of the current overall world population. In this world view, a self emerges, but this self is pre-egoic and almost completely permeable with the world and with others, so that the inner dialogue, made possible by the emergence of language at this stage, does not differentiate between what is imagined and what the modern mind would generally conceive as external, material reality. One awakens to a body, but the experience of being in magical consciousness is constituted in what mentality would subsequently demarcate into world and mind thinking and feeling together as an undifferentiated unity. Instead of a subject perceiving an object, the magical mode perceives what *is*, or at least what appears to be at that stage, swimming in a fluid, dreamlike mélange of images, emotions, and significations.

The material production characteristic of magical culture is simple tools and weapons, talismans of various sorts, and cave paintings. However, in a magical culture, the shamans are those individuals who employ what Mircea Eliade calls "techniques of ecstasy," from fasting and wilderness exposure to psychoactive plants, dance, and vocalization to perceive intimations of further stages of consciousness.[9] It appears from testimonies of these individuals that these ecstatically induced intimations would generally be located in the mythical, but may occasionally go beyond that immediately subsequent mode to experience, however briefly, the mental or the currently emerging mode, or perhaps even later stages as yet unrealized, though these more distant stages would be almost impossible to communicate or sustain in a cultural milieu whose verbal structures and premises about the nature of reality are primarily magical. And we can all recognize this stage of process by remembering our early childhood, a phase that can be grown beyond by different individuals in various cultures at a range of ages, but from which most individuals in our era eventually emerge. However, shamanic "techniques of ecstasy" can certainly be practiced in the context of subsequent stages by individuals who have attained modern mentality, especially in the integrative mode, which specifically integrates the previous modes in an emergent synthesis, incorporating the unique capacities of each stage.

It seems that for a large proportion of people in the present, though perhaps no longer a majority, their gravitational center of consciousness is located in the mythical stage, which is the stage of ancient religions and systems of thought that accompanied the entrance into history and the first signs of what we would consider civilization: writing, agriculture, cities, commerce, laws, kings, and above all, gods. This is the mode of consciousness that permeated Pharaonic Egypt and ancient Mesopotamia, and that produced the code of Hammurabi and Cuneiform tablets. This is the stage of cognizance that the ancient Hebrews first began to go beyond in their rejection of idols, and that Cortes and his crew encountered in Montezuma and the Aztecs in the 1519 meeting that would mark the incipient colonization of the Americas by Europe at the dawn of modernity.[10] Whenever a culture or a group within a culture could conceivably be described as prerational or premodern (though these potentially problematic designations are structurally equivalent to calling a child a "pre-adult"), this usually means that we are encountering the mythical stage of consciousness. In fact, contemporary fundamentalist religious movements, particularly in both Christianity and Islam, appear generally to be composed of the mythically situated masses often cynically led by individuals who have achieved enough mentality to manipulate and control those whose consciousness has stabilized in the mythical mode. However, developmentally later modes can find great value in the capacities individuated by the mythical mode of thought, as well as the archaic and magic modes, forms of knowledge and perception which must be reintegrated if we are to move past the deficient mental phase characteristic of late modernity.

Although there were intimations of mentality in the disclosures of many ancient mythical systems, the first eruption of rational consciousness on a large scale seems to have taken place during the heart of what historian Karl Jaspers has called the "Axial Age" centered on the approximately fifty-year period in the sixth century B.C.E. when many of the world's most transformative religious and philosophical figures lived, including the Buddha, Confucius, Lao Tzu, Mahavira, Jeremiah, Ezekiel, Second Isaiah, Thales, Anaximander, Pythagoras, Sappho, Thespis, Solon, and possibly Zoroaster—in other words the beginnings of Greek philosophy and science, Buddhism, Confucianism, Taoism, Jainism, and a transformed Judaic religion. This profoundly creative period built the foundations for the eventual emergence of rationality as the dominant cultural force in modernity, though it required around twenty centuries of thought, debate, war, upheaval, invention, and discovery for the mental mode of thought to begin to be articulated comprehensively, a process that appears to be nearing completion five centuries further on in late modernity. The Renaissance and Protestant Reformation of the sixteenth century, the ages of Enlightenment and Revolution in the seventeenth and eighteenth centuries, the age of imperialism, romanticism, and idealism in the nineteenth century, and through all this the development of science and technology have mediated the emergence of the mental stage as the dominant cultural mode in the West and, only in the last few decades, perhaps in the world. In the central spheres of modern culture, the attainment of rationality by the individual is the mark of entrance into full adulthood, and there seems to us something childish, and perhaps deficient or even dangerous, in a grown person who still primarily inhabits the mythical mode of consciousness but is embedded in a predominantly rationalist society.

## 6. The Emergence of a New World View

The suggestion that our culture is undergoing the collective transition to a fundamentally new mode of thought is one that has been unpalatable to the principal modern sensibility, but which irrepressibly continues to crop up, eliciting from those with minds sufficiently unencumbered by conventional assumptions the suspicion that such an emergence is possible, and perhaps even inevitable. Since at least Hegel at the beginning of the nineteenth century, and in the work of some of the most revered thinkers since then, the presentiment that a large segment of human culture is on the cusp of a transformation as fundamental as the revolution that birthed modernity has proven to be extremely persistent. The "new age" movement that began in the nineteen sixties, achieved widespread attention in the seventies, and has since undergone a trivializing reaction, in many cases for good reason, is perhaps the most prominent expression of some of the kinds of insights presented here, particularly the idea that culture is currently experiencing the emergence of a new world view.

However, the new age movement was ultimately a failure in its implied goal—to bring about a new era of human history—though I would argue that it was a necessary step for the widespread publication of the kinds of ideas that had, until then, been the province of deeply rigorous and careful theorists like Hegel and James, Bergson and Gebser, Jung and Whitehead. The great commercial success of the new age movement was also its downfall as a philosophy to be taken seriously, as complex and profound ideas were often appropriated by the lowest common denominator and flattened to fit into a modern mentality, neutered by poor aesthetic taste, simplistic, self-centered spirituality, and overly credulous commerce in tacky paraphernalia. All of these elements that many of us find so worthy of ridicule have served to diminish some of the most significant ideas of the last few centuries to caricatures in collective understanding, often buried behind atrocious pastel book covers, embedded in absurdly grandiose and imprecise language, and inextricably mixed with preposterous and unprovable assertions.[11]

While the present book is most emphatically not party to the new age movement as it is generally conceived, as Whitehead so presciently declared in 1925's *Science and the Modern World*: "Almost all really new ideas have a certain aspect of foolishness when they are first produced."[12] There are numerous thinkers and writers who may have been sympathetic to the initial impulse to birth a "new age" during that movement's earliest and most hopeful days, but who never acquiesced to that overly compromised designation. These thinkers have been quietly and consistently working to find some middle ground, to build a bridge between modernity and the emerging mode that many have intuited, and of which the new age movement is merely the most facile and publicly digestible approximation.

In particular, scholars such as David Bohm, James Hillman, Charles Taylor, Stanislav Grof, Rupert Sheldrake, Terence McKenna, and Richard Tarnas, among many others, who have all done their work primarily in the second half of the twentieth century and the beginning of the twenty-first century, have taken up the task of carrying forward the epochal philosophical endeavor initiated by Hegel, James, Jung, Bergson, Whitehead, Gebser, and all the rest. They have endeavored to produce novel concepts, forms of language, and institutions through which the emerging mode of thought can be viably articulated and propagated into collective awareness. Therefore, despite the apparently radical nature of some of the ideas expressed in the present work in relation to the main streams of academia, the project of this book is actually a rather conservative one: to synthesize and consolidate the concepts and rhetorical strategies developed by these numerous precursors, and hopefully in the process to assist in differentiating these ideas from the problematic subcultures with which they have sometimes been associated. In short, the kind of thought expressed here seems ripe for an entrance from the liminal margins into the central spheres of cultural discourse, which it has, in fact, already begun to enjoy in the work of those thinkers mentioned above, and that of many others.

## 7. The Fractal Quality of Process

Fractal geometry was essentially discovered by Benoit Mandelbrot in the nineteen sixties and seventies, based partially on the work of Gottfried Leibniz, Georg Cantor, Henri Poincare, and Helge von Koch. Mandelbrot coined the term fractal in 1975 in his foundational book, revised and published in English first in 1977 as *Fractals: Form, Chance, and Dimension*, and then further revised and expanded in 1982 as *The Fractal Geometry of Nature*. In his book, Mandelbrot elucidates the mathematical sets that produce fractals along with a conceptual framework for their understanding, which demonstrate that many objects and processes found in both nature and human culture develop self-similarly, or through the closely related concept of self-affinity, which he describes as "the resemblance between the parts and the whole." That is, coastlines, fern leaves, stock markets, turbulence, and many other complex processes and entities all recursively repeat similar structural patterns across different scales of magnitude, so that one part of the leaf magnified looks very much like the larger leaf, or the distribution of stars in one galaxy looks very much like the distribution of many galaxies in a galactic cluster.[13]

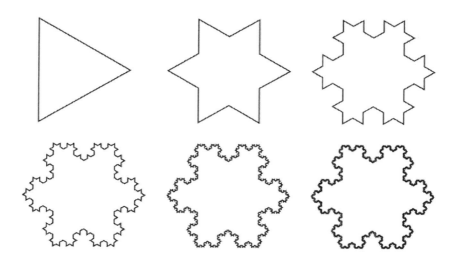

Koch Snowflake, fractal dimension of approximately 1.26

Furthermore, Mandelbrot shows that fractals possess fractional dimensionality, which, along with the fractured topology of the objects fractality describes, is why he named them as such. For instance, a Koch snowflake, a triangle with successively smaller triangles symmetrically added to the object's outer surface, at first producing a Star of David, and then increasingly resembling a snowflake with each successive iteration, exhibits a dimensionality of approximately 1.26. This mathematical object can be extended into a third-dimensional space by substituting pyramids for triangles, which exhibits a dimensionality of approximately 2.58. The degree of the object's or process' fractional dimension is significant, so that a 1.1 dimensional object traces a curved line, while a 1.9 dimensional object bends back upon itself in complex convolutions so that it almost fills a two-dimensional plane.

## 8. Forms, Archetypes, and Eternal Objects

Jungian archetypes and Whiteheadian eternal objects are both apparently rearticulations of the Platonic forms in a twentieth-century context, two inflections of the idea that there are intrinsic potentialities for meaning and relation inherent in the structure of process that manifest in all things. However, it does not seem to be the case that archetypes as described by Jung in his later years, along with associates like Marie-Louise von Franz and Aniela Jaffé, and refined by Grof, Hillman, Tarnas, and others, correlate exactly with the fundamental qualities of experience that Whitehead refers to as eternal objects. Rather, archetypes seem to be a subset of the eternal objects at their most complex order of magnitude. As Whitehead defines the general scope of his concept, any potentiality that is not preconditioned by a particular temporal occasion is necessarily an eternal object, as it can only change in particular temporal manifestations, not in its eternal, a priori form intrinsic to cosmic structure. Archetypes, however, are apparently higher-order agglomerations of qualities than the simple qualities that Whitehead mentions such as colors, sounds, tastes, and smells. Archetypes are impulses for expression that orient our relation to the world in particular domains of discourse, complex webs of metaphor organizing the meaningful connections of elements in different realms of experience. In contrast, the most basic eternal objects that Whitehead discusses, the single sensory qualia, are not intrinsically metaphorical, though they are susceptible to metaphorization when they are subsumed into emergent archetypal fields of meaning.

The archetypes appear to be one class of eternal object that are presupposed by, but not reducible to, additional, simpler eternal objects. Whereas the eternal objects constitute anything whatsoever that is pure potentiality unmanifest in time, the archetypes are more specifically personified agencies or modes of potential meaning, applicable across scale. The senex archetype, for instance, the Latin word for "old man" from which senator, senile, and senior are derived, is associated with old age, but also with slowness, distance, limit, conservatism, structure, focus, and rigor. All of these individual characteristics of the senex appear to be eternal objects that, when combined, synthesize to form the emergent archetype, which can itself be described as a more complex eternal object than the simple qualities delineated above. However, it should not be inferred from this distinction that more complex eternal objects have evolved from less complex ones, as eternal objects in general and their archetypal subset appear to be atemporal and, thus, given.[14]

## 9. Qualitative Temporality and Formal Causation

The idea that time has qualities is an ancient one, visible in the *I-Ching* (the Chinese "Book of Changes"), in the Mayan calendar of interlocking rounds, and in the various forms of astrology practiced in many premodern cultures, all of which sought to map the qualitative contours of temporality. At the dawn of modernity, Johannes Kepler and Galileo Galilei, who simultaneously confirmed the Copernican heliocentric hypothesis through the innovation of elliptical motion and improvements in telescopic technology respectively, were committed astrologers, and Isaac Newton was apparently more devoted to his studies of Biblical prophecy than to his epochal work in physics. However, in the wake of the Enlightenment of the seventeenth century, any mode of thought based on the premise of qualitative temporality became anathema to the newly emerging spirit of positivist inquiry. Although these and other qualitative approaches to time continued to be practiced at the margins of the predominant cultural networks in the eighteenth and nineteenth centuries, it was not until the twentieth century, largely in the Bergsonian concept of duration, and then even more prominently in Jungian synchronicity, that a qualitative approach to understanding time began to seem a viable proposition again in the educated sectors of Western culture. Since Jung's initial seminar on his theory in 1928, and particularly since the publication of *Synchronicity: An Acausal Connecting Principle* in 1952, the idea that time exhibits qualities has grown steadily in prominence, though it is still a minority view among most academics as of this writing.

In a representative moment of synchronicity, Jung recounts his work with a patient who seems to feel psychically constrained by her culture's rationalistic assumptions, but who is unable, or perhaps unwilling, to go beyond the limiting beliefs characteristic of modernity. In the course of her therapy, the patient describes a dream in which she is given a golden scarab, an amulet modeled on the ancient Egyptian reverence for scarab beetles. As she is telling Jung her dream, there is a "gentle tapping" on the window of the study, and Jung opens the window to find a scarabaeid beetle, the insect most like the Egyptian scarab found in that latitude, trying to get inside. Jung presents the beetle to the woman with the simple pronouncement, "here is your scarab," which sparks a revelation for the woman, who suddenly feels liberated from her disenchanted skepticism by this subjectively meaningful coincidence. This experience apparently initiated the resolution for the woman of the neurotic symptoms that seem to have been the result of cognitive dissonance between her rationally held assumptions and her intuition of the more expansive metaphysical reality revealed by such instances of formal causation. The content of the woman's dream, her recounting of that dream, the previous lack of success in her therapy, the apparent significance of the beetle's intrusion, and Jung's portentous presentation of it to her all seem to have participated in the archetypal quality of that moment.[15]

## 10. Final Causation

Teleology, the ancient idea that processes tend to develop toward ends or purposes, has generally been denied in modernity in favor of material and efficient causation, which have been enshrined as the only valid causal modes. For most of premodernity, from astrology and divination to Judeo-Christian, Muslim, and Hindu eschatologies, to various streams of Confucian and Buddhist thought, final causation was usually interpreted as divinely ordained fate. For much of human history, people felt themselves to be parts of a vast and minutely choreographed cosmic dance acting out the will of a god or gods whose reasons were unknowable. Until the nascence of the mental mode, particularly in ancient Greek thought, the prevailing world view was one that largely precluded the idea of free will.[16] For ancient people, the supposition that one could challenge the will of the gods was hubris, a laughable arrogance unsupported by the evidence of fate's apparent inevitability.[17] To a great extent, the emergence of the modern mind was a reaction against this pervasive assumption of predestination in its many complex permutations, so that Descartes' claim that the human mind, and not the mind of God, is the only thing that provides evidence of our existence (despite his attempt to reconcile this view with his Catholic faith), was a direct challenge to the hegemony of that mode of thought which located agency primarily outside the human mind. All of the ruptures, innovations, and discoveries of modernity, from the Copernican revolution to Kant's "second Copernican revolution" to deconstructive postmodernism, can partially be described as a progressive evacuation of cosmic purpose into the human mind, which has come to be seen as the sole locus of consciousness and purpose in a purely material universe.

However, although there were numerous liminal intimations of final causation's return percolating at the margins of the academically dominant positivism and materialism of the seventeenth and eighteenth centuries, including the attempt by many scientists during those centuries to reconcile science with religious belief, the idea of teleology began to reemerge in full force through the work of Hegel and the idealism that he largely mediated in the early nineteenth century. While there have been many legitimate critiques of the specific form that Hegel's vision of final causation took, and many reactions to his role as perhaps the preeminent philosopher of that century, particularly in the Darwinian view of evolution, which carefully sought to extirpate all traces of teleology from its theory, the reemergence of final causation apparently could not be contained. In particular, the stream of thought running from William James and Henri Bergson through Alfred North Whitehead and numerous others has articulated a theory of teleology stripped of its premodern limitations by means of the profoundly rigorous analytical capacity developed in modernity. In this approach, teloi are not predetermined fates to which the individual must inevitably submit, but lures or attractors toward which individual or collective entities are magnetically drawn, though the specific forms of those entities' ingression are not determined in advance.[18]

Moreover, in the transrational conception of teleology, it appears possible for an individual or culture to avoid reaching its teleological destination by choosing to ignore the deeply felt affective demands that final causes make upon a body or a body politic. Odysseus, as one of the primary figures marking mentality's nascence, through his far-flung odyssey, undergoing many trials and tribulations, was always apparently destined to return home transformed. But not all of us so completely fulfill our felt potential. Similarly, the modern mind, through its many complex and multifarious permutations, appears to be tracing a trajectory toward reunion with its ground of being in the reembrace of premodern modes of causation, though reframed and recontextualized by the individuated rational intellect. Of course, it is possible that this process may go off the rails, so to speak, though such apocalyptic scenarios seem unlikely considering the immensely long and consistent path that the vital impulse has trod thus far.

In addition to the philosophical reanimation of final causation in the nineteenth and twentieth centuries, physicist Erwin Schrödinger in his 1944 book, *What Is Life?*, suggests a complementary force to entropy, based on the work of Ludwig Boltzmann, which may be considered a previously undiscovered law of nature variously termed "free energy," "negative entropy," "negentropy," or "syntropy."[19] Although $E = mc^2$ is almost certainly the best-known formula in science, it is not as well known that this formula is the positive solution to a larger formula (expressible as $E^2 = m^2c^4$) that also has a negative solution ($E = -mc^2$) in which time can be interpreted as moving in reverse, which results in syntropy. Because time may be syntropically reversed on the micro scale at which the vital processes that produce life and consciousness occur, effects could be described as preceding causes, which draw the phenomena under consideration toward more ordered states. Schrödinger, fellow Nobel Prize winner physiologist Albert Szent-Gyorgyi, and others have suggested that this counter-entropic force may be the mechanism through which something that looks very much like final causation occurs. However, despite the fact that syntropy has been affirmed in various guises by some of the most eminent scientists of the last century given its compelling theoretical and mathematical foundations, this discovery has often been ignored in the practice of science in favor of more conventional explanations (with some prominent exceptions, such as in the work of Nobel Prize-winning chemist Ilya Prigogine and philosopher Isabelle Stengers), perhaps in large part because it contravenes the prerationally adopted premise of monocausality.

## 11. The Exponential Ingression of Novelty

It has often been observed over the last few centuries that time appears to be accelerating as trains, automobiles, and airplanes have radically increased the speed of travel and concomitantly shrunk subjective distances in space. For the pioneers who crossed North America in covered wagons, this trip was a long and perilous journey, but for us it is a several-hour flight accompanied by relatively mild discomfort. Similarly, the inventions of the telegraph, the telephone, and the internet have facilitated the acceleration of communication, so that in the mid-nineteenth century, the Pony Express, combined with the limited extent of the telegraph which only went as far as St. Joseph, Missouri, was the fastest way to send a written document from the East Coast to the West, a trip that took about ten days, whereas now one can communicate almost instantaneously through satellite video conferencing with someone in Shanghai or Mozambique. However, despite the common recognition of this acceleration, the idea that this increasing speed of experience is exponential in nature does not appear to be intuitive for most people, as our brains and our conceptual tools have evolved primarily in the context of linear phenomena.

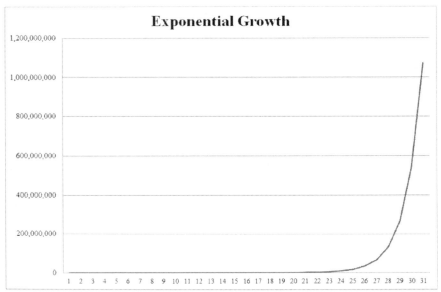

Plotted on a linear graph, this exponential progression starting with one and doubling at each integer along the horizontal axis reaches one billion in about thirty doublings.

It is unclear precisely when the quality of exponentiality was discovered, and by whom, but several persistent stories place this discovery during the first millennium C.E. in India or Persia in coincidence with the invention of Chess. A classic narrative, related by the Persian poet Ferdowsi in his epic poem "Shahnameh" sometime around 1000 C.E., tells of a mathematician named Sessa, described as the inventor of the "Game of Kings," who pleased his king so greatly by his invention that the monarch told Sessa to name his reward. The mathematician's request seemed simple and reasonable: place one grain of rice on the first square of a chess board, and double the number for each of the sixty-four squares, so that the second square would contain two grains, the third four grains, the fourth eight grains, and so on. The king, thinking this a rather modest request, quickly assented. However, when the king's treasurer calculated the total after some difficulty and delay, it turned out that the king had agreed to give Sessa more than eighteen quintillion grains of rice, which amounts to about four hundred billion tons, far more than was contained in the entire kingdom, far more even than the world currently produces in a year. In some versions of the story, Sessa is put to death for his impertinence, while in others he is made the new king. However, the key point is that this exponential growth starts out seeming fairly linear, though clearly accelerating, but by the time the doublings are well into the double digits, the growth becomes startlingly explosive.

Ray Kurzweil, the inventor of such profoundly transformative and pervasive technologies as the first omni-font optical character recognition system, the first flatbed scanner, the first text-to-speech synthesizer, and the first keyboard synthesizer capable of reproducing realistic instrumental sounds, and since 2012 Director of Engineering at Google, has been one of the primary figures in applying exponentiality to the growth of technology. In his Law of Accelerating Returns, Kurzweil demonstrates that not only technology, but the evolution of life and mind for which technology appears to be an extension, has progressed exponentially, though this acceleration is only now becoming rapid enough that individuals are beginning to have an intuitive sense of it in their lifetimes. The capacity very quickly to adapt to extreme novelty is one of the most marked qualities of the human organism, so that about three decades ago as of this writing, the internet did not exist, and a few decades before that, computers were essentially glorified calculators, but we can hardly imagine living without these inventions.

Now, as Kurzweil has often pointed out, our "phones" actually contain computers that are at least a thousand times more powerful and a million times less expensive than the building-sized supercomputers of the mid-nineteen sixties, which means that our pocket devices are a billion times more capable per dollar of computation, adjusted for inflation, than the most advanced computers were fifty years ago.[20] Kurzweil places the many innovations that have led to this situation, cross-referenced to a slew of authoritative encyclopedic sources, on a graph that traces a strikingly smooth exponential curve through periods of inflation and rapid economic growth, as well as through depressions and wars. And similarly, he places on a graph the emergence of biology through the information-conserving novelty of DNA, the emergence of mind through the information conservation of neural patterns, the emergence of computational technology through the information conservation of hardware and software, and the incipient merging of biology and technology through the embeddedness of humanity in global networks and the embedding of increasingly tiny and powerful information processors in the human brain and body. Without reproducing Kurzweil's research in detail, it must suffice to say that it is difficult to imagine a credible argument against the ineluctable mountain of data he has amassed to support his primary hypothesis. Any lingering skepticism about this phenomenon appears to be driven primarily by the hegemony of linear common sense that has been dominant in modernity. As is true of most of the concepts discussed in these pages, exponential acceleration seems to be a higher-order common-sense characteristic of the emerging mode of thought.[21]

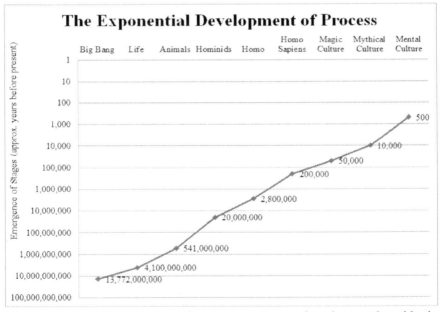

Exponential development through emergent stages plotted on a logarithmic graph. The figures given are approximate, representing orders of magnitude rather than precise dates, which continue to be the subject of debate.

## 12. The Concretion of Time

For a modern, rationalist sensibility, the suggestion that human history constitutes the process of coming to awareness of a fourth degree of freedom may seem absurd, the stuff of science fiction or of ungrounded new age speculation, not the subject of serious philosophical inquiry. However, as some of our greatest thinkers have suggested in various valences, this sense of absurdity may have more to do with the limitations of the conventional modern mentality than with the inherent implausibility of the idea itself. For a world view founded upon the premises that time is purely quantitative and linear, and that material and efficient causation are the only valid causal modes, the concretion of time would in fact be an irrational conclusion. For a world view, though, that accepts all of the other concepts introduced above into its conceptual lexicon, temporic concretion seems to be the most plausible scenario for the further development of process.

Plato, the father of philosophy, suggested that time is "a moving image of eternity," which taken at face value means that what we perceive as time is like a radically expanded reel of film, so that each still frame is a snapshot of the total situation of the cosmos at one particular point in a dimensional manifold that exceeds our current cognitive capacities to comprehend as a whole. Through this perceptual method, which Henri Bergson refers to as the "cinematographical mechanism of thought," we can trace the textures of temporality, the ups and downs, and the ins and outs of narrative development. For instance, the archetypal journey story, setting aside the complexities of frame narratives, flashbacks, and subplots, begins with the naïve, childhood embeddedness in home. Then some conflict intervenes that impels the protagonist to embark on the journey. Encounters take place along the way, consisting of all kinds of qualitative experiences, both tragic and revelatory, both languid and explosive, both violent and amorous, both expansive and contractive. And eventually the protagonist returns home transformed. This is one of the simplest forms of narrative, for which there are many convoluted permutations, alterations, and substitutions. But visualized from a spatial perspective, these qualitative temporal moments in the narrative trace a complex trajectory through time, which, if it could be seen at once in its entirety, would possess a definite shape and extension, like the lower-dimensional analogue of a three-dimensional object perceived by the denizens of a two-dimensional world. The narrative construction of time, the tracing of the qualities of temporality, is apparently a means of mapping time's contours.

Although a number of thinkers have articulated the recognition that being constitutes a process of ascending into ever more expansive degrees of dimensionality, Jean Gebser is perhaps the theorist who has most comprehensively elaborated this idea in its details in his 1949 book, first translated into English in 1985 as *The Ever-Present Origin*. In this work, through a voluminous and erudite exposition of the stages of consciousness, from archaic to magic, mythical, mental, and integral, drawing on philosophy, physics, chemistry, biology, psychology, anthropology, mathematics, art history, and other disciplines, Gebser demonstrates that what we experience as time constitutes the coming to consciousness of a further degree of freedom, perhaps equivalent to something like another spatial dimension, which we have constructed in our experience as temporality.

David Bohm, a physicist who worked closely with Albert Einstein, appears to corroborate this supposition from the perspective of quantum theory in his *Wholeness and the Implicate Order*, published in 1980. As mentioned above, it is a peculiarity of the laws of physics as they are currently understood that the equations describing the physical universe work equally well when time is reversed, and that time is only unidirectional based on probabilistic interpretations of these laws. In fact, it is this very probabilistic interpretation about which Einstein wrote in a letter to Max Born that God "is not playing at dice,"[22] by which he appears to have meant that the probabilistic interpretation of quantum theory is merely an approximation of a more encompassing theory that would reconcile quantum mechanics and relativity. These theorists and others have gestured in various valences toward what might be described as a transcendent reality intimated in premodern religious and mystical modes, though this more expansive domain would probably not be fixed and static as it was generally supposed in various religious dispensations (at least after the volatile beginnings described in the creation myths of these traditions), but enacted through the participatory process of temporal becoming.[23]

Beginning in 1984, astrophysicist Laurent Nottale, Director of Research at the French National Centre for Scientific Research, proposed the theory of scale relativity, which appears to be a viable candidate for the reconciliation of quantum theory and relativity based partially on fractal geometry, a geometry not available to Einstein, Gebser, or their contemporaries. Among many other features, scale relativity derives the result that time can be described in quantum mechanics as exhibiting a fractal dimensionality of .5, precisely one half of a full degree of freedom.[24] Although this result requires more study, when fractally extrapolated from the microphysical scale to the scale of human consciousness, it may perhaps suggest that our experience of time can be described as precisely half a dimension. If this discovery holds up to further investigation, it would seem to indicate that the human mind in its perceptual and cognitive capacity is literally halfway between an animal and something like Friedrich Nietzsche's *Übermensch*, the potentially higher-order entity whose eventual ingression into temporal actuality may have been intimated over the course of human history as spirits, gods, and the like. However, regardless of whether or not this precise fractional figure proves generalizable to the human measurement, perception, or construction of temporality on all scales, it appears plausible that fractal dimensionality, an idea only four decades old as of this writing, may be increasingly understood as the most accurate description of temporality in relation to spatiality.

# CHAPTER 1
## "WORLD VIEWS CREATE WORLDS"
### THE PARTICIPATORY QUALITY OF PROCESS

*The philosophy which is so important in each of us is not a technical matter; it is our more or less dumb sense of what life honestly and deeply means. It is only partly got from books; it is our individual way of just seeing and feeling the total push and pressure of the cosmos.*

William James, *Pragmatism*[25]

*Our world view is not simply the way we look at the world. It reaches inward to constitute our innermost being, and outward to constitute the world. It mirrors but also reinforces and even forges the structures, armorings, and possibilities of our interior life. It deeply configures our psychic and somatic experience, the patterns of our sensing, knowing, and interacting with the world. No less potently, our world view—our beliefs and theories, our maps, our metaphors, our myths, our interpretive assumptions—constellates our outer reality, shaping and working the world's malleable potentials in a thousand ways of subtly reciprocal interaction. World views create worlds.*

Richard Tarnas, *Cosmos and Psyche*[26]

The participatory quality of process implies that it is necessary to embrace the will to believe in order to mediate the production of radical novelty. To possess the courage to leap across the threshold from a known orthodoxy to a fundamentally new mode, one must understand that even our most basic beliefs about the nature of the world are mutable, collective constructions reified by consensus reality and normative discourse. Certainly, this provisional quality of our beliefs does not mean that these assumptions are not partially true, just that there are other, perhaps equally productive and valid ways of conceiving the same set of phenomena. A paradigmatic case of this partial validity of apparently incommensurable interpretations is, on the one hand, the belief often dominant in the most influential cultural networks of modernity (i.e. academia and science) that there is nothing but physical matter (reductionist materialism based on material and efficient causation) and, on the other hand, the belief that there are kinds of causality that exceed materiality (numerous streams of thought often based on formal and final causation), which are complementary to materiality. It seems clear that there is no definitive evidence to settle this controversy one way or another, as each mode of consciousness can interpret the same facts in radically different ways, or even elicit different facts from immediate experience. Thus the recognition that we participate in the unfolding meaning of the world implies that this creative act of meaning-making is constituted in a leap of faith that goes beyond the secure certainty of conventional assumptions.

This participatory insight leads to the integrative method, which seeks to reconcile such opposed assertions as are polarized in any genuine controversy, like that between the idea that the world is composed of purposeless matter and the idea that the world is animated by intrinsic meaning and purpose. The integrative method recognizes that both of these notions contain partial truths valid within their appropriate domains of applicability. If one is constructing a building, for example, the materialist, quantitative mode is indispensable, for if the construction is not based on sound measurements and solid physical principles, the building will collapse. However, if one wishes to understand the purpose of the building, the human activities that will take place inside, and the aesthetic considerations that condition the affective tone for this activity, then one is in a realm of cognizance that exceeds the grasp of physical science. Even if one believes that the emergence of human consciousness can be explained by the mere collision of atoms, this belief does not logically preclude a complementary belief that there is a teleological impulse toward novelty endemic to the fabric of the cosmos. The participatory quality of process elucidated in this chapter leads directly to "the reconciling third," the dialectical synthesis that subsumes the polarity, absorbing what each point of view asserts and jettisoning what each point of view denies. This synthesis produces a new perspective in which the premises of materialism and idealism, for instance, are both useful tools in the conceptual armamentarium, special cases of a larger reality in an analogous way to that in which general relativity and quantum mechanics can be considered partial aspects of a more comprehensive, and as yet undiscovered theory.

The mutability in our fundamental relation to experience also implies that the world is a place where things can change relatively suddenly. Like water boiling or ice melting, world views are susceptible to comparatively abrupt transformations precisely because they are not given, but are elicited by our participation in the creation of the world's meaning. However, for epochal transitions in the collective world view of a civilization, this relative suddenness is usually measured on the scale of a few generations, disrupting the generally stable cosmological continuity and steady development of previous generations. As with scientific revolutions, these rather sudden reorganizations of the entire process are predicated upon a basic discontinuity between the old and new modes of thought because they are based on different fundamental, and thus ultimately unprovable assumptions about the nature of reality.

Similarly, the participatory quality of process forms a precondition for the series of emergent developmental stages at the level of human culture mediated by discontinuous ruptures of world views. Each distinct phase in the evolution of consciousness individuates certain capacities which, until then, have been merely dormant potentiality unrealized in actual historical process. The stages of consciousness articulated in various valences by some of the theorists mentioned above, roughly definable as premodern (which can be further divided into archaic, magic, and mythical), modern, and the emerging mode, by whatever name it comes to be called, are all based on often implicit premises about the nature of reality, from which result the specific contours, the possibilities and constraints for existence of the worlds of those epochs. Where magic cultures generally perceive spirits animating the natural world as the primary reality and act accordingly, modern cultures have generally acted on the belief that the world is composed of material particles interacting through impersonal physical forces. It goes without saying that these two modes of thought produce radically different worlds, exemplified in the tribal village permeably embedded in vast, encompassing nature in contrast with the often isolated individual abiding in a modern metropolis, in which a few trees jut out of square patches of dirt cut into the sidewalk.[27] Although much has been gained by way of technological development, scientific understanding, and the individuation of the rational and intellectual capacities of humanity, the deep sense of meaning and purpose characteristic of most premodern cultures has been increasingly difficult to locate in the modern era, in large part because of this disembedding from the natural world and the imaginal, enchanted quality it evokes. Each of these emergent stages of process was able to be lived through and worked out to its furthest permutations because the lenses through which each era viewed the world cocreatively enacted the production of that world.

The radical mutability of world views implies not only that the emergence of a novel perspective can take place in the consciousness of an individual, but also that if enough members of a society undergo such a transformation, and if this new mode of consciousness is concretized in institutions and in networks of discourse and influence, then the gravitational center of consciousness of the whole society can undergo such a change of state. These dialectical transitions between world views are relatively rare, but they do seem periodically to occur, for instance in the transition from classical antiquity to the middle ages, largely initiated by the emergence of Christianity in the West, or from the medieval Christian era to the modern, largely initiated by the Copernican realization that the Sun, not the Earth, is the center of the cosmos, and mediated by the procession of insights from Descartes, Bacon, Newton, Kant, Darwin, Freud, and all the rest, which followed from this initial epiphany. The widespread intuition that we are now in the midst of a transition between eras that has been gestating since near the beginning of modernity, but has been approaching a climax in the twentieth and early twenty-first centuries, is lent plausibility by the fact that different assumptions about the nature of reality have led to drastically different ways of conceiving and relating to experience at different times and in different places.

This participatory quality of process is applicable on numerous orders of magnitude, ranging from the world view held by an individual, through the way a distinct social group understands its experience, to the way national or global cultures collectively construct reality in the vastly complex networks of legislation, politics, economics, media, and social relations. Even the objects and institutions produced by a particular world view are fractally permeated by the patterned symmetry that unfolds across these scales. For instance, in a primarily magic culture, not only the tribe and its members, but animals, plants, and objects are animated by spirits, so a spear can be as ensouled as the person, the collective, or the world itself because these entities all participate in the world soul, the *anima mundi*. For this world view, the spear's primary function is to express its archetypal purpose, the vigorously directed activity of the hunter or warrior, and its physical utility is secondary and attendant to this immaterial reality. In contrast, a society with a primarily mechanistic world view sees the body, the mind, society, and nature as essentially machines, as agglomerations of physical relations that produce the vast complexity of these entities. The whole orientation of such a society is toward the construction of increasingly powerful mechanical devices and organizational structures to utilize natural resources and to enhance what Max Weber refers to as "the rationalization of the conduct of life,"[28] the measurable, calculable, quantitative rules, roles, and mores of modern society. Both world views, the spiritual and the mechanical, contain metaphors that propagate themselves through many levels of reality, mediating the multivalent loci of becoming for these modes of relation. One cannot perceive spirits on many scales unless one believes in spirits, just as one cannot produce and perceive machines on many scales if one has not conceived of such a mode of organization. World views create worlds self-similarly across scale.

If this fractal symmetry is dependent in the human domain on the pervasive filters of belief and assumption that compose world views, the fundamental archetypal potentialities that express themselves through this process of ingression across scale are equally shaped in their concrete becoming by the world views through which they manifest. The archetypes are definable as impulses toward the coming into actuality of particular kinds of meaning. But whereas mythical world views often interpret these potentialities as gods exhibiting intentionality and autonomy, revealing themselves through both human and nonhuman activity, the modern world view has generally interpreted these formal potentialities as merely linguistic categories or organizing principles of the mind with no direct relation to what this world view conceives as a purely external and objective cosmos outside the psyche. For instance, where the ancient Greeks perceived Kronos (apparently related to Chronos, the Roman Saturn, and the senex archetype) as a transcendent personality with numerous qualities (e.g. time, death, the negative, difficulty, slowness, dryness, distance, hardness, labor, focus, structure, limit, constraint, judgment, etc.), modern scientific materialism sees these qualities as abstractions culled from unmediated experience by the human mind.

For the ancient believers in this particular form of divinity, the suffering and death ruled by Kronos were rendered intelligible and appeared intrinsically connected with more positive manifestations of this titanic personage: hard labor to construct a more solid and durable foundation for the limitation of suffering, for instance. The negative manifestation of this archetypal being, himself the archetype of negativity in this particular inflection of the mythical world view, could be appeased and even transmuted through worshipful attention and reverent submission into a more productive actuality, an activity Hegel expressed for the modern mind as "tarrying with the negative."[29]

Conversely, the logical conclusion of a purely materialist mode of thought, a mode that denies anything other than materiality, is that suffering is meaningless. Rather than impelling one to be transformed through the crucible of suffering, exclusive materialism finds, along with Hamlet, perhaps the paradigmatic modern man in his deficient phase, that the world is ultimately "a foul and pestilent congregation of vapours" and "the rest is silence."[30]

Whereas premodern world views often acted on the assumption that time is qualitative, that each moment has a quality particular to it that permeates and informs the events that occur in that moment even if they are materially unconnected, the general assumption in modernity has been that time is merely a quantitative medium for scientific repeatability. The idea that the assumptions we hold participate in the creation of the world we inhabit implies qualitative duration, as the world view that is held in one epoch produces the quality of that epoch, while during a different temporal era, a different world view produces a different general quality of experience. In a recursive, fractal operation, while the quality that characterized the premodern world was both qualitative and quantitative in an often undifferentiated unity, the quality characteristic of modernity has largely been quantitative rationality.

Even when qualitative temporality is explicitly denied and repressed as it has often been in the modern era, on a more encompassing order of conceptual magnitude, this denial of quality can be paradoxically expressed as the defining quality of the modern mind's relation to temporality. As William James particularly understood, even the denial of a certain form of belief is still a kind of belief, in this case disbelieving that time itself has contours and shades of significance that express themselves through the concrete events that occur, an active skepticism which leads to the belief that time is merely quantitative. The narrative construction characteristic of modern mentality is largely based upon the assumption that whereas quantitative phenomena, physical objects acting upon other physical objects, do not require our conscious participation for their existence, qualitative phenomena (e.g. suffering, limit, focus, judgment) require participation. In this materialist view, these are not purely measurable, objective aspects of process, while material objects are objective facts. However, one might notice that these quantitative, objective, material facts also require consciousness in order to be known at all, and there is no way to ascertain their existence independently of our particular modes of awareness. Both the quantitative and qualitative views of temporality are interpretive frameworks founded upon ultimately unprovable assumptions, both requiring our belief in some specific form of reality for their existence, and both providing explanatory efficacy for different domains of human experience. Thus, not only does the qualitative nature of temporality demand our participation, but so too does time's quantitative aspect necessitate such participation. Time in all its guises appears to be an emergent property of process elicited by our peculiarly human biases and capacities. Indeed, temporality may be one facet of a more expansive reality luring us toward its realization.

The perception of this teleological quality of temporality also depends upon the world view of the perceiver. The dominant forces of the modern West have systematically attempted to expunge and deny the possibility of final causation, partially as a reaction to the specific model of apocalyptic finalism espoused by medieval Christianity, but also as a counterbalance to the more general mythical mode of thought of which the Book of Revelation is one religion's eschatological expression. This rejection of teleology was apparently necessary for shedding the deeply constraining orthodoxies of late medieval Scholasticism, an exemplification of the mythical mode's deficient phase. Although Scholasticism was a primary container for the development of rational thought, as modes of logical argumentation largely derived from Aristotle were refined and perfected over the centuries, it was not until the advent of materialist science that these rational capacities could be individuated from the religious beliefs that had served as a womb for their gestation. Like a child separating from its mother, the rigorous analytical methods that had grown within the confining doctrines of the medieval Church were able to find a wider locus of effectuation in the practice of science. And scientific rationality has generally affirmed material and efficient causation as the only valid causal modes, like a rebellious adolescent denying formal and final causation partially because of their historical link with what the mental mode has often experienced as the repressive dogmas of its parental matrix. Although it may in fact be possible coherently to describe the evolution of life out of nonlife, and of human self-awareness and reason out of animal consciousness in reductionist materialist terms, this mode of thought does not preclude the validity of the mode which recognizes that evolution tends toward the production of novelty and consciousness. Both causal modes appear to be necessary for a mature understanding of temporal process.

From the teleological perspective, it is as if we have lived all our lives on a slight slope, but we assume that the ground beneath our feet is completely flat because we have never known any other inclination. Our physics, chemistry, and biology are formulated assuming that we are working on a flat plane (speaking in a lower-dimensional analogue) when, examined through a teleological lens, it seems that the deep cosmic structure is tilted ever so slightly in the temporal dimension toward the emergence of consciousness. Therefore, we may never be able empirically to demonstrate that there is this teleological incline until we have adjusted our whole mode of thought to take this deeply concealed, but also deeply intuitive factor into account. We need not necessarily change our physics because they work within their domain of applicability, like Newtonian physics works between the very large and the very small, though this metaphysical shift will almost certainly open up new areas of physical research. But we might also consider the possibility that our physics have been perfectly constructed to hide a miniscule slant in the nature of reality (a metaphor for a higher-order phenomenon that exceeds the scope of spatiality), which over very long periods of time produces directionality in the entire process. By holding a world view that accepts teleology, we are able to perceive the fact of final causation, whereas a world view that rejects teleology outright will see only random chance and unknowable mystery when it looks at the clear trajectory of cosmic history thus far toward increasing degrees of consciousness, a trajectory which even the most strict reductionist materialist is hard pressed to deny in good faith.

Similarly, the idea that this teleological temporal trajectory is accelerating exponentially is difficult to contravene if one examines the evidence without prejudice, though as with the rejection of teleology, the scientistic belief in exclusively static, quantitative time precludes the possibility of perceiving this apparent fact of exponential development. Again, this blind spot in the deficient modern world view, a manifestation of partial world views creating partial worlds is, to some extent, the result of the particular circumstances of modernity's inception in reaction to the specific form of finalism asserted by the Christian Church for roughly the millennium stretching between the fall of the Roman Empire and the rise of science. Unless one's world view presupposes a denial of qualitative time, the apparent fact that each emergent stage of process over billions of years has occurred at successively shorter orders of temporal magnitude is a data set best described by an exponential mathematical model, not a linear one.

However, late modernity's myopia can perhaps be partially excused by the recognition that exponential progressions are nearly indistinguishable from linear progressions for the vast majority of their trajectory. The time required for the emergence of life out of nonlife, and for each emergent gradation of complex organismic process can most accurately be plotted on an exponential graph, which only takes a marked upward turn near its asymptotic end. Furthermore, the increase in technological efficacy, measured for instance in computational power, has doubled exponentially through a number of discrete paradigms since at least the late nineteenth century. This phenomenon has emerged out of human consciousness and appears to have succeeded biological evolution as the vanguard of novelty's ingression into materiality, along with the more intangible modes of connectivity and cognizance that accompany this emergence, particularly the incipient world view itself. The modern world view has generally denied the possibility of such a trajectory largely because of the historical contingency of its origin, whereas a genuine empiricism that does not categorically and unempirically deny the possibility of the exponential quality of time will quickly recognize it as a simple fact about the nature of being.

Finally, for a world view that accepts the supposition that novel stages of process have been emerging at an exponentially quickening pace, it is only reasonable to extrapolate the exponential curve to some kind of singularity, suggested by the part of an exponential graph where the line goes nearly vertical. Even if our current "arc of history" proves to be an S-curve (a progression that briefly explodes in a seemingly exponential way and then levels off) and not a truly exponential curve, it seems plausible to suppose that the S-curve of human history is one in a series of vast epochs that together trace a larger exponential trajectory, like the multiple paradigms of computing that have woven back and forth along a strikingly smooth exponential progression over the last century. Accepting the validity of the intermeshed concepts discussed in the preceding paragraphs seems to lead inexorably to the conclusion that we are currently in the knee of a curve that plots the increasing compaction of time. Considering that time is describable in relativistic physics as a fourth dimension, this recognition leads to the suspicion that the exponential densification of time has something to do with dimensionality. As a number of the theorists mentioned in these pages have suggested, what we experience as time may in fact be a fractal dimension, the fullness of which exceeds our current cognitive capacities to comprehend. If, as one prominent interpretation of relativity theory posits, time is mathematically no different than the three spatial dimensions, then there must be an explanation for why we have full freedom of movement in space but are apparently locked into a linear, sequential movement through temporality even though this "arrow of time" is not accounted for by our most advanced physical theories.

By way of analogy, imagine that you are falling down an apparently infinite tunnel or shaft and the most you can control your rate of descent is perhaps to spread yourself out and relax your body in order to make yourself go slower or to become narrow, focused, and rigid in order to move faster. You possess full range of movement back and forth or side to side, but in the up and down axis, you are moving unidirectionally at a relatively fixed speed. This is a two-dimensional analogue of normal three-dimensional spatial experience moving through time, with the inexorable pull into the future correlating with the force of gravity in the lower-dimensional analogy. However, if the direction of movement through the shaft in this analogy really is equivalent to the other two dimensions, then there must be a way to halt one's trajectory, or even to reverse this seemingly inexorable plunge and travel back along this lower analogue of the temporal dimension. That the "crossing" property of quantum field theory describes antiparticles as traveling backward in time appears to support the plausibility of this hypothesis.[31]

For a world view that denies a priori the qualitative, teleological, and exponential nature of time, the suggestion that the purpose of life is to serve as a medium for the ascension of process into the awareness of increasing degrees of dimensionality would seem absurd. However, a world view that allows these other premises might extrapolate from this trajectory that time and history constitute a process of the world awakening, through the human mind, from a three-dimensional slumber into a four-dimensional phase space in which time becomes something like another spatial dimension for our liberated exploration. This higher-dimensional manifold is incredibly difficult to visualize, not just because our minds have only evolved to conceive three full dimensions, but because the world view of the last few centuries has been predicated on the idea that time is a linear, neutral medium.

However, as many premodern modes of thought have intimated, there may be a literally higher-dimensional reality that we cognize in a limited form as time because we have not yet developed the capacity to understand what it would mean to perceive the fourth dimension in its fullness. If this hypothesis is true, we are like half-blind moles making our way through an underground tunnel, but as we near the surface, the light gets brighter and brighter until we emerge into the full revelatory daylight illumination. I do not claim to know what this emergence into an integral (describing an integer as opposed to a fraction) degree of fourth-dimensional freedom would look like, but I will suggest in the Epilogue that an archetypal cosmology is a primary method for understanding this logically deduced, but mind-bendingly strange domain of reality.

# CHAPTER 2
## "THE CIRCLE OF THE GIVEN"
### NOVELTY AND THE WILL TO BELIEVE

*What is not yet known those blinded by bad faith can never learn.*

Heraclitus[32]

*It is the essence of reasoning to shut us up in the circle of the given. But action breaks the circle. If we had never seen a man swim, we might say that swimming is an impossible thing, inasmuch as, to learn to swim, we must begin by holding ourselves up in the water and, consequently, already know how to swim. . . . So of our thought, when it has decided to make the leap. . . . You must take things by storm: you must thrust intelligence outside itself by an act of will.*

Henri Bergson, *Creative Evolution*[33]

The recognition that we must leap outside normative assumptions in order to produce a novel mode implies that we participate in the unfolding meaning of the world because this leap would be utterly futile if our premises did not in some sense elicit the world that we inhabit. We would be leaping into nothing for no reason. However, if one were to examine any of the cases mentioned above, such as the Copernican revolution, it is clear that, had the revolutionaries not spent years entertaining their radically new hypothesis in the face of the monolithic opposition of common sense, which found the idea of the vast Earth itself hurtling through the cosmos absurd, we would still live in a world in which, for all intents and purposes, the Sun revolved around the Earth, with all of the psychological, philosophical, and cosmological implications concomitant with that belief.

And the Copernican revolution is far from an isolated case, for no matter how many times we have undergone such ruptures in thought, the majority of individuals who make up the predominant streams of a culture initially resist change in their fundamental beliefs because such transformations are often painful, requiring a kind of egoic death and rebirth initiation, whether on the scale of an individual conversion or a collective revolution. We become attached to our beliefs, as it is extremely difficult to admit that one has lived one's whole life acting on inadequate assumptions. But the adhesive bandage must ultimately be ripped off and the veil lifted. The old way of life, which was the site of all one's past glories and strivings, of one's most intimate and most public occasions, of everything one has ever known, must be left behind to some degree in order for a new world view, and thus a new world, to be born.

And this leap into the unknown almost always takes the form of a dialectical synthesis, for implicit in the monolithic premises upon which orthodoxies are founded are those elements that are repressed in order to assert these premises. This inevitable emphasis of some aspects of reality over others indicates that premises are usually one pole of a duality, one side of a seemingly unresolvable controversy. If something is privileged, something else must be maligned. In order to produce a reconciliation of opposed beliefs, therefore, one must engage in an act of will to move beyond the seemingly fundamental premises that make the opposition appear irreconcilable. For instance, it has generally been supposed in modernity that one must either believe that the nonmaterial, spiritual world is primary, as was generally the case in premodernity, or that the world is simply a vast and inherently meaningless agglomeration of material particles. However, the integrative method invites one intentionally to adopt a new and deeper premise: that both of these views, roughly definable as idealism and materialism (often correlated to, but not always identical with, religion and science), are not mutually exclusive propositions, but partially true modes of thought applicable in their respective domains of validity. One can choose to emerge from a world in which one must decide between belief and skepticism into an apparently more fundamental truth: that both of these options are forms of belief, that we cannot escape belief, and that all modes of thought have pragmatic but limited value for the production of understanding and activity. The emerging mode itself is presumably not excluded from this limitation, though the awareness of this intrinsic epistemological limiting factor "yet makes all the difference."

The discontinuity of process, the idea that fundamental change often occurs in relatively sudden jumps, is a more abstract and general recognition of the particular kind of process that transpires when an individual or a collective willfully transcends the current order to produce a radically novel phase of its developmental process. In the domain of human consciousness, conceptual ruptures are predicated upon the leap of faith undertaken by revolutionary individuals. The recognition of this multivalent quantality has itself required numerous such leaps: in the collective bound taken with the discovery of quantum theory in physics, in the contemporaneous mutation theory of Hugo de Vries, a precursor of the idea of punctuated equilibrium in biological evolution, in the recognition of phase transitions in chemistry, in Erwin Schrödinger's explication of the connection between the mutation theory and the quantum theory, in Thomas Kuhn's disclosure of the structure of scientific revolutions, and in William James' exposition of conversion experiences. In all of these instances, the revolutionary individuals or groups courageously forged beyond the accepted beliefs of their times and their milieus to elucidate this discontinuous quality in different domains, from which one can, in turn, extrapolate the recognition that processes tend to evolve in sudden saltations that punctuate longer periods of linear development.

Furthermore, the pervasive relevance of this leap outside "the circle of the given" for the ingression of novelty suggests that qualitatively new stages of process progressively emerge through pioneers willfully pushing past the current orthodoxy, whatever it may be. For instance, the invention of language in human prehistory must have required a cognitive vault by a few individuals. For a preverbal humanity that would have communicated through relatively inarticulate sounds and gestures, the comparatively sudden creation of "small mouth noises"[34] corresponding to certain facts of existence would have been profoundly novel, surely meeting with resistance from the primal collective in its mediation of conceptual thought's emergence, which is only possible through language. And this initial invention of language formed a precondition for the further emergences of narrative, religion, politics, commerce, and technology. And these inventions were the preconditions for the further stages of history. Without the persistent belief of a few exceptionally inspired individuals, this development through emergent stages would not have taken place.

And if the emergence of qualitatively new world views has consistently taken place in the past mediated by the belief of a small group of individuals, then it is reasonable to extrapolate that a further transition of world views will likely occur, and that this epochal transition will be similarly initiated by the efforts of the brave few. Although in the modern West, one is not generally in danger of being burned at the stake for holding unconventional views, as was Giordano Bruno for asserting the "many worlds hypothesis," which is now broadly accepted in science, there are real dangers that accompany the publication of unorthodox thought.[35] For instance, while there are many well-funded and prestigious institutions for the study of physical sciences and, to a lesser extent, humanities and social sciences adhering to a generally scientific, materialist orientation, there are comparatively few institutions with relatively small endowments for the study of the kinds of concepts discussed in these pages. However, this situation seems to be changing rather quickly, which is a strong indication that our culture is in the midst of the relatively sudden emergence of a new world view, a further stage in the development of process.[36]

This quality of evolutionary development that requires a vault beyond the seemingly secure knowledge of a particular time is self-similar across scale, from the individual to various orders of collective magnitude, a situation which provides evidence for the fractal quality of process. Individual intention in the act of overcoming a habitual structure seems to be reiterated fractally in the transformation of the basic beliefs of a culture, as in both cases the entity that undergoes the conversion is initially divided, containing a polarized tension, which reaching a peak of intensity produces the necessity for the adoption of fundamentally new premises about the nature of reality. For instance, if an individual sees the validity in both materialist science and teleology, but the dominant cultural attitude demands that one must choose between these two systems of thought because of their supposed incommensurability, the will to believe in a broader perspective that perceives the partial validity of both views requires a leap for the individual from identifying with one side of the controversy to identifying with a mode of thought that comprehensively encompasses the duality.

Similarly, if a culture is divided into atheistic and reductionist materialists at one end of the spectrum, and fundamentalist religious creationists at the other end, it is the function of those who see the partial validity in both perspectives increasingly to produce an integration of the individual human cells of the emergent cultural organism by articulating a mode of thought in which these seeming incommensurabilities can be reconciled. In fact, the discovery of fractality itself by Benoit Mandelbrot required a spring of assent to promulgate a revolution in mathematics against the prevailing orthodoxy, which subsequently propagated in a fractal fashion through numerous other disciplines, from geophysics, chemistry, and physiology to meteorology, metallurgy, and economics.[37]

The acceptance of the idea of archetypes in the context of a reductionist materialist world view has also required a vigorous will to believe. Jung himself, the individual who perhaps more than any other has served to return something like the forms posited by Plato to a position of prominence in cultural discourse, was excommunicated from psychoanalysis by Freud after his Viennese mentor, the individual who most mediated the previous revolution in psychological thought, had named Jung his "dear son and successor."[38] Although Jung was ultimately successful in introducing his unconventional ideas into broad discourse through a half century of prolific work, the excommunication by Freud cast Jung into nearly a decade of isolation during which he underwent his "confrontation with the unconscious," an intensely difficult but extremely productive period outside the institutional structure of psychoanalysis in which he had previously enjoyed a central role.

Even given the ultimate success of Jung's overall project, though, there is still often a lingering prejudice in the main streams of academia against the idea of archetypes as implicit potentialities in the nature of being, as they have come to be understood by thinkers like James Hillman, Stanislav Grof, and Richard Tarnas, for this idea apparently contradicts the reductionist materialist assumptions that still implicitly inform much of the academy. However, this bias appears to be in the process of dissipating as increasing numbers of scholars are coming to the conclusion that the idea that there are potentialities for various kinds of meaning implicit in cosmic structure is not necessarily incompatible with scientific materialism. Rather, it appears that archetypes, which manifest through formal causation, have been so often maligned because of formal causation's connection with premodern modes of thought against which modern science has defined itself.

The belief in formal causation, the idea that each entity or moment exhibits a particular quality constituted in the multivalent expressions of archetypal complexes, requires a similar salvo to that required for the acceptance of the validity of archetypal thought to which formal causation is closely related. For modern mentality, in which the dominant mode of Newtonian physics has primarily perceived time as a static, quantitative medium for experimental repeatability, the idea that time itself has contours, that it is a kind of trans-spatial terrain, the immensely complex ebbs and flows of which deeply condition the quality of our constantly shifting experience, has been anathema. For a rationalist and materialist world view that often simplistically perceives our highly variable affective experience as mere "moods," the insight that careful attention to lived experience can reveal meaningful correspondences between materially unconnected events requires a radical assertion that one's intuition that events expressing similar archetypal qualities tend to group together in time reflects reality and is not the product of delusion.

This qualitative aspect of temporality is observable in our most intimate experience, as most of us have gone through periods when nothing seems to go right, when one loses one's job, breaks with one's romantic partner, one's phone calls and emails go unreturned, and the world seems a sad and difficult place. Similarly most of us have experienced periods when one can seem to do no wrong, when a profusion of opportunities comes one's way, when all feedback is positive, and the world seems wide open and full of possibility. And of course, we are most often immersed in periods in which both positive and negative events and emotions are complexly intermixed. But the point to notice is that life does seem to go through relatively distinct periods, both in the experience of the individual and of the collective, not only expressed in the simple binary of negative and positive employed here for illustration, but in subtle and constantly shifting shades of multilayered meaning. And this recognition requires willful credence because it directly contradicts the stubborn myopia characteristic of the exclusive privileging of reductionist materialism in preeminent sectors of modern culture, which systematically entrains us, through nearly pervasive cultural rationalization, to deny the evidence of our own embodied experience.

The acceptance that there is an intrinsic impulse in the nature of process toward novelty and consciousness is also a belief that requires a leap of faith in the context of a modernity that has limited the construction of its entire world view to the material and efficient causal modes, excluding final as well as formal causation. But again, the evidence seems to demand such a leap, for despite the rejection of teleology by science in reaction to the particular form of apocalyptic eschatology asserted by medieval Christianity, there does in fact seem to be an undeniable trajectory in the nature of things toward the emergence of novel entities leading to ever more comprehensive forms of consciousness. However, concepts that appear self-evident to one mode of thought are often occluded by the more limited and limiting assumptions of the previous mode. The Copernican revolutionaries faced great resistance from the Church and from late medieval academics because the idea that the Earth revolves around the Sun and not vice versa contradicts the fundamental assumption of medieval cosmology that God created the Earth as the cosmic center. This was an idea that had been considered self-evident common sense for many generations, so it required a courageous and extremely risky gambit to assert the heliocentric cosmology, though this cosmological order now seems obvious to us.

Similarly, the idea that the evolution of the world can be explained purely as the interaction of material particles became a fundamental tenet of the modern world view after the progressive expunction of teleological modes of thought through the lineage of Bacon, Descartes, Newton, and Darwin. We have finally stripped any trace of explicit finalism from the practice of science, but just at this moment of the apparent triumph of disenchantment characteristic of late modernity, final causation appears to be returning with a vengeance to correct the imbalances that the dominant exclusive materialist world view has wrought. This epochal return of the repressed has been enacted by relatively few daring individuals in numerous disciplines who have chosen to desist in denying the evidence of their own bodily experience and the cosmic record in subservience to the centuries-long reactionary repression of teleology.

A further leap of faith must be undertaken to affirm the apparently exponential quality of this teleological process, though this leap is not necessary based on the evidence alone, which clearly reveals the accelerating compaction of novelty over vast spans of time when simply plotted on a graph. Rather, the leap is necessary, again, in the context of a mode of thought that has systematically denied the possibility of any directionality in the evolution of process, which is a precondition for the exponential quality of that trajectory. Although the exponential ingression of novelty appears to be simply self-evident based on the accelerating pace of the data points that mark the emergence of radical novelty over the course of cosmic history, this view is perhaps even more controversial than the idea of teleology because finalism is an ancient concept that has been instantiated in each new stage of emergence, whereas an exponential progression appears linear until near the very end of its trajectory when it starts to curve ever more steeply upward. While teleology, though it has been widely rejected in modernity due to its historical connotations (and ultimately in the service of intellectual individuation), is basically an intuitive quality of process, the exponential acceleration of that teleological movement is not intuitive based on immediately available past precedent. So the exponential quality of reality requires one of the most profound credential leaps of any of the concepts elucidated in these pages, as it not only contravenes the conventional wisdom of our era, but also our subjective knowledge extrapolated from past experience. But it seems that our task is to forge a new, more expansive form of common sense that encompasses this broader swath of reality, which is beginning to reveal itself out of modernity's demise.

Finally, the idea that this exponential compaction of novelty is leading toward an emergence into the perception of a higher, mathematically describable dimension is perhaps an even more difficult idea for the modern mind to accept than exponentiality, to the point that such a belief is often caricatured in popular media as one of the wilder and more absurd fancies of the psychedelic counterculture. However, yet again, if one examines the trajectory that the evolution of life seems to have followed thus far through ascending degrees of spatio-temporal freedom, it is simple induction to infer that this trend will most likely continue. That such an ascendance into a new degree of freedom has only occurred three times in the whole history of life on Earth, and that it has never yet occurred in collective human experience renders this supposition rather difficult to accept based on recent historical precedent, though if one's lens is widened to the evolution of life in general, it seems equally difficult to confute. Of course, it is impossible to know when this suspected emergence into the full degree of temporal freedom may occur. Indeed, the very idea of coming into full cognizance of this dimension renders the question of timing rather paradoxical. Will there be a time when time becomes transparent and we are liberated into the full experience of a fourth degree of freedom qualitatively similar to the three spatial dimensions that we now perceive? Only time will tell, but it seems that the sole way to bring about such a temporic concretion is to set one's intention toward this emergence in order to assist in its becoming. There is no scientific experiment that can prove this notion, as according to this hypothesis, human history and life itself are a vast cosmic experiment still progressing toward an uncertain conclusion.

# CHAPTER 3
# "THE RECONCILING THIRD"
## AN INTEGRATIVE METHOD

*All students of man and society who possess that first requisite for so difficult a study, a due sense of its difficulties, are aware that the besetting danger is not so much of embracing falsehood for truth, as of mistaking part of the truth for the whole. It might be plausibly maintained that in almost every one of the leading controversies, past or present, in social philosophy, both sides were in the right in what they affirmed, though wrong in what they denied; and that if either could have been made to take the other's views in addition to its own, little more would have been needed to make its doctrine correct.*

John Stuart Mill, *Coleridge*[39]

*We are crucified between the opposites and delivered up to the torture until the "reconciling third" takes shape. Do not doubt the rightness of the two sides within you, and let whatever may happen, happen. The apparently unendurable conflict is proof of the rightness of your life.*

C.G. Jung, *Letter to Frau Frobe*[40]

The integrative method implies the participatory quality of process because, if neither pole of any duality can lay claim to ultimate and complete truth, then the way one chooses to relate to each duality, whether consciously or unconsciously, is a fundamental premise that defines one's participatory enactment of the world's meaning. For instance, if one gives precedence to a view which asserts either that the world is composed solely of inanimate, mechanistic matter or of living, conscious intentionality, one must deny the opposite view. However, if one decides to believe that both of these views, roughly the materialist and the idealist, express partial truths, that each has heuristic value for illuminating certain domains of process and not others, then one lives in a world in which every point of view with some value for lived experience is available for employment, which vastly expands the possibilities for action and understanding.

Even the fundamentally oppositional modes of thought which claim exclusive knowledge of the truth against some repressed other, whether that exclusivism comes in the guise of religion, science, or some other mode, can be seen as constituting necessary stages that process must pass through, both at the individual and the collective orders of magnitude. It seems that one cannot come to the recognition, sooner or later, that one does not possess ultimate truth until one has inhabited this relatively naïve absolutist veil of illusion for at least a short time, exemplified in the "know-it-all" stage that young children pass through. Similarly, the novel mode of thought could not be in the process of emerging without the successive certainties of medieval Christianity and modern science having persisted in the West through centuries of tension, in many compromise formations, and in many domains of material manifestation and cultural discourse. The pragmatic, dialectical method that seeks to integrate opposed modes has been enacted through the long historical process to produce a recognition of the mutability of world views, an insight which now seems to be emerging into broad cultural awareness.

Furthermore, it requires a leap of faith to release one's attachment to a deeply held oppositional belief in order to allow that the belief held by one's opponent may in fact be viable. For instance, both the atheist and the devout religious believer might come to recognize that there is no conclusive evidence to prove the rightness of their respective beliefs, so even if they choose to maintain those assumptions, they will have entered the emerging mode when they hold their beliefs lightly, admitting that they have chosen their premises because they feel right to them based on the available evidence and their intrinsic inclinations. This mode is not a solipsistic relativism, which is a descriptor generally reserved for the developmentally previous postmodern mode, but an acknowledgment that one is always acting on incomplete assumptions, an insight that Socrates articulated near the dawn of the philosophical enterprise when he said "I know one thing: that I know nothing."[41] In such a relation to oppositions, while one's specific belief may not change, the frame for that belief is fundamentally altered so that one relinquishes the certainty of defining oneself against the other in favor of a broader embrace, which can be both liberating and terrifying until one becomes accustomed to this more expansive mode of thought. Rather than give one's primary attention to one's belief on one side of a controversy, such as the primacy of matter against the primacy of spirit, or vice versa, one transfers one's allegiance to the attempt to reconcile this opposition. The world is largely what we make of it, within constraints, but this power demands responsibility, requiring one to recognize that one chooses one's world view and, thus, to a great extent, that one chooses one's world.

And this leap to the emerging mode of thought is an additional piece of phenomenological evidence for the discontinuous quality of process. The decisive moment of revelatory conversion, whether in an individual or a collective, and whether over the course of a second or a century, is a moment of discontinuity between two ways of being in the world. Where before one found an enemy, one may now see a partner in dialogue. Where before the world was constructed as "us" against "them," there is now only us, and we see the temporary validity of those who seek to oppose themselves to us because we once thought as they do, because our culture and our very being were forged through such an oppositional attitude. For instance, the extreme difficulty in mathematically and conceptually translating between relativity theory and quantum theory in physics seems to be leading not toward the victory of one theory over the other, but toward their eventual reconciliation in an even more expansive theory, one concrete example of many in which the leap from one mode to another is constituted in a dialectical synthesis. And in an apparently fractal operation, the philosophical idea that opposed points of view generally exhibit partial validity seems to correspond to the mathematically precise principle of relativity (though the integrative method is not relativism as it is commonly understood), while the philosophical idea that there is discontinuity on many levels of process appears to be a multivalent reiteration of quantum theory's specific insight into the discrete behavior of subatomic particles. These two philosophical principles appear complementary in precisely the same way as the physical theories they closely mirror.

Whenever a dialectical integration of apparently incommensurable opposites occurs, the emergence of a novel phase of some process is generally mediated. Although development can take a vast number of specific forms in many different domains, it seems that processes, whether at the level of a subatomic particle, of an individual organism, or of a culture, tend to evolve through a series of stages whose potentiality for ingression is endemic to the cosmic structure. The development of species from chemical potential through varying degrees of perception and freedom of movement to their fully realized form (at least as they currently exist) mirrors the development of individuals, so that a species evolves through stages that fractally resemble fertility, infancy, childhood, adolescence, and maturity. Similarly, the evolution of species reiterates the parallel development of cultures from the archaic through the magic, mythical, and mental modes, and now perhaps the emerging mode.

The vanguard of cultural development in the West since the time of the ancient Greeks and Hebrews, but especially in the last five centuries or so, has been the mode which privileges humanity's rational, intellectual capacities, so that the majority of people have been struggling to emerge from the mythical mode of prerational belief into the mental stage even in adulthood. The center of gravity of collective world consciousness seems to have been rapidly shifting between these two phases over the last few decades in particular, one primary metric of which is the dramatic diminution of illiteracy in the world, which has essentially been reduced by half in the last forty years, from roughly 40% in the 1960s to roughly 20% in the first decade of the twenty-first century.[42] It appears to be no mere coincidence that modernity emerged during the same period as the invention of the moveable type printing press, as widespread literacy seems to be a primary indication of a culture's achievement of mentality.

We appear to be in the midst of a phase transition so that the majority of people in the world will soon primarily inhabit the rational, mental stage of development, if this tipping point has not already occurred. It seems that mentality is on the cusp of no longer being the vanguard of the evolution of consciousness, but rather the norm. Whereas prior to this epochal shift we are currently witnessing, the emerging mode was only pursued by a few exceptional individuals, relatively enlightened contemplatives, artists, philosophers, and visionaries, it seems that the collective attention of the world is rapidly beginning to reorganize around a center of gravity that seeks to develop a new mode of consciousness with integration as its primary method.

As discerned in numerous contexts, that the dialectic occurs on many orders of magnitude is evidence for the fractal quality of process. From molecules combining to create an organelle with qualitatively novel properties, to the integration of two genetic lineages in the process of sexual reproduction leading to the emergence of a child, to the synthesis of blues, country, jazz, and gospel in the creation of rock and roll, to the reconciliation of materialism and idealism, the integrative method takes two or more previously incommensurable entities and, by holding them in often tense relation produces a novel, separate entity out of preexisting elements. Benoit Mandelbrot's invention of the very idea of fractal geometry was constituted in just such a synthesis of mathematics, economics, physics, and engineering to produce a mode of thought that existed in potentia, but that had not yet been articulated in actuality until confluent circumstances, including Mandelbrot's inspired insight, produced fractality's discovery. Not only does the fact that integrations occur on many orders of magnitude prolifically demonstrate the fractal nature of reality, but the fact that the discovery of fractals was the result of a reconciliation is one instance demonstrating that this intrinsically dialectical quality of reality is a precondition for the emergence of novelty in all its forms.

Furthermore, that fractality was waiting in potentiality to be discovered through the integration of previously incommensurable entities is one indication that the dialectical quality of being is a means through which formal potentialities emerge into actuality. Archetypes only have meaning in the world because they are expressed through a process of becoming, and the dynamics of this process are only now emerging into collective awareness through the explication of the integrative method that has been occurring particularly in the last few centuries. And in fact, the integrative method itself appears to be an expression of an archetypal potentiality exemplified, for instance, in the Greek goddess Eris' Golden Apple of Discord, the source of controversy between Hera, Aphrodite, and Athena that resulted in the Trojan War and, thus, the two foundational Homeric epics of Hellenic Culture, the *Iliad* and the *Odyssey*. As has often been noted, these two epics, along with the Hebrew Bible, which it may be recalled also contains a similar origin story concerning controversial fruit from the Tree of Knowledge, are the initiatory texts of the modern West's self-conception.[43] The recognition that strife issuing into reconciliation is not only the process through which such archetypes manifest, but is itself the expression of an archetypal potentiality provides dual avenues of entry into the archetypal mode of cognizance. All things are evidently particular expressions of potentialities implicit in the nature of being, including the evolving understanding of archetypes and their dialectical mode of ingression into actuality.

That the process of integration must pass through qualitatively various temporal moments in the coming of archetypes to fruition is a demonstration of time's qualitative nature. The successive durations that constitute the dialectic all express and embody radically different characters, from the revelatory birth of the original emergent entity, itself the result of a dialectical process; through the long development of that initial epiphany into an established, concrete orthodoxy; the complementary reaction to that initial movement into its opposite; the controversial tension between the two elements of the polarity; and finally the synthesis of the polarity in a new emergence. For instance, the temporal quality that attended the initial creation of science in the discoveries and inventions of Copernicus, Galileo, Kepler, Bacon, and Newton was largely one of liberated exploration in uncharted realms faced by great resistance from the conventional institutional hierarchies and modes of thought characteristic of medieval Scholasticism. From those tenuous beginnings, the ascendancy of science continued relatively unabated through the early twentieth century (despite the romantic and idealist reactions of the nineteenth century) in the discoveries of relativity and quantum theory, until perhaps the dropping of the atomic bomb in 1945, which starkly embodied the dangers of a purely rationalist scientific mentality. This epochal event seems to have both symbolized and impelled the swinging of the pendulum away from the exclusivist privileging of intellect (a process which was already underway in jazz, and in modernist painting, dance, and literature) and back toward an embrace by mind of the intuitive, bodily, affective knowledge predominant in premodernity, an "archaic revival"[44] which perhaps found its most prominent expression in the rise of the "counterculture" in the mid-twentieth century. However, far from halting the progress of science to which it was a counterbalance, this corrective movement has begun to open up rich and profound areas of research, ultimately freeing the unmatched precision of scientific inquiry from the dogmatic exclusivity of scientism, though this liberation is still in its nascence.

The often antagonistic relationship between science and religion, and implicitly between intellect and intuition, has been one of the primary concerns of modern, Western cultural discourse. And the quality of our current moment appears to be one in which a kind of temporary stalemate has been reached between these two seemingly incommensurable poles, evident in the dichotomy of atheistic scientism and religious fundamentalism, though this polarization seems inexorably to be impelling the reconciliation of the impulses exemplified in these relational modes. This integration is partially constituted in the turning of the analytical mind developed largely through science toward understanding the qualitative nature of time as witnessed in the phenomenon of synchronicity, a modern inflection of formal causation. Whereas previously, science rejected qualitative time ultimately as a means of individuating the human intellect from other modes, now that this critical capacity has been developed to a high degree in certain sectors of society, the rational mind appears dialectically to be reembracing the concept of qualitative duration rather than denying the kinds of radical empiricism characteristic of rationality's historical enemies: religion, mysticism, yoga, meditation, alchemy, ecstatic spiritual practice, and so on. The vanguards of both materialist and idealist thought appear to be taking "the other's views in addition to [their] own," to reframe John Stuart Mill's words, enacting the return of formal causation through an integrative method.

This dialectical process is also a mode of novelty's teleological ingression into actuality, as previously incommensurable entities, whether organisms or ideas, have generally only produced a genuinely new entity through their reconciliation. From a purely materialist perspective, nothing really new can be extant because energy can neither be created nor destroyed. However, energy, and thus matter, have periodically been combined in novel ways over the course of cosmic evolution to produce qualitatively new structures and modes of organization for the temporal becoming of process. If one artificially limits one's purview to reductionist materialism, then one will find exactly what one believes it is possible to find: material particles interacting without meaning. However, if one admits that the phenomena of life, consciousness, and culture cannot be adequately explained by materialist science alone, one must acknowledge that, based on the available evidence, there does in fact appear to be a teleological trajectory toward emergent stages of organismic organization built into the cosmic structure. The controversy between materialism and idealism can be resolved by the application of an integrative method, which finds partial truth, definable as explanatory coherence, in both the material-efficient causation characteristic of science and the formal-final causation characteristic of those modes of thought which exceed the appropriate scope of scientific inquiry as it is has generally been conceived. However, this application of the integrative method leads to the conclusion that science itself should perhaps be expanded to posit a previously occluded complementary force to entropic disorder: the syntropic, teleological impulse toward novelty, consciousness, and order, particularly in the loci of the human mind and human technology.

By extension, this application of the integrative method to the evidence of cosmic evolution seems to indicate not only that there is directionality endemic to the nature of things, but that this teleological process is accelerating at an exponential rate. In the abstract, it makes perfect sense that process would be accelerating because the more dialectical integrations that occur, the more likely are new integrations to occur. Examining this largely qualitative process using the useful tools of quantitative, probabilistic analysis, if we assume a closed system of many entities in which only a few dialectical syntheses have occurred, it may require a very long time for a novel synthetic emergence to take place, which seems an accurate description of the state of the early universe, or of the early development of life. However, once the system has produced many syntheses, as has our highly complex culture over the course of human history, these loci for the ingression of radical novelty will compound upon one another exponentially, creating a cascade effect. If there are millions or billions of nodes of novelty as opposed to just a few, there will simply be many more opportunities for the polarization and subsequent reconciliation of such opposed entities. Expressed more concretely, a world with billions of people constantly interacting across continents and cultures through the nearly instantaneous technological network of the internet is much more likely to produce radically new ideas, inventions, and events than an undifferentiated primordial ooze. Like the analogy of doubling the grains of rice on a chess board so that the first few doublings (2, 4, 8, 16) demonstrate relatively slow progress, but by the sixty-fourth and final square, one has more than eighteen *quintillion* total grains (18,446,744,073,709,551,615 to be precise), the dialectical "doubling" enacted by the integrative method appears to mediate an exponential process.

Similarly, this exponential teleological process, enacted through the dialectical dynamic, seems to impel an increasing dimensional ingression at the largest order of magnitude that we can viably conceive. In the grandest fractal reiteration of the development of process through successive degrees of emergence, the cosmos itself, at least the corner that we inhabit, appears to be undergoing such a development through emergent degrees of freedom, from the one-dimensionality of the first organisms to the three-and-a-fraction dimensionality characteristic of the human experience of spacetime. If one sets aside one's usual presuppositions about the nature of being in the world based on the relatively short span of human history on a cosmological scale, and impartially examines the evidence, the conclusion of temporic concretion will appear difficult to confute. That life has developed into the perception of three spatial dimensions and that our most advanced physical understanding mathematically describes time as a fourth dimension suggests that this meta-trajectory will most likely continue.

Foregoing our normative understanding of time as a linear, unidirectional medium, an assumption not provable by the laws of physics, and instead thinking of temporality as a kind of jerry-rigged method to map a fourth dimension, it seems plausible to suggest that the emergence of time from animal timelessness, and thus human consciousness from animal unconsciousness, is a cosmic controversy that fundamentally informs our historical experience. The human intuition of divinity is that which is eternal, while many traditions have envisioned time as a fallen world, a veil of illusion to be overcome. And the evidence for the concretion of time suggests that these intuitions have not been merely fanciful wish-fulfillment, as often supposed in modernity, but are rather intimations of a mathematically describable higher-dimensional phase space that exists in potentia in the nature of being, but which we must bring into actuality by means of a dialectical process. In this conception, the integrative method is something like an engine for the teleological ingression of novelty, propelling the cosmos, through us, into the full perception of a more expansive manifold that lies waiting behind our eyes and in each particle in the universe.

# CHAPTER 4
## "JUMPS OF ALL SORTS"
### THE DISCONTINUITY OF PROCESS

*In every domain, when anything exceeds a certain measurement, it suddenly changes its aspect, condition or nature. The curve doubles back, the surface contracts to a point, the solid disintegrates, the liquid boils, the germ cell divides, intuition suddenly bursts on the piled up facts . . . Critical points have been reached, rungs on the ladder, involving a change of state— jumps of all sorts in the course of development.*

Pierre Teilhard de Chardin, *The Phenomenon of Man*[45]

*The great revelation of quantum theory was that features of discreteness were discovered in the Book of Nature, in a context in which anything other than continuity seemed to be absurd according to the views held until then. . . . The transition from one state to another is a rather mysterious event, which is usually called a "quantum jump." . . . The molecule will of necessity have a certain stability; the configuration cannot change, unless at least the energy difference, necessary to "lift" it to the next higher level, is supplied from outside. . . . It will be observed how intimately this fact is linked with the very basis of quantum theory.*

Erwin Schrödinger, *What Is Life?*[46]

The recognition that temporal process is punctuated by discrete jumps provides evidence for the insight that our premises condition the world we experience. In the domains of individual or collective psychology, if we change our beliefs, whether intentionally or impelled by the witnessing of new evidence, the world can appear suddenly and radically different to us, even though there may have been no measurable material change. The very acceptance of the discontinuous nature of process is a premise with the capacity to reconfigure one's relation to the world. If one believes that nothing ever really fundamentally transforms, that all change is merely slow, quantitative growth, diminution, or aimless drift, then this will be one's experience, perhaps until one is forced by a radical external change to recognize the quantum quality of process. However, once one has accepted the reality of this quality across scale, it seems that such transformations are much more likely to occur in one's subjective experience, and by extension in the cultural and political domains, because our assumptions partially create the conditions through which novelty is either enabled or suppressed. Once one acknowledges the validity of this discontinuous mode of thought, one perceives a layer of reality that had previously been obscure, the acceptance of the quantum perspective generalized to processes at many scales acting as a precondition for the capacity to perceive the discontinuous aspects of the world. Whereas before that world may have seemed a place of fundamentally stable continuity, now one becomes aware of the successive ruptures that punctuate normative experience.

Sudden psychological transformations often require the conscious choice to adopt a new belief, but even in cases where such ruptures seem to exceed conscious volition, something in the nature of process, perhaps one's personal unconscious, or perhaps something that transcends individuality, impels one to undertake a credential leap into a new mode of being. And collective shifts of conviction, exemplified in scientific revolutions or in the relatively abrupt transitions between world views, occur when a critical mass of the individuals who form a collective personally undergo the definitive bound into a novel relational mode. The discontinuous nature of process is a precondition for the leap of faith.

Certainly, an implicit recognition of the discrete quality of being is necessary if one is to be capable of embracing any new premise, but especially significant in this case is the often intentional character of the decision to admit that processes evolve in discrete ways. The very fact of discontinuity is a precondition for the will to believe in that particular phenomenon. And once one has accepted the generalized quantum premise, it becomes reasonable to conclude that just as revolutions in thought have occurred in the past, they are likely to occur again in the future, which can grant one courage to cross a threshold of belief. This orientation is inherently progressive, aside from one's political identification, as opposed to the more conservative mode which interprets the flow of time as an essentially stable continuity. The conservative temporal mode, even among political liberals, usually celebrates the novel achievements of the past while effectively repressing successive novelty, an attitude especially prevalent in academia. In contrast, once one has taken the leap to accept the inevitability of radical transformations, this attitude will tend to produce such transformations more consistently and successfully in one's experience.

Furthermore, this discontinuous quality of process is a precondition for the integrative method, which through the dialectical synthesis of opposed beliefs or apparently incommensurable entities produces the relatively sudden emergence of novel modes. As one may have noticed, it is often difficult to keep the concepts explicated in these pages from spilling into the discussion of other concepts. Although this difficulty complicates the articulation of these ideas, it also demonstrates how deeply intertwined these concepts are with one another to the point that one might benefit from conceiving of them as a single network of semiotic relations with roughly a dozen nodes rather than as truly separate concepts. Nevertheless, the attempt to express these ideas as a coherent system is itself an enactment of the integrative method, which seeks to synthesize concepts that previously appeared unconnected. Although it may seem apparent that the Hegelian dialectic, Jamesian pragmatism, Jungian archetypes, and Mandelbrot's fractals are all implicitly complementary modes of thought, it is not until their complementarity is articulated in its specificity, a project to which this text seeks to contribute, that the forward step is undertaken and the novel mode achieved. Although many thinkers have expressed various aspects of this emerging mode of thought, it seems that we will not witness the widespread emergence of a new world view until the kinds of insights extrapolated from the permeable pantheon of theorists constellated in this work are rendered commonsensical in the educated sectors of our culture. If we can judge by history, we will most likely reach a tipping point during which this novel mode synthesizing many disparate elements becomes pervasive in discourse over a relatively brief period. In fact, this tipping point may already be underway. Integration is itself a discontinuous phenomenon.

The developmental process of successive emergences that leads to a novel world view, whether in the individual or collective domains, is similarly predicated upon the discontinuous quality of being. It has been necessary for human culture to pass through something like the archaic, magic, mythical, and mental stages of cultural evolution in order to reach the understanding that processes in general tend to transform discontinuously. And conversely, this discrete quality of change allows the ruptures to occur that mediate the transitions between these world views. Similarly, in the experience of an individual, one must pass through these stages to reach, and perhaps even to exceed, the center of gravity of a culture's consciousness. Whereas in archaic cultures, mature people generally inhabited the archaic mode of thought, and in magic cultures, mature people generally inhabited the magic mode of thought, in a culture in which the novel world view predominates, the archaic, magic, mythical, and mental phases of development would generally be passed through on the way to full adulthood.

Even when children are simply undergoing the typical education of their culture, the emergence into each successive stage of consciousness is generally experienced as a relatively abrupt, qualitative leap into a radically expanded world. For instance, in our current cultural context in the West, one may believe as a child in the literal truth of the Bible, apparently an exemplification of the mythical mode of thought, but then one may have an experience or read a book that convinces one, perhaps sometimes even against one's will, that heaven and hell, God and Satan, redemption and sin can be understood as metaphors for natural, physiological, and psychological processes. Once the seed of skepticism is sown, even if one at first resists its gestation, one has definitively entered into the mental mode of consciousness. Similarly, when one begins to suspect that rational thought, science, and intellect are not the only valid ways of understanding the world, then one has entered nascently into the emerging mode.

But in order fully to emerge into the novel mode, it seems that one must release one's attachment to mentality, not in a permanent loss of mind, but merely in the interest of breaking oneself of the addiction to rational thought so characteristic of the modern era. Although this transition can take place in many different ways and at many different paces, in a violent or a gentle awakening, the shift from one mode to another is qualitatively similar to the discontinuous leap from dreaming to waking consciousness. However, the transition from the mental mode to the emerging one may not be as pronounced as this analogy implies, as dreams seem to embody the archaic, or occasionally the magic, mode of awareness, while we in the modern West generally awake from sleep not to the immediately subsequent magic or mythical mode, but to the further mode in which our consciousness has stabilized. The longing for the premodern is evident in the whole thrust of the twentieth century, from the volcanic eruption of destructive irrationality in the world wars to the more positive "return to the Garden" ethos characteristic of the sixties counterculture, particularly in the somatic and spiritual orientation of popular music, art, dance, and cinema, in the bodily attention produced by psychedelics and contemplative practices, and in the reembrace of premodern values and modes of thought characteristic of the "archaic revival." Philosophy of the kind found in the present work appears to be an enactment of the emerging mode becoming self-conscious, coherent, and systematic. However, the leap into the novel world view is not primarily a philosophical one, but a phenomenon that permeates all areas of experience, from sexuality, gender, race, class, nationality, and other elements of identity, to health, politics, commerce, education, and art. It may be difficult to see this transformation clearly when we are in the midst of such a fundamental rupture in human experience, but it seems to be a primary task of philosophers to articulate what this profound cultural and psychological change means for those of us who care to think about such things.

The discontinuous quality of process is evident on many orders of magnitude, which implies the fractal quality of process. When it is recognized that discontinuity occurs not only in physics, but in the domains accessible to chemistry, biology, psychology, and sociology, this recognition demonstrates that being is self-similar across scale, that the same kinds of movements recur at micro and macro orders of magnitude, over brief instants and over vast spans of cosmic time, in the most simple and in the most complex systems. For one especially apropos instance, the discovery of fractals themselves by Mandelbrot was a moment of discontinuity with the past: first fractals did not exist for the collective and then they did, and this discovery soon transformed many different disciplines. But it is also striking that a number of physicists, particularly Laurent Nottale, have suggested that fractal geometry may provide a key to the integration of quantum theory and relativity, especially considering that the special and general theories of relativity both required new geometries, those of Minkowski and Riemann respectively. It seems clear that discontinuity and fractality are deeply interconnected qualities of being. Indeed, the bifurcations found in fractal theory are apparently mathematical descriptions of discontinuity across scale.[47]

The discontinuous quality of reality also provides evidence for the assertion that there are archetypal potentialities for meaning and form implicit in the nature of being because the "quantum leap" is itself a primary expression of one such archetypal potentiality. In ancient Greek mythology, for instance, the figure of Prometheus is associated with sudden, unexpected discoveries and inventions as well as breaks and ruptures, the theft of fire from the gods his primary motif. Not only do the many expressions of the discontinuous quality of process confirm that there is a potentiality for this quality prior to the individuality of such phenomena, but the fact that various inflections of this archetypal impulse are affirmed in a large proportion of premodern cultures as a manifestation of the trickster archetype (e.g. coyote and raven in Native American mythologies, Anansi and Loki in West African and Norse mythologies, Odysseus in the Homeric epic of ancient Greece, Sinbad in Arabian mythology, leprechauns in Irish folklore, the figure of the court jester in medieval European culture, Shakespeare's Puck, and Brer Rabbit in African American culture) suggests that people in widely dispersed geographical areas were able intuitively to extrapolate this quality of reality from their experience. Furthermore, the discovery, or rediscovery, of the archetypes by Jung in the early twentieth century is an instance of the discontinuous jumps through which such profound disclosures are mediated, first in the discoverer, and then in those individuals who are converted to this way of thinking, and finally in the collective revolution of thought that such discoveries partially impel. It is suggestive that the discontinuously novel emergence of both the quantum theory and the modern formulation of archetypes occurred in the first few decades of the twentieth century, and that Jung closely collaborated with Wolfgang Pauli, one of the fathers of the quantum theory, both of which facts seem to intimate a profound implication of these two concepts.

The temporal coincidence of the emergences of the archetypal and quantum perspectives appears to be one instance of the qualitative nature of temporality, for although the two ideas were initially unconnected, their synchronic discovery and elaboration both seem to have been expressions of the quality of that era, constituted in the early emergence of prominent aspects of the novel impulse. However, this particular historical instance aside, the fact that temporal dynamics can be described as periods of steady, linear development punctuated by radical ruptures is perhaps the most direct and clear substantiation of the qualitative interpretation of time, as the periods of normative development express a quality diametrically opposed to the moments of transformative discontinuity.

Although Henri Bergson's concept of duration in *Creative Evolution* (1907) did a great deal to bring the qualitative nature of time into modern discourse, it is again Jung who is most associated with the modern elucidation of qualitative temporality in the concept of synchronicity, which was first proposed by him in the nineteen twenties. The concept subsequently received a more thorough exposition in the book *Synchronicity: An Acausal Connecting Principle* (originally published along with a monograph from Pauli under the title *The*

*Interpretation of Nature and the Psyche*) in 1952, and had become an immensely influential concept by the nineteen sixties. That a philosophical rupture concerned with qualitative time occurred in the twentieth century, after several centuries of an increasingly narrow focus on quantitative, measurable time in the dominant streams of Western discourse, provides evidence for the discontinuous quality of process. And this fact recursively illustrates the discretely transformative character of the period during which the concept of qualitative time was rediscovered by the modern mind. The two concepts, qualitative temporality and discontinuity, are so deeply intertwined that it is difficult to disentangle their causal association, as their relation is mutually confirming. Finally, the nonlocal quality of particles described by quantum theory, the synchronic entanglement of two apparently materially unconnected entities, provides a possible point of entry for the scientific confirmation of synchronicity, which is also describable as the synchronic correlation of two materially unconnected entities.

Discontinuous moments of processual development also mediate the teleological ingression of novelty into actuality, providing an indispensable apparatus for the temporal trajectory toward increasing degrees of consciousness. Although the successive emergences of novelty and consciousness do appear to trace a rather smooth curve when plotted over long periods of time, each instance of novelty's ingression appears to take the form of a relatively brief and discrete rupture. The emergence of life out of matter, of animality out of bacterial protoconsciousness, of human self-awareness out of the animal dream, and the successive emergences of world views in human history, each a profound shift and disruption of a seemingly stable continuity, have traced the stuff of the world's becoming through the evolution of vital containers for increasingly expansive modes of activity. For instance, James, Bergson, and Whitehead all broke precipitously with the Darwinian scientific orthodoxy of the late nineteenth and early twentieth centuries, which had endeavored to purge evolutionary theory of the idea of directionality, though all three are ultimately indebted to Darwin's epochal clarity of thought. Rather than merely reverting to a premodern version of apocalyptic finalism in their pioneering collective revolt against established opinion, these thinkers, along with many others, performed a dialectical reembrace of teleological cognizance by the individuated intellect, liberating finalism from its premodern impedimentia in a process that synthesized the successive eruptions of novel ideation to produce further novelty.

And if one places these moments of rupture on a timeline, one discovers that there is not only directionality in the process, but that this vector is markedly accelerating. Discontinuity is a precondition for exponentiality, each instance of processual self-overcoming tracing a familiar curve through the many vicissitudes, regressions, diversions, and periods of stasis, sweeping breathlessly upward in increasingly rapid creative advance. In this accelerating process, the old paradigm is always reframed within the more encompassing embrace of the emergent mode, so that single-celled organisms are made of matter, but they exceed the order of magnitude of mere matter's organized activity. Likewise, multicellular organisms are composed of cells, but they exhibit new capacities previously unsuspected, for as novelty compounds upon novelty, the process moves ever more quickly, the cells splitting exponentially until a critical mass is reached and the agglomeration of separate cells self-organizes to meet the crisis of exploding cell population. Without these discontinuous ruptures with the past's stable continuity, novelty would not emerge and, thus, would not aggregate exponentially.

Finally, on the widest currently conceivable scale of cosmic evolution, the exponential, teleological progression embodied in successive discontinuous ruptures traces a vast movement that has previously undergone three leaps into new degrees of freedom. According to the hypothesis of temporic concretion, temporality, the fall from the eternal, Edenic garden of animal consciousness into time and history, itself constitutes the incipience of a relatively abrupt passage into the full texture of fourth-dimensional awareness, which lies in wait in potentiality, but which, as far as we know, remains unrealized. That is, in the only self-consciousness of which we are certain, human self-consciousness, this additional degree of freedom has apparently been intimating itself as the mysteries of ages: as spirits, and gods, and natural laws, and every other vision of transcendent reality imagined and concretized in religions, philosophies, and sciences. It seems clear that the higher or deeper state of knowledge and illumination toward which humanity has long been striving is not merely a fanciful fabrication of the mind in search of meaning in an empty cosmos, not the "opiate of the masses" or an infantile illusion, as Marx and Freud would have it (though there are genuine truths about historical religion and human psychology to be found in these ideas), but a mathematically describable reality in which we are immersed from birth to death, but which is occulted in the subtle interstices of being.

That we find it necessary to employ paradoxical spatial metaphors (e.g. higher, deeper, within, beyond) for this interstitial reality suggests that this more expansive transtemporal state of being is in fact a new direction of movement beyond the three directions that we can now fully perceive, which we conceive as time. Based on past precedent, it seems likely that the emergence into the full degree of freedom in a fourth dimension currently visualized through the contrivance of temporality, should it be achieved, would at first appear fundamentally new, the birth of the embryonic human mind into a radically larger reality, opening realms to our experience that we can now only encounter in ecstatic reveries. But as with all such instances of discontinuity, just as our early animal ancestors eventually became accustomed to three-dimensional experience after emerging from the two-dimensional perceptual world of very simple organisms, we will most likely grow into the wider domain and a novel era of cosmic existence will be underway. This hypothesis may appear wildly speculative to our current common sense, but this startling result of the logical trajectory evoked in various inflections by some of our greatest minds is no more unlikely than the miraculous emergence of life itself.

# CHAPTER 5
## "A SERIES OF STAGES"
### DEVELOPMENT THROUGH EMERGENT PHASES

*There are thus at least three well characterized levels, stages or types of thought about the world we live in, and the notions of one stage have one kind of merit, those of another stage another kind. It is impossible, however, to say that any stage as yet in sight is absolutely more true than any other.*

William James, *Pragmatism*[48]

*For heuristic purposes at least, it is also useful to assume a series of stages that may be regarded as relatively stable crystallizations of roughly the same order of complexity along a number of different dimensions. . . . In reality there may be compromise formations involving elements from two stages that I have for theoretical reasons discriminated; earlier stages may, as I have already suggested, strikingly foreshadow later developments; and more developed may regress to less developed stages. And of course no stage is ever completely abandoned; all earlier stages continue to coexist with and often within later ones.*

Robert Bellah, *Beyond Belief*[49]

The stage of development that we primarily inhabit, whether as an individual or as a culture, largely determines the beliefs and premises upon which we base our decisions and through which we live our lives. If we are primarily mythical, our beliefs may construct the world as a stable, cyclical, hierarchical place of kings and subjects, of gods and the immortal souls of men. However, if we primarily inhabit the mental mode of consciousness, while there may still be hierarchies and kings and gods and divine law, these things are subsumed in the primacy of rationality and empiricism, in natural law and human politics, so that the monarch seems increasingly a quaint anachronism and the grand cathedral, however architecturally magnificent, seems an atavistic relic from an earlier age. If a person whose consciousness has settled at the mental stage and a person who primarily views the world through a mythical lens visit that cathedral together, perhaps as mother and child, the younger one may feel the full force of the divine presence, while the older, even if she senses this presence, may experience some distance from it, a skepticism that can, however, be overcome in certain cases such as through the induction of ecstatic affect, whether spontaneous or intentional. Because these two individuals primarily inhabit two successive stages of the ingression of consciousness into process, they will interpret the same circumstances, the same external facts, in fundamentally different ways. Their different world views will create different worlds.

However, whereas the mythical mind is embedded in belief, the rational mind must choose to believe or disbelieve, though as noted above, the rejection of belief is still a form of belief. What is unproblematic for premodern modes of thought becomes the primary struggle for modern humanity. Once individuals become skeptical of literal religious and monarchical narratives, it becomes the responsibility of those individuals to determine what they believe. And the answer that nascent mentality has generally adopted is the Cartesian duality of subject and object, of mind and matter, which established as modern dogma the foreshadowing Axial Age insight of Parmenides, articulated about two-thousand years earlier, that "thinking and being is one and the same."[50] The emergence of the mental mode is partially constituted in the individuation of the autonomous ego, which is understood to possess all of the conscious intentionality in the universe, while the world is disenchanted and relegated to the status of mere materiality. This is the ultimate result of the modern world view: a peripheral and accidental human mind inhabiting a vast, purposeless cosmos.

At this stage of doubt, or negation, which Whitehead describes as "the peak of mentality,"[51] one must undergo a leap of faith in order to believe anything at all, though this necessity paradoxically includes the belief in the reality of nothing but the human mind perceiving the apparently purposeless phenomena of the external world. In fact, we always already believe in premises, which determine, and are determined by the stage of consciousness that we inhabit. But it is only at the mental stage characteristic of modernity that individuals have found it necessary consciously to assert their will to believe in something beyond the bare facts given by the rational mind and the evidence of the senses. Whereas before we believed because the world could not be conceived otherwise, the individuation of premises into the categories of belief and disbelief, while temporarily throwing the modern mind into existential despair, has ultimately produced the capacity to make the conscious choice to overcome the alienation and disenchantment of the late modern mind. In a sense, the innovation of disbelief produced belief so that this duality could be reintegrated in a higher-order dialectical synthesis.[52]

As many of the theorists who have informed the present work have argued in various inflections, the primary method for overcoming the malaise produced by the exclusive privileging of mentality is the emerging mode of thought, which finds value in the premises of each stage of consciousness, in both the wonder of the child at the divine grandeur of the cathedral and in the skeptical rigor of the parent who appreciates the aesthetic construction and ambiance of the building, but who also understands its association with centuries of repression, prejudice, and violence. This is not a hierarchical valuation any more than should be that of parent and child. Though the parent does have both the power to compel and discipline on one hand and the responsibility to protect and nurture on the other, a necessarily hierarchical relationship, neither stage is inherently more valuable, as the parent was once a child and the child may one day be a parent. Both play a vital role in the family of being, not only in the parent teaching the child to act rationally and to think critically, but also, just as importantly, in the child reminding the parent of the immense value and simple joy of immersion in imaginative play. The mythical stage of consciousness without the mental can be brutal, oppressive, and unquestioning, whether manifested in the Spanish Inquisition or in *Lord of the Flies*, but the mental without the mythical can be just as oppressive in its empty, disenchanted meaninglessness. The very fact of distinct phases of process necessitates that the positive content of those stages be reconciled and integrated in the production of a new stage, the modern critical intellect and the premodern participation mystique both affirmed as indispensable and complementary human attributes.

The idea that process develops through a series of emergent stages also provides evidence for the more general principle of discontinuity, which is the dynamic that mediates the crossing of the threshold from one stage to another. As Thomas Kuhn notes in relation to scientific revolutions, shifts between paradigms punctuate the slow, steady progress of normal science so that the premises of the old paradigm, which inevitably come to appear inadequate, give way with relative suddenness to radically new premises for which the old premises become a special, limited case. For instance, the Newtonian idea that the world is made up of irreducible atoms colliding deterministically in a static, absolute space and a linear, fixed time, gives way to the quantum and relativistic recognitions that particles can also manifest as waves if observed in the right way, that electrons can jump from one energy level to another without apparently passing through the intervening energetic domain, that two particles can be connected nonlocally through entanglement, and that particles can move backward as well as forward in time. Twentieth-century physics revealed a far stranger world than Newtonian physics could have imagined (though perhaps Newton himself might have been more flexible given his penchant for Biblical prophecy and alchemy), but Newtonian equations are still vitally useful approximations for calculating trajectories and erecting buildings.

While modernity has largely been constituted in the rendering of empiricism, rationalism, Newtonian physics, and Darwinian evolution as self-evident common sense, it seems that the current emergence of a new world view is, in part, the rendering of the discoveries of various disciplines in the twentieth century commonsensical. We appear to live in a transitional moment in which the habits of thought developed over the last four or five centuries in particular, though their origins extend back several millennia, are still held as fundamental premises by the majority of educated people in the world. However, the discoveries not only of twentieth century physics, but of biology, psychology, sociology, and mathematics, have demonstrated time and again the inadequacies of modern assumptions, generally predicated on the dualistic separation of subject and object (or the denial of subjectivity altogether) and the repression of formal and final causation in favor of material and efficient causation. These are the anomalies that may herald the impending transition between eras, a leap first undertaken by an increasing number of adventurous individuals, and perhaps eventually by the central institutions of society, at which point we can be said truly to have embarked upon a novel epoch.

That there are emergent stages in many domains of process is a fundamental precondition for the specific transition between world views that we seem currently to be undergoing. If both pre-human biological evolution and human cultural evolution have progressed through a number of radical emergences into qualitatively more expansive modes in the past, it is more likely that our culture will undergo another such transition than that we have reached the end of such profound transformations. It seems that those theorists who proclaim that all the great revolutions are done and that history will most likely grind on interminably until the human race destroys the planet not only lack imagination, but they also lack an adequate understanding of the way transitions between world views have generally occurred in the past. In one sense, they are right that the current world view of late modernity has run low on vitality, has reached a stalemate of vast proportions, and that if we do not act soon, tragedy will ensue, and in fact is already occurring in the increasing extinction of species and the environmental devastation. But such crises generally seem to take place just before the period of release and transcendence occurs; it is not for nothing that the night is noted to be darkest just before the dawn. The old order must die in some sense for the new one to be born, though our particular crisis is admittedly the most pervasive in human history with the direst potential consequences if the transition is not successfully achieved.

Furthermore, that a conception of nonhierarchical stages, in which no stage is intrinsically more valuable than any other, is being recognized by a growing number of thinkers is evidence that this particular element of the emerging mode is in the ascendant. And while this formulation may seem tautological, world views, as it has often been noted, are inherently circular in their logic. That is, one cannot reason one's way from one world view to another, unless one is reasoning one's way from the mythical mode into the modern world view that privileges reason. However, as with paradigm change in science, the premises are affectively determined first principles that must ultimately be taken or left on faith, whether that faith is in reductionist materialism, as the most extreme form of mentality would have it, or in the partial validity of many modes of thought, including materialism, as integration would have it. It seems clear that the novel mode is a discontinuous step beyond the exclusive privileging of rationality, encompassing mentality in a more expansive, productive, and insightful embrace.

The recognition that process proceeds through emergent stages is also a direct, evidentiary application of the fractal quality of being, as the progression visible in the stages of biological evolution appears to be reiterated self-similarly in the development of the individual human through distinct life periods, in the development of human culture through distinct world views, and in the development of cosmic evolution through increasing degrees of dimensional freedom. The first stage can be fractally correlated with the pure, unactualized potentiality of nonlife for the emergence of life, of the unfertilized egg or sperm for the emergence of an individual organism, of archaic humanity for the emergence of culture, or of zero-dimensionality for the coming to awareness of one degree of freedom in the simplest organisms. The second stage of cosmic process, repeated self-similarly across scale, can perhaps be witnessed in the first emergence of prokaryotic life out of nonlife, in the oceanic consciousness of the fetus and the infant (which is still, for all intents and purposes, a fetus[53]), in the incipient awareness of self still unified with the cosmos characteristic of the magical world view, and in the emergence of a single degree of freedom. The third stage in this fractally reiterated progression is perhaps constituted in the emergence of organisms that can perceive and move within a plane or surface, however topologically convoluted, of individual childhood when one learns how to speak and how to begin to differentiate oneself within one's familial and cultural embedding, of the narrative location of self and soul in polarity with gods and kings characteristic of the mythical world view, and of a second degree of freedom. The fourth stage of this graduated developmental process can perhaps be observed in the coming into being of efflorescent animality, in the adolescence and young adulthood of the individual as one learns to temper one's impulses and act rationally in the world as an individuated self, in the dualistic division into subject and object, with mind privileged over (and often reduced to) materiality for the mental world view, and in the emergence into a third degree of freedom. Finally (though the trajectory may very well continue), the fifth stage of processual evolution can perhaps be witnessed on different orders of magnitude in the birth of the human species and human consciousness from animality, in the mature adulthood of the individual who no longer primarily seeks to individuate himself or herself from parents and culture, but to care for others and to contribute to society, in the reembrace of the previous archaic, magic, mythical, and mental stages as all equally valid and indispensable modes of relation by the novel world view, and in the emergence into a full perception of fourth dimensionality, of which temporality appears to be a partial approximation, expressible as a fractal dimension.

The existence of these fractally reiterated stages is itself an archetypal potentiality that manifests on many scales of complexity, which provides yet another piece of evidence for the archetypal perspective. Conversely, the development through emergent processual phases is a dynamic by which archetypes manifest. These stages are both the manifestation of an archetypal impulse and the means of manifestation for archetypes in general. As suggested above, the deeply recursive, intertwined quality of these two concepts is characteristic of all world views, which are essentially bounded systems based on certain premises, producing certain results. However, the factor that differentiates the emerging world view from the previous modes is that it subsumes all positive premises in its system, only rejecting those aspects of thought that deny other modes. For instance, the novel mode absorbs the ancient concept of a Great Chain of Being, the idea that all entities from the lowliest to the most exalted are continuously connected through links of succession, and that there are pervasive correspondences between the microcosmic and macrocosmic domains. However, this mode rejects the prejudice embedded in this premodern concept that more complex or mature forms of life are inherently better or should be privileged over simpler or less developed forms. For the mythical mind, humans were generally superior to animals, adults were generally superior to children, nobles were generally superior to commoners, and racially organized cultures with greater capacity for dominance were generally superior to less dominant cultures. In fact, this mode of thought has been an implicit factor well into modernity.[54]

By contrast, for the emerging mode of thought, the postmodern rejection of this repressive hierarchical ordering across scale is strongly reasserted, but the positive insight that process does seem to pass through distinct phases is reclaimed, though the new mode does not correlate these phases with intrinsic valuation any more than one would value the life of an adult over that of a child. Their particular capacities are each appropriate within different contexts and, as mentioned above, adults often have a great deal to learn from children, just as modern cultures have a great deal to learn from premodern ones. The reembrace of premodern values by the intellect-privileging modern mind is not merely a subject of academic and historical curiosity, but a critically important activity for our culture to undertake if we wish to survive and progress into the next phase of human existence. The archetypes that are expressed through the developmental process are not pregiven essences that essentialize cultural difference and justify domination, a misinterpretation that has often been the fallacious basis for their critique. Rather, archetypes are potentialities for ingression that manifest in many domains on many scales of conscious awareness in many different valences.

Furthermore, these successive stages of process support the notion that time can viably be perceived as qualitative, as each of the stages, on whatever scale, is precisely a temporal period qualitatively different from those periods that come before and after. For instance, the temporal quality of the mythical stage partially consists in a privileging of a qualitative approach to time, though perhaps it would be more accurate to say that qualitative and quantitative time are relatively undifferentiated just as astrology and astronomy were long considered one artful science. Subsequently, the temporal quality characteristic of modernity has partially consisted in the repression of a qualitative conception of temporality in favor of an exclusively quantitative conception. And finally, the temporal quality partially characteristic of the emerging mode appears to be the acknowledgment of the validity and value of both the qualitative and quantitative approaches to time, though these two aspects of temporality have been individuated, and can now be understood as applicable in their appropriate domains. In this way, qualitative temporality has come into conscious awareness through the developmental processes mediated by qualitatively different stages of ingression.

That these stages of process obtain is an enactment of the general trajectory of being toward novelty and consciousness. It seems to be the case that novelty is generally mediated through these stages, whether on the level of the individual person who makes the transition from the mental world view to the emerging one, and therefore finds herself able to produce a novel description of the new world view, or on the level of a culture, whose gravitational center of consciousness undergoes a shift from the modern to the emerging, potentially allowing that culture to discover solutions for many problems, both philosophical and practical, that previously appeared insoluble. For instance, in a world view that reifies a radical separation of subject and object, of self and world, the idea that we should collectively care for the health of our planet, though an eminently rational consideration, is not an urgent concern for the majority of people.

Although many of us have a more or less firm conviction that something should be done about climate change and the pollution caused by the burning of fossil fuels, the political, economic, and technological obstacles seem dauntingly immovable. Because the consensus reality of the main streams of Western culture in the second decade of the twenty-first century is still primarily rational, even though many of us maintain vociferous opinions about this issue, the collective organism of our culture, which appears to have stabilized at the mental stage of development, is simply incapable of caring for what it constructs as the objective, nonhuman world sufficiently to generate the will to leap these hurdles. However, if enough individuals in our culture are able intentionally to overcome the Cartesian division between mind and world to enter into the more expansive world view, this "slightest change of tone" would "yet make all the difference," and a tipping point would most likely be reached when the emergent entity of our culture would also make the shift to the novel mode. If this transition was to occur on a collective scale, the political, economic, and technological factors would probably align with relative suddenness to produce the solutions that we know are possible because the will to act would suddenly be evident. It is not modernity's fault that it cannot bring itself genuinely to take responsibility for the environment, as the privileging of human intellect over nature, including the human body, lies at the very root of the modern world view. However, the emerging world view, in its reembrace of premodern epistemologies and modes of thought, cannot help but feel compelled to care for the Earth from which it emerged and in which it is embedded, just as one feels compelled to care for one's aged parents, or for one's own body. The very limitations of the previous world view appear to be leading us inexorably toward the overcoming of those limitations.

An examination of the stages of process also reveals the exponential compaction of time in its trajectory toward novelty. As noted above, the first stage of biological evolution, the pure potentiality of nonlife, was unchallenged until billions of years ago with the emergence of prokaryotic life, while the evolutionary emergence of animals occurred hundreds of millions of years ago, the emergence of hominids occurred millions of years ago, and the emergence of humans occurred hundreds of thousands of years ago. The steps of cultural evolution follow a similar progression, so that the archaic world view predominated for hundreds of thousands of years, the magic for tens of thousands of years, the mythical for thousands of years, and the modern for hundreds of years. It might not be too much to suggest that the emerging world view may predominate for mere decades before a new transition looms. Although I am not in the business of predicting the future in its specificity, but rather of tracing the general trajectories that animate our present moment, my intuitive sense aligns with that of thinkers like Ray Kurzweil, Hans Moravec, and Terence McKenna that the exponential compaction of temporality will be mediated through the exponential growth of technology.

This accelerating progression through stages on different orders of magnitude appears, at first glance, to be contradicted by the developmental process of the individual human organism, as conception takes only a few minutes, gestation requires about nine months, childhood and adolescence each last a few years, and adulthood stretches across decades. However, the qualitative experience of these stages appears to be inversely proportional to these quantitative measures, so that the fetus lives in an apparently timeless womb, exemplified in the eternal Edenic state. Subsequently children, who can perceive the passage of time to varying degrees over the course of their growth, possess a notoriously vague conception of death, and can often seem to be living in a kind of eternal present. Adolescents and young adults, though usually more aware of time than they were as children, generally feel that they "have all the time in the world," as it is often said, for deep bodily recognition of temporal limit has not yet become a reality for them. Finally, for the adult who objectively lives the longest, time seems to accelerate as the awareness of mortality becomes increasingly present. For instance, it appears to be the general consensus that the subjective, qualitative experience of the fourth decade of life, one's thirties, seems to go by much more quickly than the seemingly boundless expanses of time that one experienced as a child in one's first decade. Thus, in all of the primary iterations of the developmental nature of process through emergent stages that have been traced across different levels of complexity, these stages seem to advance exponentially.[55]

Finally, the broadest currently conceivable manifestation of these stages is the ascendance of process through successive degrees of freedom. If one imagines the cosmos as something like a potential organism, these are the stages through which that development occurs.[56] It seems that the world comes to know itself through the emergent awareness of different orders of dimensionality in its creatures, beginning with the zero-dimensional potential for awareness of pre-life, and proceeding through the single-dimensional awareness of very simple organisms, the dual-dimensional awareness of somewhat more complex organisms, the three-dimensional awareness of animals, and the primarily human awareness of time. Although human history may appear to us a vast temporal expanse, enacted through the lives of countless individuals over yawning millennia, on a cosmic scale this history can perhaps be seen as a relatively sudden phase transition from the awareness of three dimensions to the incipient awareness of four dimensions. The whole span of cultural development, from the discovery of fire, the invention of language, and the building of the pyramids to quantum theory, space travel, and the internet, may be analogous to water boiling, mediating the transition from a liquid to a gas.

Although in our subjective experience this process has stretched across many individual lifetimes, for cosmic process it marks the relatively brief and abrupt emergence from one stable stage into another. In this broad view, time seems to be merely a partial approximation, a conceptual tool employed by a three-and-a-fraction-dimensional species to perceive a four-dimensional manifold, a domain which exceeds the current ability of our minds intuitively to grasp except through metaphor and mathematics. However, it seems likely that this limitation to three-and-a-fraction degrees of freedom is not a permanent, essential condition of existence in the cosmos, as it has often been assumed to be by many brilliant scientists and philosophers, but a step in a process toward a deeper, more expansive participation in the world's becoming. While it seems unlikely that a mere philosophical innovation of the kind traced in these pages could alone effect such a profound transformation of human experience, it appears far more likely that such an outlook, acting in concert with exponentially accelerating technology, could in fact produce such a fundamental rupture.

# CHAPTER 6
# "AN EXTRAORDINARY THRESHOLD"
## THE EMERGENCE OF A NEW WORLD VIEW

*It is not difficult to see that ours is a birth-time and a period of transition to a new era. Spirit has broken with the world it has hitherto inhabited and imagined, and is of a mind to submerge it in the past, and in the labour of its own transformation.*

G.W.F. Hegel, *The Phenomenology of Spirit*[57]

*We find ourselves at an extraordinary threshold. One need not be graced with prophetic insight to recognize that we are living in one of those rare ages, like the end of classical antiquity or the beginning of the modern era, that bring forth, through great stress and struggle, a genuinely fundamental transformation in the underlying assumptions and principles of the cultural world view. . . . Something is dying, and something is being born.*

Richard Tarnas, *Cosmos and Psyche*[58]

The idea that our culture is on the cusp of collectively adopting a new world view based on radically novel premises is an exemplary instance of the recognition that the assumptions we hold about the world largely determine the quality of that world. If we choose to believe, as many continue to do, that the world is composed solely of matter, and that the mind, which is a chance epiphenomenon of that matter, can never know the external world directly, then modern mentality will inevitably experience a sense of alienation after an initial liberation from the constraints of the previous, mythical world view. For this habit of mind followed to its logical conclusion, the world seems meaningless and purposeless, the individual apparently nothing more than an accidental, peripheral, and insignificant collection of atoms trying to make the best of a bad situation. No matter how hard exclusive mentality tries, along with the existentialists, bravely to forge meaning in the face of the void, it will always fall back to the baseline experience of being a stranger in a strange land, the inescapable qualitative result of asserting the Cartesian duality a priori. However, if we instead take as our premise that the human mind is situated in the body, which is evolved from and permeable with the world, then we will inevitably come to understand that, far from being peripheral and insignificant, the human mind, as the most complexly conscious entity of which we know, is in fact the stuff of the world coming to awareness of itself. Based on what is, in my view, a rather more plausible premise, we concrescences of cosmic content participate in the creation of the world's meaning, and all of the other insights articulated in this book seem to follow from this initial recognition.

In order to accomplish the transition from one world view to another, from late modern disenchantment and alienation to reenchantment and participation, all that is required is for one to decide. Once one understands that the dualistically constructed choice of modernity is not truly between belief and disbelief, but between two ultimately unprovable beliefs roughly describable as reductionist materialism and vital idealism, then one can transcend the incommensurability of this polarized decision to make a third choice. This "reconciling third" affirms the validity of both modes of thought within their appropriate domains, and judges each mode of belief by the fruit it produces for lived experience. Although the affective tone associated with altering one's most fundamental assumptions about reality can be radically different in individual cases, a terrifying leap into the void for some and a gentle relaxation into a wider embrace for others, it seems that one must make the decision, whether consciously or unconsciously, to undergo this transition if one hopes to move beyond deficient mentality. And once one decides to partake of this conversion, one's entire relation to experience shifts dramatically, though this transformation may not be readily apparent to observers. Whereas before the vicissitudes of life seemed unintelligible and perhaps even cruel, the adoption of the intermeshed premises of the emerging mode grants meaning to the texture of one's experience, though it certainly does not eliminate suffering. Rather, it lends a significance and nobility to suffering that renders the inevitable pain easier to bear.

The integrative method is thus indispensable for the emergence of a new world view. Whereas modernity, for instance, has generally privileged rationality over affective and intuitive knowledge, the novel mode perceives these two epistemological domains, very roughly privileged in the modern and premodern eras respectively, as equally necessary for a balanced approach not only to the formulation of philosophical understanding, but to the living of life. Similarly, by affirming both the positive content of the materialism prevalent in modernity as well as the positive content of the metaphysical and teleological intuitions of premodernity, one can perhaps come to a deeper understanding of the evolution of process, for in order to practice this seemingly paradoxical dual affirmation, one need only jettison the negative content of each perspective. Although one would affirm the value of materialist science such as the Darwinian view of evolution by means of natural selection, one would reject the tendency of Darwinists to deny the possibility of teleology, in which case Darwinism is an eminently useful theory for describing certain aspects of the development of process but not others.

Conversely, one might affirm teleology because it is apparent, based on the available evidence, that process does in fact tend in the direction of consciousness, but one could put aside the idea that this teleological thrust must only take place in the form of eschatological Christianity, for instance, an assertion which effectively denies all other forms of finalism. However, in the emerging mode, one can also affirm the historical contingencies that rendered the negative content of both Darwinism and Christianity valid and even necessary within their developmental contexts, but which no longer obtain. Whereas the heady finale of modernity, describable as deconstructive postmodernism, has primarily consisted in critiquing, problematizing, destabilizing, dismantling, and deessentializing the supposed certainties of modernity that have served to exclude and repress that which has been identified as other, the novel mode absorbs the necessity of such careful and even fervent critical rigor in the service of affirming whatever content does not detract from some other positive content.

The discontinuity of process is both an exemplary facet of the emerging mode and a dynamic through which this new world view is apparently emerging. As noted above, while modernity can to a large degree be described as the ideas of Newtonian physics become common sense, the theories of relativity and quantum mechanics can be seen as deeply related to the novel mode so that the results of the quantum theory that are strangest and most counterintuitive to the modern mind, from nonlocality to complementarity to the atomic electron transition, the "quantum leap" itself, seem intuitive to the new mode of consciousness. For instance, as also mentioned above, nonlocality is so strikingly similar to Jungian synchronicity that Jung and Einstein discussed the subject over dinner on several occasions, and Jung and Pauli copublished a book and explored this issue in their extensive correspondence that stretched over the course of two decades.

One suspects that should the practice of science overcome its largely unexamined prejudice toward formal causation, something like nonlocality may actually be discovered as a kind of mechanism for synchronicity, though it seems probable that at such a deep level of reality, the distinction between mind and matter, or between formal and efficient causation, might break down, so that neither phenomenon would take primacy over the other. Rather, they may be shown to be the result of the same underlying potentialities expressed in actuality, two aspects of the same phenomenon. Similarly, Niels Bohr's principle of complementarity, witnessed in the wave-particle duality, is conceptually very much like the integrative method itself, as two kinds of entities that long seemed incommensurable, waves and particles, are shown to be different manifestations of the same underlying entity, and each face can be elicited by employing different methods of measurement and observation, each method a special case partially valid in its appropriate domain. And quantum discontinuity seems to correlate with the emerging realization that processes on many levels of ingression undergo sudden, discrete transformations. The definitive emergence of the novel world view on a broad scale would recursively confirm the discontinuous quality of reality by providing a strikingly clear and universal example of such an occurrence.

The widespread collective emergence of a novel mode would also confirm the development through emergent phases characteristic of diverse gradations of process. Although it may perhaps be difficult for the majority of individuals not immersed in the study of earlier ages clearly to evaluate the claim that qualitatively new stages have emerged in the past, the larger the number of individuals who are able discerningly to assess this issue, the greater will be the momentum of the recognition at large, which appears to be fairly self-evident unless one holds the rejection of metanarratives as a fundamental premise. In fact, this rejection of metanarratives is itself a metanarrative, an untenable paradox unless one limits this "hermeneutics of suspicion" to its appropriate domain, critiquing the hierarchical essentialization characteristic of the mythical and modern modes.[59] However, when a critical mass of thinkers has been able to release the privileging of this deconstructive capacity over more constructive modes, then those who do not make philosophy their business might begin to be able to accept the logic of such a further emergence based on past precedent, and a cascade of public opinion may occur, which would serve to propel our culture's conscious center of gravity into a more expansive world view. Paradigms are circularly self-confirming and incommensurable with one another, so in order to undergo a revolution in science, or in one's general mode of thought, the individual or the culture must reach a peak of dissatisfaction with the old paradigm and, at the same moment, come upon new evidence and new modes of explanation that serve to facilitate the entity's crossing of the epistemological threshold into a new realm of cognizance.

As with progression through discrete phases, the emerging mode also appears to represent the rendering of fractal geometry as common sense, though it was only discovered by Mandelbrot half a century ago. It seems to be the case that until an idea is articulated in a robust way, which for the modern mind often means mathematical formalization, it is not a viable candidate for acceptance into the collective conception of reality. Although Mandelbrot's insight that the same structures and dynamics tend to be reiterated self-similarly across scale is one that had been partially expressed many times in various valences over the previous centuries, it was not until Mandelbrot gave this intuition its mathematical formulation as well as its name that the concept of fractality was able to transform many disciplines and to permeate collective awareness. And the recognition that the novel mode is applicable on many orders of magnitude provides evidence for a more expansive view of fractals than their limited mathematical and scientific applications might initially suggest. The emerging world view, itself an expression of the fractal dynamic, is also a locus of ingression for the widespread admission of fractality into normative discourse.

One of the primary premodern intimations of fractality, now reemerging, is the concept of archetypes, as they can be described as specific structural potentialities expressed by multivalent actualities in many different domains across scale. Whereas the modern world view has privileged material and efficient causation at the expense of the other two kinds of causation, the novel mode is partially constituted in a renewed recognition of the forms that give formal causation its name. Archaeologically unearthed and carried back into the light of rational consciousness by Jung, Grof, Hillman, Tarnas, and many others, the concept of the archetypes signifies the reembrace of the intuition of spirits prevalent in magical consciousness and of gods prevalent in mythical consciousness on a more complexly individuated order of understanding. The character of the emerging mode, which finds value and truth in earlier modes, resurrects those premodern intimations within a transrational context, so that the inclusive quality of the new mode is a precondition for the reawakening of an archetypal perspective.

From this archetypal insight, it follows that if the Platonic forms are being reanimated under novel conditions, then their channel of animation, formal causation, must also necessarily be revived by such a theory. The emergence of the new world view is both a precondition and a result of the return of temporal quality to collective awareness. In fact, the quality of the contemporary moment appears to be that of the novel mode becoming self-aware, partially constituted in the recognition that the character of one temporal period can be radically different than that of the previous period. It is impossible to determine a direction of linear causation between these two concepts, the recognition that we are undergoing the collective emergence of a new world view and the qualitative nature of temporality, precisely because this co-emergence is ascribable not to linear, efficient causation, but to correlational, formal causation. That is, both concepts are manifestations of an implicit archetypal potentiality. The quality of our time appears to be that of awakening from the dream of psyche's separation from cosmos, and of quality's separation from quantity.

Similarly, the emerging mode is a precondition for the renewed expression of teleological thought in the context of the skeptical rigor established over the last few centuries, exemplified in philosopher Thomas Nagel's coming out of the teleological closet, so to speak, in *Mind and Cosmos* in 2012. And conversely, the novel mode is itself an exemplification in historical development of the trajectory toward more comprehensive conditions of consciousness mediated through the previously predominant perspectives. This is the very character of teleology, which depends upon the simultaneous cocreation of a number of mutually supporting factors for novelty's ingression. In a recursive formulation, a telos of cultural evolution (though presumably not the final end) appears to be the emergence of the new mode, which acts both as evidence for teleology and the platform for its return to broad cultural acknowledgment.

And that this mode appears to be emerging into collective awareness only about five centuries after the birth of modernity, which required thousands of years to be born from the crucible of the mythical mode, which in turn required tens of thousands of years to emerge from the magical world view, which in turn required hundreds of thousands of years to be born from archaic humanity, provides a clear exemplification of the exponential ingression of novelty. These orders of temporal magnitude plotted on a graph depict a smooth upward curve that shows no sign of abating. Thus, the exponential acceleration of time is not only evident in the emerging mode that contains it, but appears to be the primary fact of existence that is allowing this new world view to emerge so soon after the dawn of modernity on the scale demarcated by the previous world views. Based on the underlying assumptions of modernity, particularly the linear quality of time, exponential ingression is counterintuitive, even seemingly absurd. But bolstered by the other concepts that appear to constellate the novel mode, exponentiality seems poised to become a more comprehensive sort of givenness.

Finally, if one accepts all of the previous concepts as integral elements of an emerging world view, one is inexorably led to the idea of temporic concretion, as exponential growth implies a singularity that enacts a leap from the described system into some sort of transcendent domain. And while the affective quality of this suspected transformation may perhaps be that of ecstatic, mystical rapture, like waking from a dream into a radically expanded world, the probability of such a leap's occurrence is based not only on a solid conceptual foundation, but also on a solid mathematical one. If we synthesize the ideas of qualitative temporality, teleology, and exponentiality with the description of time in our most advanced physics as a fractally partial fourth dimension, then the only direction of egress offered to the radical compaction of time is to produce the conceptual and technological tools for the perception of a qualitatively new degree of directionality. Once the exponential function of time goes vertical, so to speak, it will have nowhere left to go in the three spatial dimensions and the apparently fixed dimension of temporality, so it seems plausible that it may build itself an escape hatch, through us and our inventions, into the wider cosmos. That it is almost impossible for us intuitively to visualize what this emergence will look and feel like in any specificity is perhaps evident in the generally vague and paradoxical quality of nearly every spiritual or mystical revelation. Like the Tao, the Nirvana of Buddhism, the nonduality of Advaita-Vedanta Hinduism, or the Judeo-Christian and Islamic conceptions of Heaven, this higher degree of freedom is that which cannot be truly understood until one has merged with it.

# CHAPTER 7
## "SYMMETRY ACROSS SCALE"
### THE FRACTAL QUALITY OF PROCESS

*As is the atom, so is the universe; as is the human body, so is the cosmic body; as is the human mind, so is the cosmic mind; as is the microcosm, so is the macrocosm.*

*Ayurveda*[60]

*Self-similarity is symmetry across scale. It implies recursion, pattern inside of pattern. . . . Serious cognitive scientists can no longer model the mind as a static structure. They recognize a hierarchy of scales, from neurons upward, providing an opportunity for the interplay of microscale and macroscale so characteristic of fluid turbulence and other complex dynamical processes. . . . The laws of pattern formation are universal.*

James Glick, *Chaos*[61]

Numerous theorists have articulated the insight that Benoit Mandelbrot describes with mathematical precision in the more abstract, conceptual domains of relation between individual organisms, species, and cultures. Processes and entities on many orders of magnitude have been described by some of the greatest minds of the twentieth century as something like the scalar repetition of an underlying function, perhaps expressible as an archetypal potentiality. It appears that the assumption of fractality is the basis for understanding this otherwise secluded quality of process. Mentality carried to its logical conclusion is exemplified in the postmodern suspicion of anything that even remotely resembles hierarchy because of its contingent historical association with the premodern Great Chain of Being, which posits correspondences between microcosm and macrocosm, but which conflates a hierarchical valuation with these resonances. By contrast, the emerging impulse seems to be in the process of embracing fractality as a mode of thought which conserves the profound insight that the same patterns of organization are repeated on many levels of complexity in many domains, but that strips this understanding of the privileging of emergent entities as superior to the entities they subsume. Rather, the adoption of the fractal premise allows one to see that all previous modes of organization, expressed in an individual, a culture, or a species, are contained within the later, emergent modes as indispensable components of the whole.

Late modernity, whose overriding concern has been to describe the phenomena of being in their atomistic particularity, whether of the individuals that form the collective or of the genetic traits molded by natural selection, has generally eschewed modes of thought that seek a larger coherence, exemplified in the postmodern rejection of metanarratives which, as discussed above, is itself an unconscious metanarrative. The transition from recognizing that there are specific instances of fractality in abstract geometrical constructions to the recognition that fractality is a pervasive dynamic for the ingression of potentiality into actuality requires a leap of credence outside the circle of modern givenness. For as so often seems to be the case, although the evidence is overwhelming in support of the more general application of fractality, the dominant mentality of modernity takes the Newtonian understanding as its primary metaphor, which excludes the possibility of the perception of the mode which supersedes it. As Mandelbrot himself expressed it in a 1999 article in *Scientific American*, like typhoons, these perceptions are "in effect, defined out of existence"[62] by the reductionist mode. It is apparent, then, that in order to perceive something that essentially does not exist for one's world view, in this case the more expansive application of fractality, one must decide, for whatever reason, to admit the possibility of the existence of that domain of process.

The acceptance of fractality is itself an example of the integrative method in action, as it affirms self-similarity, which is a mathematically precise articulation of the positive content posited in the Great Chain of Being. However, along with the postmodern, fractality rejects the negative claim implicit in the Great Chain, which is that more-exalted or highly developed entities possess greater intrinsic value than humbler or less-developed entities, so that the modern city is not understood, by the emerging mode, as qualitatively superior to the magically oriented tribal village, and the adult is similarly not understood as qualitatively better than the child. The integrative method leads one to affirm the basic modern value of the equality of individuals, though this value has often been imperfectly instituted, while also affirming the fundamental premodern premise of universal interconnection.

Whereas in the mythical mode, for instance, the self may be permeably embedded in a hierarchy ruled by God the Father, modernity has largely constructed itself as consisting of individuals with naturally equal rights vying for survival and dominance in a Darwinian free market. And while modernity has fallen well short of its ideal of equality, which appears impossible based on inadequate atomistic and mechanistic premises, the novel mode perceives the self as both an autonomous individual and as an entity fractally embedded in a cosmic symphony of becoming. In this symphonic totality, the conductor, perhaps analogous to the human mind (or some more transcendent entity), is the focus and primary form of agency in the whole, but far from the only indispensable element, or even the most important one, as a conductor without an orchestra is merely waving his arms. Fractality provides both a mode of ingression and an individual expression of the integrative dynamic.

One aspect of fractals not yet discussed in detail is the phenomenon of bifurcation, which occurs in certain dynamical systems, such as those mapping turbulence. These bifurcations trace the progression of mathematically definable processes, in which the initial trajectory undergoes a sudden qualitative transformation. These kinds of dynamical processes are self-similar, as one can zoom in or out in one's view of a bifurcation diagram to find strikingly familiar instances of this phenomenon at many different scales. And similar to the electron transitions that transform relatively stable atoms, or the changes of state that transform chemical processes, bifurcation points are abstract mathematical moments of rupture where a steady system enters with relative abruptness into a qualitatively new phase of its topological trajectory. In addition, the concept of reverse bifurcation, introduced in 1980 by mathematician Edward Lorenz, appears to be a process through which diverse trajectories are initially differentiated through normal bifurcation, and then reconciled in an emergent unified system, which seems even more closely to reiterate the quality of discontinuous emergence through dialectical synthesis.[63]

As mentioned above, there are also promising areas of research into the fractal quality of spacetime in quantum mechanics. Laurent Nottale's theory of scale relativity suggests that fractal geometry may be a key to unifying the three forces of quantum theory with the force of gravity described by general relativity. Therefore, fractals and the quantum quality of process appear deeply intertwined in the more restricted, mathematically formalizable sense employed by this particular branch of contemporary physics. However, this interconnection also suggests the more general conclusion drawn by a wide array of thinkers that the repetition of patterns on different orders of magnitude manifests in actuality through the dynamic of discontinuous ruptures mediating the transition from one discrete scale of being to another.

The fractal dynamic suggests that processes which occur on many scales, such as quantum discontinuity or bifurcations, mediate the development of these diverse orders through successive stages of ingression, so that the emergence of the adolescent into adulthood is self-similar to the emergence of the human species from hominidity in the biological domain, and to the emergence of the novel world view from the modern in the cultural domain. In fact, the idea of emergent phases of becoming depends upon the broader concept of fractality because it is the dynamic through which this potential progression is mediated on many orders of magnitude. Whereas it has often been argued in late modernity that the apparent similarity of the developmental processes of individuals and cultures is merely an analogy without deeper significance, this determination generally appears to be based on the inadequate assumptions of pre-twentieth century science, for which such an idea is pure speculation incompatible with the reductionist conception of reality. However, in an era when fractals have so quickly come to permeate our most advanced scientific understanding but have not yet become intuitively apparent for many people, including those laboring within the inherently conservative institutions of academic and scientific orthodoxy, the recognition of fractality's broad application to different orders of developmental magnitude partially constitutes the work of bringing the foundational insights of the emerging mode to self-awareness and, thus, commonsensicality.

Whereas for the modern mind, what can now be understood as fractality was thought to be the residue of an irrational, unscientific, and flagrantly hierarchical conception of being, the new world view appears to be reembracing the core positive element of this premodern idea through its reimagining in the numerous applications of fractal geometry. Although it is the rational world view within which the theory of fractals and its employment in chaotic, dynamical systems has been produced and enacted, this product of late modernity appears to be a precondition for the widespread emergence of the novel mode of understanding. Without the pillar of fractality holding up its section of the edifice, large aspects of the emerging world view would appear to be merely examples of regression to credulous prerationality. However, as discussed above, paradigms change when all of the necessary factors align, so that the old mode becomes intolerably constraining just at the moment (on the scale of decades or even centuries) when the necessary conceptual tools emerge to provide a way of transcending assumptions that previously appeared irrefutable.

Fractality also provides a means of ingression for archetypes, as these potentialities endemic to the structure of being manifest self-similarly in many different domains on many different orders of magnitude. For example, the idea of fractality itself is an expression of an archetypal potential that finds articulation in the mythical mode as the Great Chain of Being, and particularly in its doctrine of correspondences between microcosmic and macrocosmic entities, but which is expressed in the mental mode as mathematical laws describing the Mandelbrot set or Julia sets. Although superficially these two conceptions seem directly opposed in that the Great Chain is a religious, cosmological hierarchy, while the Mandelbrot set is an equation that produces aesthetically pleasing visual representations and profound descriptions of physical processes, the emerging mode suggests that the same archetype can manifest in apparently opposite ways, revealing a deeper coherence.

The archetype associated with the Greek god Ares (correlated with the Roman Mars and numerous other gods of war), for instance, manifests as both violent aggression and energetic vigor, while the senex archetype manifests as both limiting constraint and rigorous focus. Critiques of the archetypal perspective have often hinged on a misunderstanding of this issue, arguing that archetypes essentialize certain roles like the hero or the mother, when a more sophisticated conception of archetypes, with the fractal dynamic implicit, suggests that "archetype" is merely a word for the insight that the phenomena of experience tend to cluster around certain nodes or axes of meaning and form. As in the empirical investigations of the psyche undertaken by twentieth century depth psychology, one can learn to perceive these impulses that manifest in multifarious actualities across scale by developing what James Hillman refers to as an "archetypal eye," which combines conceptual and aesthetic discernment, intellect and intuition.

The concept of fractality is also a precondition for qualitative temporality, as formal causation is precisely constituted in the expression of archetypal forms in many instances across scale. Two materially unconnected entities can participate in the same archetype synchronistically in the same moment, or at different times, so that one can undergo a subjective experience that feels qualitatively connected to something that happened when one was a child, for instance. Rather than the earlier event directly causing the later event through efficient causation, the two experiences instead bear an affective resonance with one another because of their mutual participation in the same archetypal complex. The factor of these experiences that is foregrounded is their qualitative meaning as opposed to their quantitative temporal relation on a linear timeline. Whereas modern science would generally interpret this experiential self-similarity as a projection of the mind onto phenomena, effectively defining the experience's validity out of existence, the archetypal perspective allows one to perceive such instances of affective and structural resonance as the human mind participating in the cocreative elicitation of the world's significance. And this quality of formal causation is just as true of two events occurring simultaneously, whether the two archetypally similar events occur externally or whether one external event appears to correlate with an internal state. In each of these cases, the events can be understood as fractally participating in the same archetypal potentiality.

Furthermore, the concept of the "strange attractor" in chaos mathematics appears to be a formalization in fractal terms of the ancient idea of final causation, describing the way dynamical systems change over time, tracing and retracing involuted topological manifolds exhibiting fractal dimensionality. Diagrams depicting strange attractors start as seemingly random curves, but distinct shapes quickly emerge, such as with the Lorenz attractor, which resembles a figure eight traced by a recursively curved, nearly flat, tape-like planar figure with a fractal dimensionality of about 2.05, or the Henon attractor, which looks vaguely like a crescent moon and has a fractal dimensionality of approximately 1.25. Terence McKenna has suggested that temporal becoming itself constitutes the filling in of a fractal dimension pulled toward increasing completeness by a transtemporal strange attractor, a notion directly relevant to the concretion of time hypothesis.

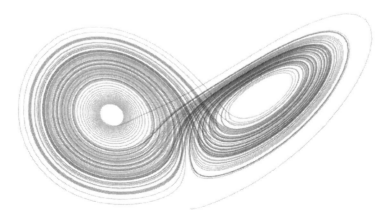

Lorenz Attractor, fractal dimension of 2.05

The broader fractal quality of reality appears to be a means of the teleological ingression of novelty into actuality, as the processes that occur at one stage of development tend to reiterate themselves on increasingly expansive scales of magnitude. For instance, the idea of teleology itself was expressed in a mythical context by medieval Christianity in the Book of Revelation, in which Christ returns as the exclusive divine mediator of judgment and salvation. By contrast, for the novel mode, this Christian narrative can be seen as one metaphorically partial expression of a deeper and more general tendency of being to be drawn ever onward toward increasingly comprehensive forms of consciousness, a concept that has been expressed in numerous religious and philosophical contexts over the course of millennia. While the rejection of the exclusive form of Christian finalism by the rational modern mind appears to have been necessary for the individuation of the autonomous intellect, the specific form of eschatology espoused by the medieval Church can be seen through the lens of fractality as one facet of a larger and more universal truth.

From this insight, it follows that the exponential ingression of novelty is also mediated through fractality, as the increasingly brief stages of development self-similarly subsume the earlier stages within them. The emergence of rational thought on a wide scale in modernity is structurally similar to the current novel mode's emergence, which employs intellectual rationality and intuitive affectivity in a higher-order confluent synthesis. And each successive synthesis constitutes a temporal compaction, as the dialectical reconciliation of intellect and intuition is a more pragmatically effective way to approach experience than through intellect alone, so that the insoluble issues for pure mentality, such as the "mind-body problem," are readily resolved by the emergent attention of intellect to bodily knowledge. Of course, new, deeper kinds of challenges emerge with the novel mode that are perhaps not even expressible in a coherent way by pure mentality. For instance, the question of how to assist those who feel themselves to be constrained by the hegemony of pure reason in making the leap into the emerging world view is a difficult one to tackle, fractally reiterating the struggle of mentality to offer rationality to those who begin to experience their mythical world view as limiting without ineffectively imposing modern values on premodern cultures.

As witnessed in the still prominent debates between positivist science and religious fundamentalism in American culture, it is not possible to convince someone who believes in the literal truth of a mythical disclosure through reasoned argumentation, as the mythical mode does not especially value reason. Rather, the most successful strategy appears to be to articulate rationality in an attractive, or even seductive way, forging texts and institutions for use by those on the cusp of transition from one mode to another. And this strategy can apparently be fractally reemployed in the increasingly aesthetically savvy, enticingly inclusive texts and communities that propound the emerging orientation. But the key point is that, although a self-similar strategy may be employed at different stages, the more encompassing a world view is, the more quickly will it make itself viably available to the preceding mode of consciousness because each stage appears to comprehend on a qualitatively greater order of magnitude the precise factors that drive the evolutionary dynamics of processual transformation. This temporal densification of experience based upon novel premises facilitates exponential progression.

Finally, the fractal self-similarity of moments of process' self-overcoming is visible on the scale of dimensionality itself. The transition from the two-dimensional consciousness of relatively simple organisms to the three-dimensional awareness of animals is driven by the same dynamics that appear to be drawing the full perception of a fourth dimension to emerge through the fractal dimensionality of time. As in the example of the late nineteenth-century novel *Flatland: A Romance in Many Dimensions* by Edwin Abbott Abbott, beings who could only perceive in two dimensions would find ingenious ways to relate to the intrusion of three-dimensional objects. For instance, if a species of organisms existed only on a flat plane, like the surface of a pond, through which passed a human hand, the denizens of this hypothetical two-dimensional world would first perceive five miniscule fleshy ovals appearing seemingly out of nowhere, as if by magic. As the hand passed through the surface, the five ovals would grow larger and then merge into one fleshy, kidney bean-shaped entity. These hypothetical beings, which I am anthropomorphizing as an aid to visualization, would be astonished by this unthinkable appearance of a higher-dimensional object, transforming in seemingly supernatural ways. If given long enough, these creatures, improbably assuming that they possess sufficient cognitive capacity, would construct elaborate theories to explain how such a thing could occur, though all of these theories would be mere metaphors for the three-dimensional reality that we humans take for granted. Some might even assert that such an experience of a higher-dimensional manifold is impossible according to the laws of nature and, thus, the product of delusion. Eventually, after many generations, some of these organisms might perhaps undergo a physically mediated evolutionary leap that would allow them to perceive the full hand, which would mark that species' entrance into a more expansive order of dimensional existence.

Of course, this is not a precise description of how two-dimensional creatures became three-dimensional creatures, for we can only speculate about the subjective, interior experience of this primordial transformation lost in the proverbial mists of time, even given our ability to observe such organisms under microscopes. But the fractal self-similarity that can be extrapolated from this hypothetical emergence is that we humans have long experienced intimations of a more expansive reality, a reality that seems to defy the logic of the world as we understand it in three dimensions. So we have constructed ecstatic shamanic practices and religions and philosophies and scientific theories to attempt to find some point of access into what appears to be describable as a higher-dimensional manifold. Many of our most brilliant and accomplished thinkers would deny this possibility as naïve metaphysical delusion. Nevertheless, bolstered by self-similarity with the lower-dimensional analogue, it appears plausible to suggest that the changing conceptions of time through human history, from magic timelessness, to the cyclical, qualitative temporicity of the mythical mode, to the quantitative linearity of modern, rationalized time, have constituted successive approximations of a mathematically formalizable transcendent domain which the emerging mode, in its synthesis of quantitative and qualitative time, appears to be on the verge of allowing to be revealed to itself through the combined efficacy of conceptual and technological innovation. If we can radically expand the processing power of our minds in addition to widening the scope of our world view, which seems likely given our current computational and cultural trajectories, we will soon be able intuitively to cognize four-dimensional entities that we can currently only describe through mathematics and lower-dimensional analogies.

# CHAPTER 8
## "A POTENTIALITY FOR ACTUAL ENTITIES"
### FORMS, ARCHETYPES, AND ETERNAL OBJECTS

*Any entity whose conceptual recognition does not involve a
necessary reference to any definite actual entities of the
temporal world is called an 'eternal object.' . . . An eternal
object is always a potentiality for actual entities; but in itself, as
conceptually felt, it is neutral as to the fact of its physical
ingression in any particular actual entity of the temporal world.*

Alfred North Whitehead, *Process and Reality* [64]

*Let us then imagine archetypes as the deepest patterns of psychic
functioning. . . . All ways of speaking of archetypes are
translations from one metaphor to another. Even sober
operational definitions in the language of science or logic are no
less metaphorical than an image which presents the archetypes
as root ideas, psychic organs, figures of myth, typical styles of
existence, or dominant fantasies that govern consciousness.*

James Hillman, *Re-Visioning Psychology* [65]

The archetypal eternal objects are preconditions for the participatory
quality of process, as archetypes are the very potentialities in whose
temporal unfolding the human mind participates. An archetype such as
the senex can find expression in many valences, so that related to
unconsciously, one might experience unintelligible suffering, whereas
related to consciously, whether as an ancestor spirit in the magic mode,
as a stern father god in the mythical mode, as the psychoanalytic "reality
principle" in the mental mode, or as the senex archetype in the emerging

mode, suffering can be transmuted by careful attention, for instance, into the building of stable structures, whether of metal and concrete or of abstract conceptual relations. And this kind of attention finds different expression depending on the world view of the person experiencing this archetype, so that the ancestors or gods might be appeased through a ritual or a sacrifice in the magic and mythical modes, one might learn to endure suffering by the rational sublimation of instant gratification in the mental mode, and an individual inhabiting the novel mode might submit to the necessity of pain and labor in order to integrate the hard-won gifts of the senex archetype, whether through ritual, sacrifice (presumably metaphorical), rational sublimation, or some combination thereof. One's world view largely determines the constraints and possibilities of one's relation to the archetypes, through which these potentialities find their means of expression.

However, the primary difference between the modern interpretation of the impulse embodied in the senex archetype and the diverse interpretations of the other world views is that the magic, mythical, and emerging modes generally perceive this quality of being as existing both outside and inside the mind (this distinction is not even intelligible for the premodern modes), while the mental stage of development generally sees the senex as a purely psychological phenomenon with no cosmological correlate. All of the other modes accept the validity of formal causation, whether explicitly or implicitly, while the modern categorically denies this kind of causality. Therefore, in order to make the transition from the disbelief in formal causes necessitated by modern premises to the emerging understanding that, if something exists, there must be a potentiality in the nature of process for that thing to have come into being, one must assert one's capacity to choose one's own fundamental premises about the nature of reality despite the inculcation of reductionist materialist assumptions in modern schools and academic institutions. In fact, it seems to be the case that "the will to believe" only becomes an issue beginning with mentality, which holds skepticism of nonmaterial modes of relation as one of its fundamental tenets. By contrast, it would be absurd for people embedded in a magic or mythical world view even to consider needing to assert their credence, as it is only in the mental mode that a belief becomes something that one can decide to adopt or reject. Prior to mentality's inception, the spirits or gods are real, tangible presences, perhaps even more real than the material world that they seem to inform and animate. However, the emerging mode is able to hold both of these realities in its purview at once, though each mode of thought, the archaic, magic, mythical, and mental, finds different emphases in different situations.

94

In one's daily work, one might focus one's attention on intellect, as it is necessary to do in order to write a work of philosophy for instance. However, whereas the modern world view is often compulsively fixated in the rational habit of mind, for the emerging mode, rationality is a tool that one can employ in its appropriate domain of applicability, and put aside for other activities in which other modes might be more productive. If one is attending a rock concert or a religious ceremony, one might choose to embrace the magic or mythical modes of relation in order to experience the full efficacy of the pounding drums or the solemn chanting. One common instance of this transition can be observed in the necessity of "getting out of one's head" in order to dance with any conviction. The Western dances popular during the earlier centuries that spanned the height of modernity, such as waltzes or quadrilles, can seem stiff, formal, and overly structured to a sensibility raised on the modes of bodily movement that have accompanied swing, rock and roll, soul, hip-hop, or electronic music in the twentieth and early twenty-first centuries. In fact, as I suggested in my previous work on the philosophy of rock and roll, these forms of music and movement seem literally to have been training the modern body to overcome its addiction to mentality in the embrace of a more expansive mode. It is no accident that the "hip" countercultures of the twentieth century have often been associated with archetypal modes of thought.

The integrative method, which affirms the positive content of all modes, is exemplified in the conscious reembrace of archetypes by the rational mind individuated in modernity. And conversely, the emerging mode itself is apparently the expression of an archetypal impulse toward integration, synthesis, and reconciliation. In premodernity, this archetype was associated with the *hieros gamos*, or sacred marriage, closely related to the alchemical *unio oppositorum*, the union of opposites. For the explicitly rational modern mode, this quality appears to be expressed in sexual reproduction, in political and economic unions, and in the integration of races, cultures, and scientific theories, though the modern mind generally declines to acknowledge any deeper coherence among these integrative instances. However, it appears to be with the novel mode that the archetypal impulse toward the integration of seemingly incommensurable polarities becomes self-aware in its inclusive acceptance of all forms of thought and modes of relation that do not detract from the freedom of expression sought by other modes, a situation which recursively serves as evidence for the efficacy of archetypal thought in the practice of integration.

The archetypal perspective is also a precondition for the recognition of discontinuity in domains other than those described by physics, for although the numerous expressions of this principle have often been recognized in modernity, from atomic electron transitions and phase transitions to scientific revolutions and psychological breakthroughs, the underlying coherence of these specific manifestations has been difficult to assert based on modern assumptions of the particulate division of entities in all domains (though one might notice that the modern assertion of this very principle of atomicity across scale paradoxically violates its own premise). However, by means of the archetypal perspective, the emerging mode reveals the separation of entities asserted by rationality to be the expression of one archetype, describable as the senex, which organizes boundaries and limits of all kinds, while the novel world view admits all the archetypes delineated in premodernity into its conceptual pantheon. The root of the word "rationality" itself is "ratio," meaning the quantitative calculation of proportional difference. Although it is often necessary to analyze, reduce, separate, and differentiate processes in order to understand phenomena, it is often equally necessary to perceive the efficacy of qualities across scale, including discontinuity, which makes possible sudden leaps to novel domains of ingression such as the paradigmatic Promethean discovery of fire, and all of the subsequent discoveries that ensued, from the archetypes themselves to quantum field theory.

Furthermore, it is the concrete expression of archetypal potentialities that occurs through emergent stages of process. In all domains of ingression, from the development of individuals to that of cultures, species, or the cosmos itself, the complex interactions of the originary impulses for becoming can be fruitfully described by the relations of archetypal potentialities. Archetypes appear to constitute the initial conditions of the universe, though whereas modern science has interpreted this phrase in a purely materialist mode, except of course for mathematical and natural laws which are archetypes snuck in through the back door of the modern edifice, initial conditions for the emerging mode are precisely those potentialities for relation, whether material or formal, that result in the multivalent profusion of our world. And conversely, the developmental process itself is the expression of an archetypal complex, so that the very idea of development is understood in qualitatively different ways at different phases of its ingression. Whereas in mythical cultures, the developmental process is generally perceived as a static hierarchy from the lowest forms of matter to the Godhead, this compound archetypal impulse is interpreted by the mental mode as the development of the organism, which is only metaphorically connected to the development of the species, the culture, or the cosmic structure. Finally, the emerging mode reintegrates these differentiated scales of development to recognize them as the multifarious, nonhierarchical expressions of an archetypal complex perhaps described by the interaction of the archetypal impulse toward expansive ascendance with the archetype of discontinuous leaps, punctuating static periods of stable continuity, also expressive of an archetypal potentiality, and driven by the evolutionary impulse toward transformation, as well as the archetypal tendencies toward unification and reconciliation.

Specifically in the cultural domain, the archetypes appear to be finding a new container for their more complete expression in the novel mode, which strips the premodern gods and Platonic forms of their association with essentialized hierarchy, liberating the archetypes from the constraints of their particular cultural manifestations to begin to see them in themselves as potentialities for multivalent ingression. Consequently, the emerging mode itself is not only the expression of the archetypes mentioned above, but it is also preconditioned by the idea of the archetypes themselves as they serve to mediate between the material physicality characteristic of modernity, based on material and efficient causation, and the metaphysicality more characteristic of premodernity, based on formal and final causation. While the archetypes constitute the formal causes that give formal causation its name, the novel mode appears partially to be constituted in the recognition that the ingression of potentiality occurs largely through material substrates, from the emergence of proteins and cell biology, to the emergence of the human mind, to the emergence of that mind's extensions in artificial intelligence, the internet, and incipient nanotechnology. In this light, formal and efficient causation are intimately and inextricably intertwined, the Janus-faced aspects of interiority and exteriority, of psyche and cosmos. Though we might assert that qualitative consciousness pervades all matter, at least in potentia, it also seems likely that there is no consciousness or quality without some material or energetic substrate, however subtle. The emerging mode is predicated upon the archetypal reconciliation of the very idea of archetypality with materiality, a dizzyingly recursive operation characteristic of the emergence into a higher-order domain of process.

Fractality is also predicated upon archetypality, as archetypes are the initial potentialities that the fractal dynamic expresses, not only in mathematical sets and their aesthetically dazzling visual representations, which seem to have been waiting in the nature of process to be discovered and synthesized by Mandelbrot half a century ago, but in the broader definition of fractality. This pervasive quality of process facilitates the self-similarity across scale of archetypal qualities like expansion, contraction, rupture, dissolution, transformation, and reconciliation, all associated with various mythological figures, a domain of correlation traced in more depth below. Conversely, as with all aspects of process, the fractal repetition of patterns on different orders of conceptual magnitude is itself the expression of an archetypal complex, perhaps definable as the archetype of web-like interconnection and the dissolution of boundaries in combination with the expansive, encompassing archetype. Fractality, partially describable as an encompassing web of interconnection across many different scales of being, can perhaps be seen as an expression of the relation between these two archetypal potentialities.

Qualitative temporality is predicated upon the archetypal understanding, as formal causation is the mode of ingression that takes its very name from the forms. The qualitative nature of time is defined in the Jungian concept of synchronicity as the meaningful nonmaterial correlation of two or more events that participate in the same archetype or archetypal complex. Whereas the modern mind constructs time exclusively as one material thing leading to another through efficient causation, the emerging mode perceives the conjunction of qualitatively similar events at the same moment, or of qualitatively similar moments separated in time, as being connected interiorly, while efficient causation is exclusively exterior. For instance, in premodern modes, the sight of two birds flying across the horizon could communicate something to the perceiving human, perhaps seeming to signal an acknowledgement of a decision the person has made to marry. Or perhaps the watcher is undecided and the sight of the birds seems to be the decisive factor in this decision. Either way, something in nature, the sky spirit perhaps, would be experienced as communicating its wisdom to the observant individual. For the modern mind, this mode of thought would be considered childish or pathological, the product of anthropomorphic projection, wish fulfillment, or the pathetic fallacy. However, for the novel mode, the vision of the birds spurring the decision to wed could be described as constituting a cocreative mutual participation of the birds and the human mind in the underlying archetypal quality of that moment, which would be one of union.

It seems unlikely that the birds in this scenario would be aware of the person's dilemma, consciously communicating their opinion through the trajectory of their flight. Rather, it makes more sense to say that the durational quality of reality would have constellated a morphic field of significance in the system constituted by birds, watcher, landscape, and dilemma to produce the affective quality of union, which has a real effect on the lives of the people involved. If it had been a different time, perhaps the two birds would have flown away from one another, possibly impelling the decision to call off the wedding. But for the emerging mode, this is not necessarily a projection of human concerns onto nature. Rather, the watcher could be described as having projectively elicited this communication from the total affective field of his embedded, relational experience, which would then be one of separation or division. In this way, the modern idea that the individuated human mind possesses autonomous agency is reconciled with the magical conviction that agential spirits external to the individual human are communicating through the subtle movements of nature. Whereas for the modern mind, these two interpretations seem contradictory because modern rationality has fallaciously conflated human agency with the evacuation of intentionality from the world outside the mind, both views are affirmed and integrated in the emerging approach. However, it should be noted that archetypes and the temporal qualities they inform are multivalent and can be interpreted, or misinterpreted, in many complex ways. One must employ rigorous discernment to determine if one is reading and enacting the quality of a moment in the most efficacious manner, or if one is falling into delusion or projection, using the archetypal perspective as an excuse for choices motivated by fear or selfishness rather than as a tool for more profound self-knowledge. Archetypes are not deterministic, and they can manifest in many ways, both constructive and destructive, though these manifestations seem always to be appropriate to the archetypal character of a particular duration.

Furthermore, archetypality implies teleology, which is merely another way of stating that formal causation implies final causation. These two kinds of causation are so deeply intermeshed that one can viably speak of formal-final causation, as the formal potentialities are the origins of the teloi toward which final causation is luring the process of becoming. They are alpha and omega, divorced from that phrase's specifically Christian connotation, the eternal objects of which time is the medium of becoming and the ends to which those archetypes are inexorably drawn. In fact, it seems plausible to assert that archetypes and teloi are expressions of the same transtemporal entities, articulated in their unrealized potentiality as forms, and in their ultimate purpose as final causes. It could perhaps even be suggested that archetypes and teloi as perceived by human consciousness are lower-dimensional intimations of higher-dimensional entities, casting their shadow across human history, impelling the ingression of novelty ever onward toward more encompassing actualities. Therefore, it may be an understatement to say that archetypes imply teloi as they may be different facets of the same transtemporal states of being.

And the process of the archetypes' ingression into actuality, lured by their correlative ends, appears to be accelerating. In the early stages of cosmic evolution, before even the formation of stars and planets, the archetypes would have been almost completely unrealized. However, as the pace of cosmic development has exponentially increased, each subsequent stage has emerged an order of magnitude more quickly, and the potentialities for becoming implicit in process have been progressively drawn toward emergent orders of consciousness. The archetypes may have first become conscious to some degree in animal awareness, though still only in dreamlike images, pure affect, and the felt correlation of qualitatively similar experiential episodes. Subsequently, the emergence of human consciousness appears to have marked the coming to self-awareness of the archetypes, the sources of all agency, first in spirits, then in gods, then in the human mind, and now, in a dialectical reembrace of the previous modes by individuated intellect, as archetypes that can manifest in experience as immanent spirits, as transcendent gods, and as egoic consciousness and its concomitant unconscious. In this view, the archetypes appear to be spiraling upward, outward, and into the depths (all three-dimensional analogies for a more expansive process than our current language can easily describe), expressing themselves not only as agencies external to the human self, or as the exclusive agency of the human mind in an inanimate world, but in the relationality between self and world. We seem to be vessels of the archetypes' accelerating self-overcoming.

Finally, this archetypal self-overcoming appears to be mediated through the densification of temporal experience. Just as a dimensionality of 1.1 would appear very similar to a straight line, but a dimensionality of 1.9 would trace a complex curve that nearly fills a second dimension, the implicit project of human history appears to be a self-similar filling of a fourth-dimensional phase space based on a three-dimensional platform through the discernment of qualitative temporality, which traces the increasingly convoluted curvature of time. Whereas the cyclical temporicity of the mythical mode can be visualized as a closed loop, constraining the possibilities of egress, the emergence of linear time via the mental mode is an opening of that loop to a higher degree of freedom, but only at its beginning and end, intimated as the alpha and the omega. For the emerging mode, the qualitative perception of time mapped onto the quantitative temporality of modern science, an activity made possible by the archetypal perspective, might be imagined as a temporal string woven continuously back upon itself, each duration along the temporal thread revealed to correlate with other, apparently distant moments to produce a textured fabric of labyrinthine entanglement that can be placed conceptually over the higher-dimensional contours. In this analogy, though we do not yet possess the perceptual and cognitive capacities directly to know the topological curvature of this fourth-dimensional manifold, we can perhaps perceive the outlines of this phase space through the qualitatively interwoven fabric of historical temporality, and particularly through the method of archetypal cosmology presented in the Epilogue.

# CHAPTER 9
## "A FALLING TOGETHER IN TIME"
### QUALITATIVE TEMPORALITY AND FORMAL CAUSATION

*Chance happenings have a tendency to fall into aperiodic groupings. . . . Therefore it cannot be a question of cause and effect, but of a falling together in time, a kind of simultaneity. Because of this quality of simultaneity, I have picked on the term 'synchronicity' to designate a hypothetical factor equal in rank to causality as a principle of explanation. . . . Synchronicity therefore means the simultaneous occurrence of a certain psychic state with one or more external events which appear as meaningful parallels to the momentary subjective state—and, in certain cases, vice versa.*

C.G. Jung, *Synchronicity*[66]

*"Secular" time is what to us is ordinary time, indeed, to us it's just time, period. One thing happens after another, and when something is past, it's past. . . . Higher times gather and re-order secular time. They introduce "warps" and seeming inconsistencies in profane time-ordering. Events which were far apart in profane time could nevertheless be closely linked. . . . Once events are situated in relation to more than one kind of time, the issue of time-placing becomes quite transformed. . . . Narration is one way of gathering time. It shapes the flow of time, de-homogenizes it, and marks out kairotic moments.*

Charles Taylor, *A Secular Age*[67]

The supposition that the assumptions we hold condition the kinds of meaning we can elicit from experience is supported by the insight that different times exhibit qualitatively different experiential characters, as the premises on which we base our world view are almost always adopted for affective reasons, and thus our assumptions often shift with the shifting of our felt experience. During a certain period, one may have the sense that the world is contracting, that one's possibilities are diminishing, and one's responsibilities are weighing heavily on one's shoulders. However, it is almost inevitable that a relatively sudden and often unexpected shift will eventually occur that fundamentally alters the character of one's lived experience, so that one suddenly feels liberated, expansive, successful, and lucky. Although this is merely one of many possible affective shifts, which can be described archetypally, it is such fundamental changes in the quality of experience, both subjective and objective, that condition our relation to the world.

And it is the same with transformations of a culture's world view, so that all of the factors described thus far in the transition from one cultural mode to another are both predicated upon, and productive of a widespread shift in collective sentiment. For instance, the belief that the Earth is the center of the cosmos is more appropriate for the mythical world view because that mode requires a fixed, stable cosmos to feel at home, whereas the modern world view is partially constituted in, and driven by the recognition that the Earth hurtles around the Sun because the mode of thought that makes this world view feel most in control of its environment, a generally modern value, is the rational, skeptical mode, which rejects metaphysical doctrine in much the same fashion as adolescents rebel against parental strictures. And just as when adolescents become adults, they often realize that there was more value in their parents' mode of thought than they had previously imagined, an individual who enters into the emerging mode might recognize the validity of metaphysics, though usually not in the specific form of exclusivist premodern religion.

Consequently, the insight that we do not generally decide to adopt new beliefs for primarily rational reasons, but because of profound alterations in our bodily experience is also dependent upon the qualitatively mutable nature of that experience. For instance, mentality may cling to the exclusive validity of scientific rationality just as surely as the mythical mode clings to the exclusivity of its religious beliefs. There is a deeply felt need for those beliefs, which are each appropriate (i.e. efficient) at one stage of development, such as ancient Mesopotamia for the mythical and seventeenth-century Europe for the mental, but inappropriate (i.e. deficient) at another stage of development, such as the

United States in the twenty-first century for the mythical and some point in the future when the emerging mode will presumably have become normative for the mental. As with scientific revolutions or conversion experiences, the anomalies and incommensurabilities amass until a tipping point is reached, and many relevant material, technological, cultural, and psychological factors synchronically emerge to produce the transformation of the individual or collective consciousness. It appears that only once the conducive temporal quality has arisen can one choose to make the leap into the new reality or to cling to the old assumptions despite increasingly uncomfortable dissonance between affect and intellect, a dissonance that can result in schizophrenic or dissociative disorders when not integrated.

The integrative method also depends upon temporal quality, as ideas or impulses must ripen in contradiction with one another for relatively long periods before they can be reconciled through the universal affirmation of positive content characteristic of the novel mode. And as discussed above, such reconciliation appears to be the expression of a specific qualitative, archetypal complex that can perhaps be partially described as the expansive and the discontinuous qualities of existence acting in concert, whereas mutual polarization and incommensurability are qualities perhaps more associated with the archetypal complex formed by the conventionally authoritative and the radically novel archetypes, the dialectic of father and son, or of senex and puer. And furthermore, the dialectical reconciliation of qualitative temporality, privileged in a relatively naïve and undifferentiated mode in premodernity, with the quantitative conception of time prevalent in modernity is an exemplary instance of the integrative method, which asserts the value of both modes of cognizance.

Without the quantitative approach to temporality, the contemporary world would simply revert to a premodern state, so that the trains would cease to run on time, if at all, the commercial exchange of goods and services would become impossible to conduct on its current scale, scientific and technological advance would essentially cease, and the vast machinery of our civilization would break down, most likely resulting in mass famine, disease, and war—not a desirable scenario. However, without the qualitative approach to time, the world becomes exactly what it seems to be in deconstructive postmodernity: a vast, disenchanted machine devoid of soul, meaning, or purpose. The synthesis of these two modes seems capable of producing a technologically sophisticated civilization that understands itself to be embedded in a world of profound significance, so that the great achievements of modernity, from the harnessing of electricity and the invention of computers to techniques for healing the body and for growing food, would be conserved, but they would be resituated within a new context of existential intelligibility, in which the alienation, stress, depression, distraction, waste, and vacuity often characteristic of our primarily postmodern culture could increasingly be shed in favor of the collective project of birthing a new mode of consciousness from the crucible of human history. If this scenario seems at all implausible, consider that there was a time when life did not exist, and then it did, or a time when consciousness as we understand it did not exist, and then it did. Clearly, we live in a world in which things that have never before been extant suddenly come into being.

Although the majority of our experience is spent enmeshed in long periods of static linearity when not much changes at the level of first principles, periods that display the quality of radical novelty periodically occur, disrupting the stable continuity to produce a fundamental rupture that thrusts the process, whether of an individual organism, a collective, a species, or the cosmos, into a qualitatively different duration. For instance, while there had been precursors to modern, Western mentality in the ancient Greeks and Hebrews, and in the limited kind of rationality, severely constrained by dogmatic assumptions, characteristic of some medieval Christian Scholastics, from Augustine to Aquinas, the broad emergence of the modern world view can be marked as having occurred with relative suddenness in the few decades surrounding the year 1500. This is the period when Copernicus was formulating his heliocentric hypothesis, Columbus, Magellan, and Vasco da Gama were exploring the globe, Leonardo, Raphael, and Michelangelo were creating their masterworks, and Martin Luther was initiating the protestant reformation by posting his ninety-five theses on the door of the Wittenburg church. Such moments of compact transformation are only adequately explicable by reference to the qualitative nature of temporality, perhaps expressing a period during which the archetype associated with discontinuity is emphasized in collective experience. Apparently, something in the quality of that moment demanded such an efflorescent emergence.

Each stage of process, which is both demarcated and produced by such perinatal ruptures, is equally dependent upon the principle of qualitative temporality, as each successive stage exhibits a distinct temporal quality. The thousand years in the West before the emergence of modernity, roughly definable as the middle ages, can be described as a philosophically static era founded upon the hierarchical structure of God, angels, kings, nobles, subjects, animals, and objects. Although there were many profound and complex debates about the interpretation of scripture and dogma during this millennium, the questioning of first principles was generally considered heresy punishable by death, and thus such questioning rarely occurred. By contrast, the last five-hundred years can partially be described as an increasingly volatile period of discovery, invention, exploration, and innovation. Although many of the qualities of the mythical world of premodern Christianity were subsumed in the modern, the liberation of thought from the constraints of Catholic dogma produced a fundamentally different quality of experience during the epoch now apparently drawing to a close. The qualitative nature of time is a precondition for the possibility of fundamental change, though as with modernity, each new era eventually becomes a conventional orthodoxy offering diminishing returns. In such moments, a novel dispensation is required to renew the vigorous productivity of process in its vernal juvenescence.

The emerging epoch will presumably subsume many of the qualities of modernity, but recontextualize them in a novel qualitative approach through the reembrace of premodern modes in addition to modern ones. Whereas for modernity, the mind-body problem, climate change, the acidification of the oceans, political gridlock, and many other issues appear insoluble, the qualitative experience of the new world view may generally be more optimistic about these problems because it appears to possess both the conceptual and affective tools necessary to solve them that modernity does not on a collective scale; not only the rational and technological capacities to engineer solutions developed by mentality, but the implicit compassion and sense of responsibility for the other, whether human or nonhuman, that is fundamentally lacking at large for the modern world view, if not always for the modern individual, based on the unsustainable Cartesian dualism. The emerging world view is doubly dependent on qualitative temporality: as the precondition for any novelty's emergence, and as a vital conceptual component of that world view in particular.

Qualitative temporality is also a precondition for fractality in its broad definition, as the recognition that the same patterns of meaning are repeated self-similarly across scale presupposes the temporal qualities of which actual instances are the expression in time. It appears that this particular conceptual relation is most clearly expressed by reference to archetypality, which forms the middle term between these two aspects of process, as qualitative time and fractality both imply one another because they are mutual modes of ingression for archetypal potentialities. Whereas temporal quality describes the ingression of archetypes in time, fractality describes the ingression of the qualities associated with particular archetypes across scale. Therefore, it could be said that synchronic duration indicates the temporal loci of archetypal self-similarity across scale, like two axes of a graph depicting the process of scalar-temporal becoming.

The points on this metaphorical graph, a quantitative analogy for qualitative phenomena, would then represent the archetypes manifesting self-similarly in time. Qualitative temporality is a precondition for the ingression of archetypes, as formal causation is the causal mode through which formal potentialities manifest in materially unconnected events in the same moment, or in qualitatively similar moments at different times. For instance, if the young prospective groom who witnesses two birds flying across the horizon as he ponders his impending marriage interprets this experience as confirmation of union, then all of the elements in that moment may be participating in the *hieros gamos* archetype, while if he interprets this experience as something in the nature of process, constituted in the relation between his mind and the world in which he is embedded, communicating that the marriage is doomed, then this decisive moment may be manifesting the archetypal quality of division endemic to that temporal span. However, it would probably be wise for this young man to consult with his elders and spend time contemplating if he is reading this synchronistic communication in its most efficacious form. Nevertheless, it almost goes without saying that formal causes depend on the activity of formal causation for their ingression.

Qualitative temporality is also a precondition for teleology, as in order for there to be qualitatively emergent instances of novelty and consciousness evident in process over time, then time must necessarily be capable of changing qualitatively. Whereas the quality of the billions of years before the appearance of life on Earth was relatively static in terms of creative advance, at least in our localized quadrant, each period of life's emergence into a more expansive order of magnitude has constituted not only a quantitative densification, but a qualitative elaboration of consciousness and novelty relative to pre-animate materiality. Similarly, whereas the era of predominantly mythical cultures was a fundamentally unchanging world of cyclical time and static hierarchy, though there were many surface fluctuations marked partially by the rising and falling of empires and dynasties, and this world view certainly developed and matured over the millennia of its predominance, the modern world has traced a progressive ascent toward increasing scientific and technological mastery accompanied by a concomitantly increasing disenchantment and sense of existential alienation from the ground of being, producing many more instances of qualitative novelty than the mythical era. A currently emerging epoch would presumably mediate an even more expansive efflorescence of qualitative novelty through the reembrace of premodern modes of thought, which would serve to expand radically the modern mind's epistemological armamentarium, and thus to increase by an order of magnitude the potential instances of qualitative advance. In this way, temporal quality and the quantitative growth of novelty appear to be mutually interdependent aspects of process.

Considering that quantitative growth and qualitative emergence are often complementary, if one traces the quality of successive temporal periods over the course of cosmic development, one will not only find that there is a clearly visible trajectory toward the emergence of novelty and consciousness, but that this trajectory is progressing exponentially, not linearly. Each successive stage, from nonlife to proto-life to complex animality to humanity, constitutes a quantitatively more brief and compact era of qualitative ingression. The recognition of the qualitative nature of temporality by the emerging mode is a precondition for the recognition of the exponential ingression of novelty over time, as the very thing that is being exponentially compacted is the quality of temporal experience, though always mediated through quantitative materiality. This accelerating densification of novelty in time is apparently being facilitated largely through the exponential growth of technology and, particularly, of computational power and interconnectedness. Quantitatively measurable exponential growth generally correlates with concomitant qualitative transformations.

Just as the emergence of the human prefrontal cortex made possible the perception of time, our engagement with one another through our devices, connected by a vast network of nodes increasingly situated in a cloud of shared processing which appears fractally to reiterate the structure of the human brain, is opening new modes of qualitative experience to our purview, from collectively written and organized repositories of human knowledge to platforms for unprecedented social interaction. Our devices direct us on the roads and answer spoken questions, they can hold whole libraries of books, music, and film, and they can even connect us visually as well as aurally across great distances in real time. We take all of these things for granted, but they were science fiction a decade or two ago. And the pace of change appears to be accelerating so that it seems likely that, in the relatively near future, we will have the capability of being immersed almost constantly in some form of "virtual" or "augmented" reality overlaying our physical reality, intimately interacting with spatially distant people, and with artificial intelligences increasingly indistinguishable from human minds.

Currently emerging technologies such as powerful computers embedded in eye glasses, or even contact lenses, may constitute a significant step in this trend toward technology moving ever closer to our bodies and, eventually, disappearing from our sight as conspicuous technological instruments. The skepticism (as of this writing) about the potential for this particular technology's broad adoption strikingly echoes the skepticism leveled against the first wristwatches when they were introduced in the mid-nineteenth century, which were denigrated as a feminine fad until their widespread adoption by men in the nineteen twenties after their use in the First World War. However, whether or not this particular technology finds wide adoption, it seems likely that the distinction between reality and virtual reality, or between human and artificial consciousness will become increasingly difficult to parse in the coming decades as we incorporate ever more miniscule machines into our bodies and our environments, and the machines become as intelligent, creative, interesting, and supple as us hairless apes. Although it is one of the great capacities of the human mind to become accustomed to novelty very quickly, this capacity can also blind us to the explosively accelerating transformation of the quality of our current lives relative to past transformations.

While the suggestion of an emergence into the perception of a fourth-dimensional manifold may also seem like science fiction in the current cultural context, following the exponential trend line of technological growth that has been occurring since at least the late nineteenth century, it seems plausible that our minds may become interfused by nanotechnology in the coming decades, powerful computers too tiny to see with the unaided eye, so that we will be able to think, perceive, and communicate many times faster and with greater depth and clarity than we can now. Just as the dramatic increase in size of the neocortex over a relatively brief period facilitated the human perception of time, which hardly exists for even the most intelligent nonhuman animals, the fourth degree of freedom appears to be a domain of process that exists in potentia, but which we are unable completely to perceive on our current neuronal platform. But the incorporation of increasingly organismic technology into our bodies will most likely allow us to visualize and, thus, to perceive a fourth dimension, which is describable as a higher order of relationality.

Although this claim may perhaps seem implausible based on our current intuitions about the nature of reality and our minds, as has been noted, these intuitions are generally based on a linear mode of thought, not an exponential one. We implicitly assume that the world will change about as much in the future as it has in the past, but if we trace the actual trajectory of those past transformations, we find that the most likely scenario is an increasing concretion of time driven by exponentiality.

However often we sheepishly glance at our colleagues and recheck our calculations, perhaps chagrined that our careful study has produced such seemingly preposterous results, the conclusion remains the same: we are in the knee of an exponential curve in which the density of time itself is accelerating through our still-evolving minds. Although we cannot know precisely how the world will look to us once the curve has gone vertical, carrying us up and out of our current perceptual and conceptual limitations, we can perhaps prepare for this singular emergence by refining our world view, consolidating the positive contributions of human history and setting aside the negative as historical contingency. It seems that if our trajectory is toward a more complete understanding of time, then the collective study of time's qualities is perhaps the most efficacious way to construct a viable model for our eventual self-overcoming.

# CHAPTER 10
## "THE TELEOLOGICAL INTRODUCTION OF NOVELTY"
### FINAL CAUSATION

*The essence of life is the teleological introduction of novelty.*

Alfred North Whitehead, *Adventures of Ideas*[68]

*The world is an astonishing place, and the idea that we have in our possession the basic tools needed to understand it is no more credible now than it was in Aristotle's day. That it has produced you, and me, and the rest of us is the most astonishing thing about it. If contemporary research in molecular biology leaves open the possibility of legitimate doubts about a fully mechanistic account of the origin and evolution of life, dependent only on the laws of chemistry and physics, this can combine with the failure of psychophysical reductionism to suggest that principles of a different kind are also at work in the history of nature, principles of the growth of order that are in their logical form teleological rather than mechanistic.*

Thomas Nagel, *Mind and Cosmos*[69]

That a teleological mode of cognizance is apparently in the process of returning to a position of prominence in cultural discourse is an instantiation of the participatory quality of being, as the admission of final causation into one's world view has the capacity radically to transform one's relation to one's most intimate experience. The return of final causation is literally the return of the possibility of intrinsic purpose to the mental mode of thought that has carefully expurgated all such purpose from the cosmos, and thus found itself pursuing a "search for meaning" in a seemingly meaningless world. It is by now clear that the modern world view generally only acknowledges material and efficient causation, an exclusivity which produces a world of particles colliding unintelligibly, set in motion by a prime mover, whether in the guise of the clockmaker God of nineteenth century Deism, or in impersonal natural laws that provide the initial conditions for the Big Bang, winding down entropically toward increasing disorder, with life and human consciousness as accidental and peripheral epiphenomena. However, if one adopts the premise of final causation, which is so readily apparent in the evolutionary record in its movement toward increasing degrees of consciousness that no amount of scientific evidence can viably disprove it unless one credulously asserts the first principle of exclusive materiality, then the world becomes a place in which everything happens for a reason, though what that reason may be is often the work of an individual life or, indeed, of an epoch to determine.

Belief in final causation, in the context of modernity's anti-teleological bias, requires a leap of faith, though no more so than disbelief in teleology when differentiated from its historical context. This particular instance of credential assertion is another piece of evidence for the necessity of the will to believe in general. As soon as we are conscious, we must believe something, for acting is always acting upon some implicit assumption about reality, even if that assumption is purely negative, denying the very possibility of legitimate belief. For those of us educated on modern assumptions, the embrace of teleology is fraught with peril, as most academic institutions in our era are fundamentally driven by materialist premises, even though the novel modes of thought are slowly, but with increasing speed, being smuggled into the halls of academe, particularly in the humanities. Although many scientists privately hold a belief in some form of teleology, and some brave souls have even asserted this belief publicly, the fund-granting bodies, the departments, and the journals and publishers of scientific discourse largely reassert an anti-teleological bias, so that the increasing number of scientists who find themselves impelled to study teleology are forced to do so at the margins of scientific activity. However, as more and more scientists, philosophers, and thinkers of all sorts consistently and rigorously proclaim their belief in final causation despite how this commitment might limit their career prospects in the short term, the more institutions are supporting work done in this area so that we may soon witness a tipping point in which academic culture will begin to look more favorably on finalism.

However, it seems to be the case that a simple assertion of teleology against reductionist materialism is no more integrative than the opposite assertion. In fact, the adoption of pure finalism in evolution against the pure belief in efficient causation appears to be a transitional reversal, as oppositional assertion itself is more characteristic of the mental mode than the emerging one. This halfway point between the often pure materialism of modern science in theory and the embrace of all kinds of causation is perhaps a dialectical necessity most prominently exemplified in the movements associated with new age spirituality at the liberal end of the spectrum, and religious fundamentalism at the conservative end. These two seemingly opposite movements often have in common a rejection of materiality in favor of spirit, which largely constitutes a regression to premodern modes.

If one asserts the efficacy of teleology to the denigration of Darwinian selection, for instance, one is simply reversing the privileging operation, which appears to be a necessary, but incomplete step in the reconciliation of materialist and teleological approaches. Rather than reject Darwinism outright, one might affirm that evolution does occur through the mechanisms of natural and sexual selection on the micro-scale, but that on the macro-scale, these variations are tilted ever so slightly toward the emergence of consciousness and novel order, the "teleological incline" hypothesis discussed above. However, whether or not this specific way of integrating materialist and finalist modes of thought in evolution obtains, it seems clear that the mode which affirms the partial validity of all previous modes, subsuming their positive contributions within its encompassing embrace, is the most viable path forward at the current juncture.

The return of final causation also gives weight to the discontinuity of process, as the dialectical leap of faith that leads one to adopt the premise of teleology is a primary example of the revolutionary rupture in action. In fact, discontinuity on the scale of evolution, both biological and cosmic, depends upon the notion of final causation, for otherwise such discontinuous jumps in process would have nowhere to leap, just as the atomic electron transition itself requires the potentiality of increasingly encompassing discrete energetic levels to which to vault. Similarly, an assertion that the transition from the mythical mode to the mental mode, for instance, constitutes the qualitative emergence of a more encompassing layer of being into actuality would be unintelligible without the recognition that process appears to be moving inexorably toward the telos of increasingly expansive modes. Teleology calls forth discontinuity to mediate its ingression. And this relationship between final causation and discontinuity appears to be a generalized expression of the mathematically formalizable relation between the fractal strange attractor of chaos theory and fractal bifurcations and, perhaps especially, reverse bifurcations.

Furthermore, final causation is a direct precondition for the development of process through emergent phases, as these novel stages of ingression across scale are primary loci of teleology's trajectory, mediated through discontinuity. These stages can be described as fractally reiterating the Kuhnian phases of normal science punctuated by scientific revolutions, though whereas Kuhn appears to remain ambivalent about whether there is directionality in the process of science, it seems apparent that relativity and quantum theory subsume classical Newtonian mechanics within their more encompassing enfoldment. These two bastions of twentieth century physics can unequivocally be described as a qualitative advance on Newton, though not as more valuable within their specific domains of applicability, as Newtonian equations can be employed to calculate trajectories that would be impossible for the far more complex equations of quantum theory given our current computational capacities. Furthermore, it appears that whichever final theory is ultimately deemed triumphant in the reconciliation of quantum mechanics and relativity, whether some form of string theory with its extra dimensions, Laurent Nottale's application of fractal geometry to quantum gravity in scale relativity, loop quantum gravity, some combination of these approaches, or some other innovation, this theory will represent a qualitative step beyond the current state of physical understanding. Perhaps it is not too much to suggest that this step may constitute a further reconciliation of quantitative physical science with qualitative modes of thought, a supposition variously articulated by the majority of the founding fathers of twentieth century physics.

The parallels between twentieth-century physics, quantum theory and relativity, and philosophy, particularly of the premodern and Asian varieties, have often been remarked upon. However, it is striking to note that, not only did Jung develop the concept of synchronicity partially through several conversations with Albert Einstein, and through extensive correspondence and collaboration with Wolfgang Pauli, but that these scientists, as well as Max Planck, Werner Heisenberg, Niels Bohr, and Erwin Schrödinger, a large portion, perhaps even a majority of the greatest physicists of the twentieth century, all expressed the notion in various valences that quantum theory and relativity could be conceived as mathematically formalized expressions of ideas that had been intuitively grasped by premodern philosophers and mystics. Although our collective modern common sense is still based primarily on Newtonian mechanics, the atomistic and mechanistic form of classical physics, thought expressive of the qualities elucidated in relativity and quantum theory, from discontinuity and nonlocality to complementarity, relativistic time dilation, and the spacetime continuum, can be seen as an integration of the modern quantitative and the premodern qualitative modes.

Such a large-scale reconciliation of quantity and quality, of material-efficient and formal-final causation, in the emergence of a new world view would itself be driven by the teleological ingression of novelty, which proceeds through the dialectical and discontinuous syntheses of previously incommensurable modes. Not only is the concept of teleology an indispensable component of the emerging mode, but it is also a precondition for such a mode's emergence. That some of the late twentieth century's most noted thinkers, including the prominent atheist philosopher Thomas Nagel and influential philosopher and cultural historian Richard Tarnas, have come out in support of the teleological mode of thought that was previously so odious to the rational modern mind suggests that a profound sea change is underway in Western intellectual culture's understanding of the most basic premises of existence. Although William James, Henri Bergson, and Alfred North Whitehead, whom many consider the most important American, French, and English philosophers of the twentieth century, respectively, asserted the validity of teleology, and Gebser, Teilhard, Tarnas, Nagel, and many other prominent philosophers have concurred, there still appears to be a deeply ingrained anti-teleological prejudice in academia, and particularly in science, though this bias seems to be in the process of dissolution as the work of these philosophers and others becomes increasingly well known, both within and without the disciplinary boundaries of philosophy.

The fractal quality of process is yet another aspect of the dynamics of transformation driven by the teleological impulse. The quality of self-similarity partially finds justification in teloi, which draw the particular manifestations of archetypal potentialities across scale toward their becoming. In the same way that fractality is instantiated by the manifestations of archetypes in different domains of actuality, fractality is also evidenced by its efficacy in final causes which, after all, appear to be the complement of formal causes. Furthermore, the historical emergence of the concept of fractality was apparently driven by the teleological impulse, which demands the emergence of novel modes of thought out of concepts that previously appeared unconnected, or even contradictory. Mandelbrot's theory subsumed Leibniz's exploration of recursive self-similarity in one dimension, the Cantor set, the self-inverse fractals introduced by Klein and Poincare (though not under that name), the Koch curve, the Sierpinski triangle, carpet, and curve, the Julia sets, Hausdorff's introduction of the idea of non-integer dimensionality, the Levy C curve, and the Peano curve. The theory of fractals appears to have been implicit in these concepts and mathematical structures, teleologically drawn toward synthesis by the telos of what we now refer to as fractality, which acts as a strange attractor for the coming to consciousness of the very processual quality that elucidates such luring entities.

As discussed above, formal and final causes are deeply implicated with one another. Final causation is a precondition for formal causation just as archetypality is a precondition for teleology. The idea that the things of the world are being drawn toward a transtemporal destination, though the particular contours of their ingression are not determined in advance, implies that those multifarious entities are the manifestations of atemporal potentialities in the nature of process. The classic example employed by Aristotle, and then by Hegel in final causation's modern reanimation, is that of the acorn and the oak tree, fractally reiterating the relationship between form and telos. Just as the acorn contains the formal potential for the oak tree, though not its specific shape which can only be developed through the long temporal process of becoming, the oak tree is the purpose and end which gives the acorn its meaning and function in the world. Without the telos of the oak, the acorn is merely a nut for the enjoyment of squirrels, though even the purpose of providing sustenance for tree-dwelling rodents could perhaps be considered that particular acorn's telos. The idea of formal causes is unintelligible without the idea of final causes.

It clearly follows that, if the archetypal forms depend upon final causation, then the formal causation to which they lend their name also depends upon teleology. The ends toward which archetypes are drawn largely condition the way those archetypes are qualitatively expressed in temporality. For instance, in the case of the woman for whom Jung's presentation of the scarabaeid beetle produced a revelation, all of the elements that participated in the scarab archetype—the woman's divided psychological condition, her dream, the beetle tapping at the window, Jung's presentation of the beetle, and the woman's breakthrough into a more expansive mode—were drawn toward this conclusion by the woman's urge toward self-overcoming, which itself is an individual expression of the teleological self-overcoming apparently endemic to the nature of process. In other words, synchronicity is driven not only by formal causation but, through a simple transformation, by final causation.

Teleology is also a precondition for the exponential quality of process, as the recognition that time is accelerating toward increasing novelty depends upon the idea that there is a trajectory toward novelty implicit in the nature of being. The data points plotted on a graph depicting the major events of cosmic development trace a smooth upward trajectory from nonlife to proto-life to various degrees of plant and animal consciousness to human consciousness and then on to the external, and incipiently internal augmentation of that consciousness through technologies and their complementary modes of thought. Such a graph demonstrates that the directionality of process is increasing at an exponential rate, so that animality emerged an order of magnitude more quickly than life, human consciousness emerged another order of magnitude more quickly than animality, and world views and technologies are emerging at increasingly rapid orders of magnitude, so that the current vanguard of evolutionary development can be traced over the course of decades rather than centuries, millennia, or aeons.

Finally, the teleological ingression of novelty is a precondition for the concretion of time, as the progression through ascending levels of dimensionality appears to trace an expansive trajectory toward ever-more-encompassing stages of the world's self-awareness. It seems that temporic concretion can be understood as the most fundamental expression of final causation that it is possible for the current material substrate of our minds to cognize, so that the deepest urge of being which we can currently conceive is apparently to make its way toward greater degrees of spatio-temporal freedom through the unimaginably vast permutations of cosmic becoming. In this light, humanity's relatively brief history appears to be a transitional moment between cosmic eras, mediating the emergence from third-dimensional animal perception into fourth-dimensional awareness.

Followed to its logical conclusion, this dimensional ascendance would entail the capacity intentionally to navigate temporality in some sense that we cannot yet grasp, but perhaps by means of such a complete collective immersion in the qualitative nature of time that the intimate correspondences of different moments marked on a linear timeline expressive of the same archetypal qualities will seem equally significant to our culture as quantitative clock and calendar time. This teleological coming to consciousness of the full fourth degree of freedom may take place through technologies such as full-immersion virtual reality in which we could record experiences in their cognitive and sensual completeness in order to share them with others, so that it would be impossible to differentiate the original experience from its copy, in which case the question of which experience is more real would become genuinely problematic.[70] Similarly, we may soon be able to reconstruct, through massively amplified computational capacities, the experiences of people and times long gone, which would be practically indistinguishable from actually traveling back in time. Or perhaps some technology will emerge that we have not yet suspected. However, I will suggest in the Epilogue that an archetypal cosmology is an exemplary strategy for tracing the contours of this more expansive manifold.

# CHAPTER 11
## "AN EXPONENTIALLY ACCELERATING PROCESS"
### THE INCREASING INGRESSION OF NOVELTY

*Not only does the universe have this preference for novelty, but each acceleration into novelty has proceeded more quickly than the one which preceded it. So for instance the slow cooling out of the universe led to the slightly more rapid appearance of organic chemistry, which led to the quite rapid evolution of higher plants and animals, which led to the hysterical pace of human history, and I see no reason to suppose that the process of acceleration will ever slow down. . . . It's an exponentially accelerating process.*

Terence McKenna, *Interview on Coast to Coast AM*[1]

*A specific paradigm (a method or approach to solving a problem; for example, shrinking transistors on an integrated circuit as a way to make more powerful computers) generates exponential growth until its potential is exhausted. When this happens, a paradigm shift occurs, which enables exponential growth to continue. . . . If we examine the timing of these epochs, we see that they have been part of a continuously accelerating process.*

Ray Kurzweil, *The Singularity is Near*[72]

The exponential ingression of novelty provides support for the participatory quality of process, as the assumption of linearity produces radically different results than the premise of exponentiality. For the modern mind, whose intuitive sense of the world is grounded in classical

Newtonian mechanics, our current rate of population growth seems unsustainable as, based on linear projections, food and energy production will soon be unable to keep pace with the explosive growth of the world population, which is temporarily exponential (it appears to be leveling off). However, food and energy production are also growing exponentially, so that unless the process truly goes off the rails in a mass pandemic or a nuclear apocalypse, the production of food and energy will not only keep pace with population growth, but progressively exceed demand so that the average standard of living for individuals in the world will continue measurably to grow.[73] Whether scientists, academics, corporations, and lawmakers work on the assumption of linearity or exponentiality will have a great impact on the decisions they make for the directions of research and development, and the legislation that governs these endeavors. Acting on the assumptions characteristic of the modern, linear conception of development will tend to produce greater scarcity and unsustainability, while acting on the more subtle and accurate assumption of exponential growth will generate a precondition for effectively meeting the great challenges faced by our civilization. Exponential development appears to occur whether we know it or not, but while a linear world view poses the danger of prolonging the mode of thought characteristic of deficient mentality and all of the destructive tendencies which accompany that mode, from wealth inequality to environmental degradation, the more individuals who adopt the premise of exponentiality, the more rapidly will we be able to make the transition to an exponentially sustainable world.

However, making the transition from a linear to an exponential understanding of growth in time requires a leap of faith, whether for the individual or the collective. No matter how much rigorously compiled and analyzed evidence is arrayed in support of exponentiality, even the rationality privileging modern mind does not ultimately make its decisions based on logic alone, but on its affectively driven premises. This is a great paradox of modernity: that a world view which sees itself as eminently rational is still founded upon the prerationally adopted notions of Cartesian dualism, and Newtonian atomism and linear, absolute time. It is only within the constraints of these assumptions that science could be forged from the relatively undifferentiated mass of physical and metaphysical speculation characteristic of premodernity. However, these constraints have been largely instrumental, and do not appear to describe the lived quality of temporal process, which is generally understood more deeply by premodern modes than modern ones.

While theorists of exponential growth employ the mathematical and empirical methods of science, they place this mode's utility within the context of a broader approach, which sets aside the unprovable premise of linearity in favor of the more realistic exponential model of temporal development. And as with the adoption of all genuinely novel ideas, this conceptual shift requires not just improved logical reasoning, but the courage to accept a radically new premise when the old one it is subsuming has become unproductive and limiting. These thinkers have undertaken a credential bound based on their affective proclivities, though bolstered by reams of convincing evidence, despite the common resistance to this mode of thought in the central networks of intellectual culture by individuals who are often more gifted at climbing the hierarchical rungs of academia or publishing than in comprehending the far-reaching consequences of radically novel concepts. However, the success of the emerging mode partially depends upon those exceptional academics, publishers, and journalists who possess both a broad vision and the position authoritatively to assert that vision's validity. We are not passive observers of the emerging world view, but active and integral participants.

Exponentiality is also a precondition for the integrative method, which has emerged only in the last few centuries in philosophical discourse (though presaged in various streams of premodern thought), and which now appears to be rising into collective awareness. The exponential ingression of novelty over the preceding millennia has finally made possible, through the accelerating successive emergences of world views, accompanied by the accelerating development of technology, the recognition on a wide scale that seemingly incommensurable modes of thought can be reconciled through the confrontation and subsequent synthesis of opposites to produce an emergent mode. Although this insight was variously articulated by Hegel and by John Stuart Mill in the nineteenth century, and elaborated by James, Jung, Bergson, Whitehead, Gebser, and their many associates and successors, it seems that it was only after the era of postmodernism, which appears to have been largely constituted in a broad recognition of the core insight of relativity (that entities can only be defined in relation to other entities), that the novel mode could truly emerge into collective awareness.

Postmodernism has allowed the intellectual culture of our era to begin to see that its fundamental ideas about the world, and about our identities in the world which seemed fixed and immutable, from essentialized gender roles, sexual identities, and racial characteristics to Cartesian dualism, monocausality, and linear temporality, are far more malleable than we had previously imagined as we gained unprecedented access to other cultures and other ways of thinking within our own cultures. But the postmodern insight concerning the radically constructed quality of reality is now being turned on its head in the novel insight that all modes of thought have value insofar as they do not impinge on other modes and that, in fact, all modes are complementary and necessary for the construction of an intelligible and comprehensive world view. For instance, although the entire philosophy of the Nazis, as a limit case for negativity and evil in the modern world, can be rejected without hesitation because it is founded upon the denial of the most basic rights of others, one can recognize that their visual aesthetic was really quite striking, though its associations are certainly horrific, an enduring reminder of the darkness to which humanity can descend. In this way, although one might condemn the primary negative assertions of any mode of thought, it appears that there is always some value, however minor or occulted, in every mode that has found some success in the world.

Furthermore, discontinuity is supported by exponentiality, as the data points that trace exponential growth are generally mediated through discrete jumps, providing yet another piece of evidence for the discontinuous quality of process. Conversely, the discovery of energetic quantum discontinuity in early twentieth-century physics was made possible by the exponential ingression of novelty, so that the quantum revolution occurred only four-hundred years after the Copernican revolution, and two-hundred years after the birth of classical physics in the mind of Isaac Newton. By contrast, the similarly epochal revolution just previous in the West occurred perhaps with the birth of Christianity fifteen hundred years before Copernicus, or possibly even in the heart of the Axial Age a half-millennium before that. The fact of accelerating phases of ingression has similarly facilitated the mathematical formulation of the premodern intuitions of discontinuity, expressed in many valences, from Promethean inspiration to Christian transfiguration, which has subsequently allowed discontinuity to begin to be applied not just in the mathematically formalizable domain of physics, but also in the conceptual domain of philosophy as an essential element of the novel mode.

The exponential quality of being is also exemplified in the development of process through emergent stages, so that the increasingly brief time claimed by the predominance of each world view—hundreds of thousands of years for the archaic, tens of thousands for the magic, thousands for the mythical, hundreds for the mental, and now perhaps even fewer for the new world view—provides a primary locus of effectuation for temporal acceleration. Similarly, the subjective span of each stage in the life of an individual, which appears to be inversely proportional to the measurable time that those stages endure so that childhood seems eternal, adolescence seems very long, and mature adulthood seems to pass ever more quickly, appears to be describable as an exponential process, and thus individual development is another domain for exponential acceleration. And conversely, the exponential progression of world views has itself made possible the reembrace of the core insight of the premodern Great Chain of Being that there are distinct gradations of process, though it strips this concept of its hierarchical valuation.

It follows that the emerging mode itself has been made possible by the exponential acceleration of world views, which has allowed this mode to begin to emerge into collective consciousness so soon on a cosmic scale after the emergence of modernity. And this emergence is partially constituted in the concept of exponentiality itself, which has served both to provide evidential instantiation for the other concepts characteristic of this new world view, and has acted as a means for the timely ingression of these concepts into collective understanding. The exponential growth of technology in particular has progressively drawn the world together, so that there is greater communication and interconnection between far-flung individuals and cultures than there has ever been before, producing increasing opportunities for the elicitation of novelty through the tension of difference (though, as has often been noted, there may also be a concomitant diminution of connection in more local, physically present spaces). This process is building on itself so that the more nodes of interconnected novelty there are in the total system, the more novelty that system will produce until a tipping point is reached and the new world view presumably emerges triumphant.

The recognition of the fractal quality of process has also been facilitated by exponentiality, so that acceleration of the inauguration of successive world views has produced a flood of novel ideas, first in the work of Leibniz, and then in Cantor, Koch, Julia, and the rest during the late nineteenth and early twentieth centuries, which made possible Mandelbrot's formalization of fractality in the mid-twentieth century. Since Mandelbrot, the applications of fractals have exploded in what appears to be an instance of exponential growth. And furthermore, the quality of exponentiality can be observed self-similarly across scale, so that the exponentially accelerating evolution of nonlife to life to human consciousness fractally reiterates the accelerating development of premodern to modern to the emerging world view, as well as the subjective development of the individual from infant to adolescent to adult. That this exponential progression is repeated in these different domains provides one primary class of evidence for fractality.

Similarly, exponentiality constitutes a dynamic of ingression for archetypal potentialities, so that whereas the idea of eternal forms was barely actual in archaic humanity, the pace of development through the magic perception of spirits, the mythical knowledge of gods, the Platonic recognition of forms, and Jung's revivification of the forms in the idea of archetypes has occurred with increasing rapidity, and this acceleration appears to be continuing. In addition, the quality of exponential growth itself appears to express an archetypal complex, perhaps correlated with the archetype associated with the evolutionary drive in synthesis with the archetype associated with discontinuity, which serves to instantiate the archetypal perspective. In a recursive formulation, exponentiality, which has made possible the individuated ingression of archetypal thought, has itself mediated the recognition of exponential growth as an archetypal potentiality, which in turn provides support for the archetypal mode of cognizance.

Qualitative temporality also finds support in the exponential quality of being, as exponentiality is constituted in the qualitative experience of time's acceleration, though intimately correlated with quantitative growth. The increasing compaction of novelty can also be described as the accelerating occurrence of qualitative change in the temporal process. And in a different valence, one quality ascribable to temporality in general is exponentiality, so that it seems to be the nature of time to move ever more quickly in a way that appears to describe an exponential curve, of which the transition from the mental mode to the emerging one is perhaps the knee. In the inverse explanatory trajectory, the exponential acceleration of world views has made possible the reembrace of formal causation by the individuated rational intellect through the densification of innovations associated with physics, depth psychology, and philosophy, issuing particularly into the work of Bergson, Jung, Gebser, and Tarnas. Exponentiality is an instantiation of qualitative time which, in turn, has been able to find its current dialectical reanimation because of the accelerating ingression of novelty into process.

The teleological introduction of novelty and consciousness also relies on exponentiality, as linear progression toward a telos would apparently be unsustainable. In such a scenario, the development of life into animality and of animality into human consciousness would require the same amount of time as the development of inanimate matter into vital organization. But each emergence is constituted in an order of magnitude greater connectivity, which multiplies sites of novelty, thereby producing the next emergence an order of magnitude more quickly, so linearity appears unreasonable in this context. The same archetypal progression from the nascence of a new mode to that mode's senescence and subsumption into the following mode occurs with increasing rapidity in each stage because each emergence provides many more opportunities for dialectical synthesis than the previous stage, and so exponentiality is implied as soon as one recognizes the teleological principle, and vice versa. And in a by now familiar operation, the exponential acceleration of world views has also facilitated the reemergence of final causation after teleology's repression in service to the individuation characteristic of modern science. Exponentiality is a necessary factor in the abstract dynamic of teleological directionality, as well as in the recognition of that dynamic in historical time.

And certainly, exponentiality is an essential element in the concretion of time hypothesis, as it is the primary dynamic by which the densification of temporal experience occurs, and thus a precondition for the emergence of the world's self-awareness through the human mind from three spatial dimensions mapped onto the fractal dimension of time into a more complete perception of a fourth degree of freedom. The incipient fourth-dimensional awareness apparently evident in episodic mammalian consciousness lasted for millions of years, so that the nascent temporal awareness that can be witnessed in dogs, for instance, is limited to a sequence of specific events: when their human companions get up from the dinner table, this may signal that it is time for their treat. However, if the humans in the house happen to eat lunch one day at the dinner table, although the dogs may never have received a treat at this time, they will still insist enthusiastically on collecting their reward when the person from whom they usually obtain their meaty bounty gets up from the table, even though it is the wrong time of day, and even though it is light outside where it is usually dark. Similarly, dogs seem not to have a conception of how long their humans have been gone, for they clamor just as excitedly when one returns from a ten-minute trip to the corner store as when one returns from a two-week vacation.

However, once the human prefrontal cortex evolved after millions of years of animal evolution in a low-resolution temporal domain, say a fractal dimension of very roughly .1, the human perception of time has advanced at an exponentially increasing pace over the ensuing hundreds of thousands of years. Techniques for the qualitative perception of time, from premodern astrology and the *I-Ching* to the modern ideas of duration and synchronicity, as well as techniques for the increasingly precise quantitative measurement of time, from astronomy and calendars to sundials and clocks of the mechanical, digital, and atomic varieties, have mediated the progressive elaboration of the temporal domain. The collective human perception of time can now perhaps be described as exhibiting a fractal dimensionality of .5, which is the figure Nottale derives for the temporal dimension in quantum systems. Through exponential technological growth, it seems plausible to suggest that this temporal acceleration may result in the emergence of human consciousness into an integral degree of fourth-dimensional freedom.

# CHAPTER 12
## "THE CONCRETION OF TIME"
### PROGRESSIVE DEGREES
### OF SPATIO-TEMPORAL FREEDOM

*Our epoch is concerned with the concretion of time. And our fundamental point of departure, the attempt to concretize time and thus realize and become conscious of the fourth dimension, furnishes a means whereby we may gain an all-encompassing perception and knowledge of our epoch. . . . Time has us because we are not yet aware of its entire reality.*

Jean Gebser, *The Ever-Present Origin*[74]

*Since quantum theory implies that elements that are separated in space are generally non-causally and non-locally related projections of a higher-dimensional reality, it follows that moments separated in time are also such projections of this reality. . . . This leads to a fundamentally new notion of the meaning of time. Both in common experience and in physics, time has generally been considered to be a primary, independent and universally applicable order, perhaps the most fundamental one known to us. Now, we have been led to propose that it is secondary and that, like space, it is to be derived from a higher-dimensional ground.*

David Bohm, *Wholeness and the Implicate Order*[75]

The concretion of time constitutes evidence for the participatory quality of process, as the assumption that temporality is a partial approximation of a fourth degree of freedom, whether adopted by the individual or the collective, has far-reaching consequences, many of which are extremely difficult for us even to imagine given our current perceptual and cognitive capacities. However, what seems clear from the work that has been undertaken concerning this concept is that many of the questions and conflicts that appear insoluble to a modern world view, which presupposes the premise of time as a linear, quantitative medium, appear far more approachable based on the premise of an emerging fourth-dimensional awareness, even though we may not be able fully to inhabit this awareness for a long time to come. However, the pragmatic belief in the possibility of this ascendance into an additional degree of freedom would make all the difference in bringing into actuality the conceptual and technological tools and methods for this collective self-overcoming.

The concept of temporic concretion is perhaps a limit case for the will to believe, as the adoption of this premise marks a definitive break from the assumptions of modernity. Although the individual premises that together lead inexorably to this conclusion are fairly well established in twentieth-century thought, though still often minority positions, the idea that human history and the awareness of time have been leading all along toward our collective emergence into a higher-dimensional manifold is difficult to swallow for all but the most intellectually adventurous among us in our current cultural milieu. But this has been the case for all truly novel ideas in human history, such as the heliocentric hypothesis, the cosmological foundation for the modern world view itself. Although it seems natural to us now that Copernicus, Kepler, and Galileo would feel confident in the idea that the Earth revolves around the Sun, and not vice versa, as this supposition is almost universally accepted in our time, these Copernican revolutionaries were embedded in a world that believed heliocentrism was the height of absurdity based on many millennia of thought and discourse about the nature of the world. Although the heliocentric hypothesis had been proposed by Aristarchus in antiquity, this suggestion was generally assumed to be a historical curiosity unworthy of serious consideration by the medieval ecclesiastical and academic authorities.

It was not until Kepler's innovation of elliptical motion nearly a century after Copernicus first introduced his hypothesis that a plausible geometrical model was adduced for the movement of the planets around the Sun. The heliocentric hypothesis constituted a radical leap of faith for these men, as the discovery of a coherent mathematical explanation for their certainty required the unproven belief to persist through multiple generations. In fact, this intentionality is a primary factor in making such a discovery possible. The temporic concretion hypothesis appears to require a similarly abiding credence, for though we do not yet know precisely through what means this suspected dimensional transition may occur, and the physical, mathematical, and conceptual basis for understanding time as a fractal dimension is still very new and in the process of being worked out in greater detail, this notion seems more plausible to a growing number of our most forward-thinking minds than the current collective assumption of static temporality, just as the heliocentric hypothesis seemed intuitively to make more sense to those at the vanguard of sixteenth- and early seventeenth-century thought.

The hypothesis of temporic concretion is also an exemplification of the integrative method, as it seems to be the ultimate result of the reconciliation of quantitative and qualitative modes of temporal cognizance, correlated with material-efficient and formal-final causation respectively. On one hand, the description of time as a linear succession of moments is valid because this quantitative mode has been incredibly productive in the development of scientific and technological accomplishment in the modern era. However, in light of the concretion of time hypothesis, linear temporality can perhaps be seen as a special and vitally useful case of a larger reality, just as Newtonian physics has come to be viewed as a special case of relativity and quantum theory. On the other hand, the predominant premodern description of time is qualitative, so that events that are materially unconnected or separated in time can be understood as corresponding through their participation in the same archetypal qualities. This qualitative temporal mode has also been incredibly productive in elucidating the complexities of human experience, explored for many thousands of years by shamans, sages, contemplatives, and yogis, and expressed in some of the great ancient religious and philosophical texts and inventions, from the *I-Ching* and astrology to alchemy and the Mayan calendar of interlocking rounds. And this mode of thought can also be seen as a special case of a larger reality, just as formal and final causation account for half of the Aristotelian causal quaternity.

The concretion of time is an instance of quantum discontinuity at the largest imaginable scale, as the transition from three-dimensional animality to four-dimensional awareness appears to be in the process of being mediated through human history. Nietzsche's evocation of humanity as a "bridge . . . between beast and overman" appears to be an intimation of the recognition that, viewed from a wider perspective, what seems to us a vast expanse of historical time is actually a relatively brief phase transition from one stable continuity to another.[76] In relation to the countless aeons that led to the birth of human consciousness, the duration required for the discovery of fire, the creation of language, and the invention of religions, philosophies, sciences, and technologies is a mere instant, so it seems plausible that this increasingly rapid pace of development may level off and enjoy a more stable existence once dimensional ascendance has been achieved. However, this is pure speculation based on the apparently discontinuous quality of this transition, as the emergence into the full perception of a fourth dimension appears to be beyond the event horizon of a temporal singularity, which we can feel luring us ever closer, but cannot yet conceive in its integral wholeness.

The developmental quality of process through emergent stages also finds exemplification in temporic concretion, as the ascendance through successive phases of dimensionality is the most expansive conceivable expression of this processual tendency. The zero-dimensional perception of nonlife gives way to the one-dimensional perception of early organisms, which issues into the two-dimensional perception of somewhat more complex organisms, the three-dimensional perception of animals, the three-and-a-fraction-dimensional perception of modern humans, and finally the four-dimensional perception toward which we are apparently being drawn. Each phase in the process is a profoundly significant qualitative expansion of consciousness, so that our transition from the partial dimensionality of time to the awareness of the full fourth dimension, though it may not be quite as drastic as the full-dimensional step from nonlife to life, or from bacteria to animals, could conceivably be on the order of the transition from the most intelligent primates (or, more accurately, our common ancestor) to archaic *homo sapiens*.

Although the state of being that we seem on our way toward inhabiting may appear godlike to us mere mortals, we surely seem similarly transcendent to our dogs, for instance, who appear to have a vague sense that there are things occurring in human life in which they will never be able to participate because of cognitive constraints. We take this difference for granted, while the emergence of yet more expansive states seems like wild and ungrounded fancy. But this appears only to be a function of the human mind's limited ability to intuit future radical novelty, as the simple recognition that such a dimensional transition has already taken place three times over the course of cosmic history inevitably leads one to the conclusion that it is more likely that this trajectory will continue than that it will end with our current mode of existence.

And the notion that we are in the midst of a dimensional phase transition appears to be a primary premise of the emerging world view, for as Gebser particularly demonstrates, the novel mode of thought is largely constituted in the coming to consciousness of time as a full integer. If, as Gebser suggests, zero-dimensionality fractally correlates with the archaic mode, one-dimensionality with the magic mode, two-dimensionality with the mythical mode, and three-dimensionality with the mental mode, these nested progressions may converge in the emerging mode. The realization of four-dimensionality on the scale of human culture would manifest as the emergence into collective awareness of the temporal dimension as a full integer. If this sounds tautological, it is because the emergence into a more expansive domain always requires the adoption of new assumptions, so that the premises and the world view that they produce emerge together as a seamless whole, like a child emerging from the womb. It is not possible, therefore, to deduce logically either the emerging world view or its accompanying qualitative densification of temporal experience from modern premises. Rather, like Bergson's swimming metaphor given epigraphically above, one must leap into the new medium in order to verify the reality of that medium.

In discussing temporic concretion, it becomes increasingly problematic to separate the concepts presented in the previous chapters from one another, as perhaps for this concept more than any, those previously explicated ideas are all necessary to speak with any clarity or precision about the prospective concretion of time. Whereas the other concepts have been demonstrated extensively through more specific forms of evidence in various disciplines, those previous concepts are themselves the primary evidence for temporic concretion, which consequently depends upon the considered adoption of these other directly adduced concepts as premises for its own validation. Fractality is given its widest locus of exemplification in the concretion of time, which appears self-similarly to reiterate the emergence of the novel mode from the crucible of the modern, of human self-awareness from animality, and of the individual from adolescence into mature adulthood. While the transitions to human self-awareness and mature adulthood have already occurred in our collective experience, and thus are proven facts, and the emerging world view has been adopted in its various inflections by many individuals if not yet by a majority of our culture, temporic concretion is a purely hypothetical extrapolation from these other ingressions of which it is apparently a fractal reiteration. Only if the emergence into a full fourth degree of freedom occurs in actuality will the application of fractality to dimensional ingression itself be proved with any certainty, but this will be striking proof indeed.

The advent of temporic concretion would also provide a locus of exemplification for the archetypal perspective, as the archetype of the number four, the "quaternity" of Jungian thought, is central to the process of individuation. For Jung, the Trinity of Father, Son, and Holy Spirit left out a "fourth function," alternately identified as

Satan/evil/shadow, as Christ's relationship to the Church, or as the feminine and the body, though it should be noted that this attribution of the feminine has been decoupled from the biologically female in the wake of feminist postmodernism. Nevertheless, in all these inflections, the fourth element is that which has been repressed and identified as "other" in the long trajectory of Judeo-Christian patriarchy, culminating in modernity. For Jung, this fourth element is the "archetype of wholeness,"[77] which may produce a reconciliation of the traditionally conceived transcendent masculine divinity with embodied feminine immanence.

Following Jung scholar Jolande Jacobi and Gebser, this return of the repressed fourth element can ultimately be described as the reembrace of premodern epistemologies and modes of causation, and most significant for the present discussion, of the qualitative approach to time by the mentality that privileges the quantitative temporality characteristic of scientific materialism. And this dialectical synthesis of modern and premodern modes of temporal cognizance can be understood as the incipient emergence of the fourth dimension in its wholeness, so that the first dimension is archetypally correlated with God the Father, the second with Christ the Son, the third with the Holy Spirit, and the fourth with the feminine womb and ground of being, the relationality of Christ and Church. It seems strikingly significant, therefore, that Pope Pius XII initiated the epochal recognition of the Assumption of the Blessed Virgin Mary in 1950, in Jung's view completing the quaternity (for which the psychologist sent a letter of congratulations to the Pope), two years before Jung published *Synchronicity*, and one year after Gebser published *The Ever-Present Origin*. This midpoint of the twentieth century appears to have been an axis of transformation, which synchronistically mediated the symbolic reembrace of the archetypal feminine by the primary Western institution that had perpetrated its repression, as well as the nascence of temporic concretion as a viable mode of thought.

Both the historical circumstances of temporic concretion's emergence and the concept itself depend particularly upon the qualitative nature of temporality. In light of the dimensional hypothesis, the tracing of time's qualities is a primary method for mapping the fourth-dimensional manifold of which temporality appears to be a fractional approximation. As in the lower-dimensional analogy of a 1.9 dimensional object, which can take the form of a convoluted curved line doubling back upon itself continuously to trace the contours of a two-dimensional surface, attention to qualitative time appears to be a method for effectively folding time back upon itself, weaving together qualitatively similar moments separated in linear temporality, but connected by their participation in the same archetypal form. Formal causation may find its ultimate expression as the threadlike medium for the fabrication of a qualitative temporal knit. Although this woven web may currently resemble loose yarn strewn across an invisible complex terrain, describing some contours but leaving large gaps in its coverage, as an increasing number of the scholars who currently study exclusively quantitative modes of thought turn their attention to qualitative time, the loose thread may eventually be woven into a whole cloth, fitted so snugly to the previously unperceivable surface that the two will be indistinguishable. The figurative meaning of fashioning a garment "out of whole cloth" as a fictional fabrication is not lost here, but it is recontextualized as the world-constituting narrative construction of novelty. In this way, the study of time's qualities may find its fulfillment in the emergent perception of an integral fourth degree of freedom, so that the metaphorical cloth woven through the process of human history may, in fact, constitute the fabrication of the fourth dimension in its actuality, whereas this wholeness is now largely potentiality, at least for human consciousness.

This lower-dimensional analogy for the progressive densification of temporality implies teleology, as the full collective perception of the fourth degree of freedom appears to be the telos toward which the process of temporic concretion is moving, the needle guiding the temporal thread into an increasingly ordered entanglement. This more expansive degree of freedom is apparently an attractor drawing human activity into its wake of significance, casting its shadow back across history, granting purpose not only to the long dialectical evolution of world views, but to the far longer ascent through progressive stages of dimensional ingression. This final cause appears to be the source of the widespread eschatological intimations of premodernity. Indeed, temporic concretion may have been intimated in the Messianic expectations of Judaism, in the Christian apocalypse marked by the Second Coming of Jesus Christ, and in the Islamic Day of Judgment which, according to the Prophet Mohammed, will be preceded by the appearance of ten signs, one of which is Christ's Second Coming. The Hindu prophecy of Kalki, the tenth and final incarnation of Vishnu, whose coming will mark the end of the *Kali Yuga*, the fourth age of human history, may constitute another such premodern intimation. Viewed from a dimensional perspective, these ancient eschatologies articulated by some of the world's great religions may have been early intuitions of the end of exclusively linear temporality and the inception of transtemporal freedom within a mathematically describable higher-dimensional phase space.

And this progressive densification of temporality appears to be accelerating, which, if the concretion of time proves a viable description of reality, would instantiate the exponential ingression of novelty into process. Although cosmic history leading up to the emergence of the modern world view does appear to have traced an exponential curve, it is only in twentieth century technology that this exponential growth has become visible over the course of an individual human life. Whereas in previous centuries, the rate of novelty's ingression could viably be interpreted as linear growth, it is becoming increasingly apparent that the total processing power of our civilization is doubling approximately every two years and that we are in the knee of an exponential progression which, when it goes vertical, may mediate a discontinuous leap of cognitive and perceptual capacity as radical as the relatively sudden emergence of the human prefrontal cortex from the platform of the primate brain.[78]

Of course, processing power is not the only indication of creative advance, as intelligence without wisdom is meaningless and inhuman. It appears that the collective adoption of a world view which embraces not only rational intellect, but premodern intuitive, affective, somatic, and spiritual modes, as well as premodern epistemological and causal conceptual modes, is a vitally important component of the concretion of time. If exponentially accelerating technology constitutes the hardware of the human-machine civilization, then the emerging world view may provide the software, a more comprehensive operating system for the mindful engagement with this explosion of processing capacity. Not only has the quantitative growth of computing and information technologies facilitated this emerging world view, but the progression of world views has made that quantitative growth possible, and has given it form and meaning. In particular, the archetypal cosmology discussed in the Epilogue appears to be a primary method for tracing the qualitative meaning of temporality.

# EPILOGUE
## "A THIRD COPERNICAN REVOLUTION"
### ARCHETYPAL COSMOLOGY

*Despite what might appear to the more literal-minded as a reversion to premodern geocentrism, this idea actually deepens Kant's insight that his proposal for a "transcendental idealism" constituted a second Copernican Revolution, only here, with a third revolution, it is not the human subject that provides the epistemological meta-point of view, but the Earth as a whole (though still mediated, of course, through human knowing). Such recognition allows us to honor to the fullest extent Kepler's insight—terra stella nobilis—that the Earth is a noble star, and in one sense the noblest among our solar system, in that it is through human consciousness as it has evolved on Earth that the new structure and unfolding meaning of the cosmos is revealed.*

Sean M. Kelly, *Coming Home*[79]

*Could it be, then, that our continuing endeavours to push back the frontiers of both the cosmos and the psyche betray a single, deeper motive? Perhaps our quest within, to explore the human psyche, and our quest without, to explore the universe, are but different expressions of the ubiquitous spiritual quest, as old as humanity itself, to discover our ultimate origins, to come into conscious relationship with the source and ground of all being. If so, then archetypal patterns, reflected in the structural order of the cosmos and manifest simultaneously in the depths of the human unconscious, might serve to illuminate our way.*

Keiron Le Grice, *The Archetypal Cosmos*[80]

When I first read Richard Tarnas' 1991 book, *The Passion of the Western Mind*, its breadth and depth of insight set the one-volume history of philosophy apart from other accounts I had read. Employed as a text at numerous universities, and praised by various academic luminaries, *Passion* presents the great thinkers and visionaries who forged the Western world view, from the ancient Hebrew and pre-Socratic to the postmodern. It was the first book that allowed me fully to inhabit the realization, as a young man not yet twenty, that people in other times really did conceive the world in radically different ways than how most of us collectively construct our experience in the late modern West. The epilogue to Tarnas' book explicates, through a number of historical streams including romanticism, idealism, and depth psychology, the emergence of what Tarnas refers to as a "participatory epistemology," a philosophical approach that seems capable of overcoming the radical alienation of the individuated modern subject. This participatory perspective acknowledges that if human consciousness is evolved from and embedded in the world it seeks to know, then the mind can be understood as the world coming to know itself. This insight, toward which the book built like a vast symphonic crescendo, appeared simultaneously epiphanic and self-evident, allowing me to become conscious of dynamics that I had only intuited, not yet possessing the verbal and conceptual tools to articulate them.

A half-decade later, during the second year of my doctoral studies, I was deeply involved with poststructuralists like Jacques Derrida and Michel Foucault when it began to dawn on me that, although these theorists are brilliant and fascinating, they are almost exclusively oriented toward problematizing and deconstructing the privileging hierarchies characteristic of modernity. The more I read, the more I began to see the postmodernism that they exemplified not as an end, but as a necessary step in a dialectical process like the one Tarnas describes, a clearing away of the previously dominant world view's assumptions to make room for the emergence of a qualitatively new mode of thought that subsumes the earlier modes. At this point, I reread *Passion*, an activity which ignited in me the realization that I could adopt the kind of theoretical orientation articulated by Tarnas, along with that of the other theorists mentioned in the preceding chapters who I was also reading in the course of my studies. I therefore decided to embrace the ideas of thinkers from Hegel, James, and Whitehead to Jung, Bergson, and Gebser as my primary hermeneutic approach, though this theoretical commitment sometimes put me at odds with the predominant milieu of an extremely skeptical New York academia in which I was then immersed.

As I inquired more deeply into Tarnas' work, I made a startling discovery: an essay he had written in 1987 entitled "Introduction to Archetypal Astrology." At first, I was astonished that the man who had written *Passion* could take seriously something as patently ridiculous and naïve as astrology. However, as I read the essay, written with the same elegant prose and rigorous reasoning as the book that I valued so highly, I found it necessary to begin to reconsider my position on this ancient idea that posited a meaningful correlation between the movements of the planets and events in human experience. In the process of reading Tarnas' exposition, it became clear that I knew very little about the way astrology actually worked, and that I had based my opinion of this interpretive method more on received modern prejudice and hearsay than on any real evidence. The kind of astrology Tarnas described hardly resembled the horoscopic predictions of the sort found in newspapers, or the horary astrology practiced by psychics in little shops above storefronts with neon signs in the window.

Still undecided, I was apprehensive as I acquired a copy of Tarnas' *Cosmos and Psyche* when it was published in January of 2006, reading it with a sense of real urgency. However, those five hundred pages of gracefully composed narrative, carefully reasoned argumentation, and meticulously compiled evidence proved a revelation, one that has been confirmed many times over in my subsequent research. At the beginning of *Cosmos and Psyche*, Tarnas gives sixty pages to tracing the larger historical and philosophical context within which the discipline that has come to be known as archetypal cosmology can be understood, analyzing the evolution of world views, the radical shift in the underlying assumptions held by humanity that took place in the aftermath of the Copernican revolution, and the relatively sudden emergence of the disenchanted cosmos of modernity. Tarnas then offers several hundred pages of evidence for four planetary cycles, which to my mind convincingly demonstrate that the angular relationships of the planets to one another consistently correlate with certain categories of events in human history, in both individual and collective domains of experience. These events bear specific archetypal qualities that seem to correspond with the planets that have moved into particular geometrical alignments with one another during any given period, especially the dynamic or "hard" aspects: the 0° conjunction, the 180° opposition, and the 90° square.

Before briefly citing a few of the more striking correlations, it is important to note that, from Tarnas' perspective, the planets do not cause events in human experience. Rather, the planets appear to be like hands on a vast clock that correlate with the archetypal quality of each moment in the solar system that they constitute. The extensive evidence presented by Tarnas implies the ancient conception of a cosmos so deeply and fundamentally ordered that both the movements of the planets and events on Earth correspond to the qualitative contours of temporality. Tarnas suggests that this correlation can be illuminated by the Jungian concept of synchronicity, which can in turn be described as a modern inflection of formal causation: an archetypal potentiality manifesting in two materially unconnected but meaningfully correlated events. The relation of the planets to human experience does not appear to be deterministic or concretely predictive. Rather, the movements of the planets appear to be more generally predictive of the archetypal "weather" at any given moment. Although, as discussed above, the archetypes are multivalent and can manifest in many different, sometimes even opposite ways, they apparently do so consistently within the constraints of each archetype's domain of significance. Moreover, these manifestations seem to be enacted cocreatively through the participation of human consciousness.

For instance, through the study of natal charts (which depict the positions of the planets at the time of an individual's birth) since Uranus' discovery in the late eighteenth century, a consensus among astrological researchers has emerged that the planet appears to be associated with sudden change and awakening, with the Promethean spark of innovation and discovery, and with revolution, discontinuity, rupture, and unexpected revelations or breaks. The archetype correlated with the planet Uranus seems to liberate the other planetary archetypes with which it comes into relationship, coinciding with the corresponding planets moving into specific alignments. Through a similar process, Pluto was found to be associated with the Dionysian underworld of instinct, sex, the will to power, the evolutionary drive toward transformation, and elemental intensity and massiveness. The Plutonic archetype appears to potentiate and titanically empower the other planetary archetypes with which it comes into dynamic relationship.

The archetypal complex of Uranus and Pluto combined can manifest as the profound empowerment (Pluto) of the impulse toward innovation and discovery (Uranus), observable at the inception and publication of numerous milestones in the history of thought, including those wrought by Copernicus, Kepler, Galileo, Descartes, Newton, Marx, Darwin, Freud, Einstein, and many others. The same planetary combination also seems to coincide with major historical periods of political and social revolution, and of movements toward emancipation, including the nineteen sixties (1960-1972), the French Revolutionary era to which the sixties have often been compared (1787-1798), the wave of revolutions that swept across Europe in the mid-nineteenth century (1845-1856), and our current era of worldwide revolutions and mass demonstrations, from the Arab Spring to the Occupy movement to Black Lives Matter to mass protests in Hong Kong, Mexico City, and Standing Rock, North Dakota (2007-2020). These eras all seem to demonstrate a heightened impulse toward radical change, innovation, and liberation of all kinds, but also toward violent upheaval, disruption, and the destabilizing of existing structures and institutions. Tarnas devotes sixty pages exclusively to tracing a cascade of such correlations with Uranus-Pluto alignments.

In a 2010 article written for *Archai: The Journal of Archetypal Cosmology* as an update to *Cosmos and Psyche*, Tarnas notes that several eminent scholars and commentators, including Nobel Prize-winning economist Paul Krugman and Harvard historian Niall Ferguson, have discussed two previous historical periods in the last two-hundred years that especially resemble the "Great Recession" initiated by the global economic crisis of 2007-2009. As Tarnas observes, these are the only three periods during those centuries when there has been a "T-square," a vast right triangle, formed by Saturn, Uranus, and Pluto relative to the Earth: the Long Depression that began in 1873-1876, the Great Depression of 1929-1933, and the Great Recession that occurred during the 2007-2012 alignment. Tarnas shows that eras during which this three-planet combination occurs tend to be particularly conducive to the sudden and unexpected collapse of existing structures of various kinds. Among many other phenomena, this archetypal complex is correlated with accidents and mistakes that lead to crashes and breakdowns of massive and destructive character, the Saturn archetype negatively inflecting the Uranus-Pluto correlation with dramatic ruptures. Similarly, these three planetary archetypes in combination tend to coincide with periods characterized by intense (Pluto) polarization of reformist-revolutionary (Uranus) and conservative-reactionary (Saturn) tendencies in many different realms of human experience, public and private—a phenomenon vividly witnessed in the recent American political context and in numerous conflicts in the Middle East and around the world.[81]

There are many such correlations traced in *Cosmos and Psyche*. However, one of the sections I found most striking, which Tarnas describes as "a test case for the entire perspective," focuses on the heart of the Axial Age discussed above, approximately the first half of the sixth century B.C.E. when Buddha, Confucius, Lao Tzu, Mahavira, Jeremiah, Ezekiel, Second Isaiah, Thales, Anaximander, Pythagoras, Sappho, Thespis, Solon, and possibly Zoroaster all more or less simultaneously walked the Earth.[82] It turns out that this era which saw the inception or transformation of a large proportion of the world's great religious, philosophical, and artistic traditions was centered on the sole close triple conjunction in human history of Uranus, Neptune, and Pluto, the only three major planets discovered in the modern era, during the eighteenth, nineteenth, and twentieth centuries respectively, at least until the 2005 discovery of Eris and several other trans-Neptunian objects.[83]

Furthermore, the synthesis of meanings attributed to these planets is precisely evocative of an epochal, titanically transformative (Pluto) revolutionary awakening of a new form (Uranus) of spiritual consciousness and cultural vision (Neptune)—in this case of unique historical magnitude and enduring significance. Although I approached Tarnas' book with a healthy degree of skepticism, *Cosmos and Psyche* provided satisfying explanations for how and why these particular qualities came to be associated with the planets by contemporary astrologers, as well as for a number of other concerns that I initially harbored. However, the project of this epilogue is not to reproduce Tarnas' work, but to place it within the novel context traced by the other twelve concepts elucidated in the pages above, a number of which Tarnas discusses, but which are here synthesized with the ideas of thinkers to whom he does not extensively refer.

The participatory quality of process is a precondition for the archetypal cosmological perspective, as the premise that the planets are intelligibly correlated with events in the human realm bears radically different fruit than the modern assumption that both planets and people are mere agglomerations of matter rushing meaninglessly through uniform space and time. This reductionist materialist belief leads inexorably to the existentialist dilemma, constituted in the necessity of creating meaning in the face of an ultimately meaningless world. However, a world view that accepts archetypal cosmology into its conceptual lexicon will instead perceive events in human life as appropriate expressions of the archetypal complexes associated with planetary transits at specific moments. For instance, everyone undergoes their Saturn Return between the ages of about twenty-eight and thirty-one, when Saturn makes one full circuit in relation to the Earth and conjoins its position (within approximately fifteen degrees) at the location it inhabited when each individual was born. In psychology, these years are often referred to as the "Age Thirty Transition,"[84] which generally mediates the distinct emergence into mature adulthood. It is common to experience heightened difficulty and constraint during this period, just as in the previous Saturn alignment to itself, the 90° square that occurs around age twenty-one to twenty-three (Saturn reaches these axial alignments approximately every seven years), many of us are undergoing the fraught transition from college to "the real world" of work and adult responsibility.

Although these Saturn transits manifest in many different ways for different individuals, inflected by whichever other transits are occurring, expressed through each person's individual character and cultural embedding, and modified by one's degree of conscious participation, these periods are widely recognized as highly significant moments of passage across a threshold into a new phase of experience. For an individual who rejects the astrological hypothesis out of hand, the difficulties and constraints often experienced during these periods may simply seem circumstantial. However, for an individual who accepts the validity of the archetypal correlation with planetary motion, the pain, pressure, constriction, and recognition of limit that are often experienced under Saturn transits can be understood as qualities that are meaningful and necessary for these periods of maturation and initiation, Saturn representing the hard reality and necessity that forges one into what one will become. And the more one brings attention to these correlations in one's experience, the more one may see that the movements of the planets do in fact seem to correspond consistently with the affective qualities and archetypal characteristics of the events that occur during particular periods.

Of course, for disenchanted modern culture, astrology is a limit case of superstition and credulousness. It is not for no reason that, in 1975, a group of 186 scientists, including eighteen Nobel Prize winners, found it necessary to purchase space in the journal *The Humanist* to denounce astrology. Indeed, based on the assumption of the exclusive validity of material and efficient causation, the rejection of astrology is only logical and right, not to mention that very few astrologers practice their art with the level of scholarly rigor achieved by Tarnas and his milieu. The acceptance of the archetypal cosmological perspective requires one of the largest leaps of faith it is possible to undertake in our culture. Although astrology was pervasive in premodernity, being perhaps the most widely practiced mode of abstract thought besides religion itself, it has been rejected by the modern world view because it embodies everything that modern mentality found necessary to deny in order to allow the individuation of the rational, autonomous human intellect. Premodern astrology is generally fatalistic, while archetypal cosmology asserts the individual's free will to participate in the manifestation of the formal potentialities associated with planetary motion. Similarly, premodern astrology contains a bewildering mass of received claims about forms of correlation, including aspects, transits, signs, houses, elements, qualities, rulerships, nodes, parts, decans, and dignities, so unwieldy that it is difficult to assess this form of the astrological perspective's validity without spending years of one's life even to determine if it is worth the devotion of one's time.[85]

In contrast, archetypal cosmology has thus far focused almost exclusively on the angular relationships of the planets (aspects and transits), which many contemporary astrologers have found to be the most significant forms of correlation, and which provide a coherent and relatively manageable body of quantitative knowledge for empirical investigation. Although it is probably true that astrology cannot be considered a "hard" science like physics or chemistry, in the specific form of archetypal cosmology, it can be as rigorously examined as social sciences like psychology, sociology, and anthropology for which there is a subjective element. In order to undertake such an examination, though, one must first make the decision to adopt the astrological hypothesis, however speculatively, as one cannot assess the potential validity of any system of thought without first admitting that it may be true. In fact, the very opposition of skepticism and belief is associated with the Saturn-Neptune archetypal complex, for which Tarnas traces a slew of correlations in intellectual and cultural history in two articles published in *Archai*, rigorously examining the evolving conflict between science and religion, doubt and faith, through the lives and works of a wide variety of world-historic figures.[86]

Archetypal cosmology is also an exemplification of the integrative method, as it is a primary locus for the integration of the individuated, rational modern intellect with epistemologies and modes of causation more characteristic of premodernity. While the archetypal cosmological perspective affirms the basic astrological hypothesis that an underlying correlation exists between planetary movements and human experience, it rejects the denial of free will often characteristic of premodern astrology. Instead, archetypal cosmology explores the notion that planetary transits consistently correspond with the expression in actuality of certain archetypal potentialities, but that these potentialities can manifest in drastically different ways, though always appropriate to the specific archetypes that are constellated. Thus, although Saturn-Neptune transits can correlate with skepticism (Saturn) about belief (Neptune), this archetypal complex can also manifest as the testing and strengthening (Saturn) of faith (Neptune), or of hard work concretely to implement (Saturn) the ideals of compassion and unification (Neptune).

For instance, while C.S. Lewis, whose *Mere Christianity* is a classic defense of Christian faith, and Bertrand Russell, whose *Why I Am Not a Christian* is a classic refutation of that same faith, are diametrically opposed in their views, both men were born during hard-aspect alignments of Saturn and Neptune (an opposition and a square respectively), both books were published during alignments of Saturn and Neptune (a conjunction and a square respectively), and both books participate in the archetypal complex associated with these two planets in their sustained attention to the duality of belief and doubt. And certainly, premodern astrology is not the only mode of thought whose negative content must be rejected in order to produce an emergent dialectical synthesis of this particular polarity, as rational mentality's exclusive privileging of reductionist materialism must also be shed according to the radical, universal affirmation of positive content characteristic of the integrative method.

Archetypal cosmology is preconditioned upon the discontinuity of process, as the relatively sudden reemergence of the archetypal perspective into academic discourse, beginning in earnest with Jung and coming to fruition in the field of archetypal cosmology, constitutes an *enantiodromia*, an abrupt volte-face in the evolution of historical process. Whereas for the modern mode of thought, astrology is anathema, for the emerging mode, the potential validity of this novel approach to astrology must necessarily be affirmed if the integrative method is carried to its logical conclusion. And conversely, discontinuity is itself an expression of the Promethean archetype associated with the planet Uranus, which correlates with sudden breakdowns and breakthroughs, with revolution and revelation, disruption and rupture. For instance, the atomic electron transition described by quantum physics appears to participate in the same archetypal potentiality that made possible the sudden emergence of quantum theory itself, first in Planck's work on black-body radiation in 1900 and then in Einstein's 1905 paper on the photoelectric effect, both published during an opposition of Uranus and Pluto, which often correlates with transformative (Pluto) discoveries (Uranus), in this case concerning discontinuity (Uranus). Planck's and Einstein's discoveries eventually resulted in the 1927 Solvay Conference, which marked the coming to prominence of the Copenhagen interpretation, the predominant interpretation of quantum mechanics for much of the twentieth century, during a conjunction of Jupiter and Uranus, which correlates with the sudden (Uranus) success and elevation (Jupiter) of a radically novel (Uranus) mode of thought, in this case specifically having to do with discontinuity (Uranus).

Similarly, development through emergent stages can be expressed in archetypal terms, so that for this processual dynamic, Jupiter is associated with expansion, elevation, progress, and growth; Saturn is associated with the specific structures and constraints of each stage, with maturation, and with the boundaries that delineate the thresholds that must be crossed; Uranus is associated with the sudden crossing of these

Saturnian thresholds, with revolutions in thought and the spark of inspiration that introduces radical novelty; Neptune is associated with the dissolution of boundaries, the subsumption of the previous stages into the emergent stage, and the movement toward an unrealized ideal; and Pluto is associated with the vital evolutionary force that impels the process toward self-overcoming through death and rebirth, whether of the messiah figure, of the individual ego, or of the collective world view. And these archetypally mediated stages of process are the phases that an individual or a collective must pass through in order eventually to be able to adopt the method of archetypal cosmology, which is a dialectical synthesis of premodern modes of cognizance with modern mentality.

Archetypal cosmology appears to be deeply intertwined with the emerging world view, as the novel mode must be attained in order for the validity of archetypal cosmology to be affirmed, just as the emerging mode itself requires a more expansive cosmology for its ingression. A radically new world view needs a new cosmology as its container, just as the new cosmology requires the adoption of the new world view for its efficacy. The two are intimately interconnected and, thus, both novel world view and archetypal cosmology can apparently only emerge in their fullness in coincidence with one another. Whereas premodern cosmologies and modes of relation are profoundly connected in their qualitative and archetypal character, and modern cosmology and mentality are entwined by virtue of their quantitative and material character, the emerging cosmology and world view are coextensive in their integration of premodern and modern cosmologies and modes of causation.

The novel mode and its accompanying cosmology affirm the complementarity of quality and quantity, and of formal-final and material-efficient causation, while setting aside as historical contingency the negative assertions of mythical premodernity (static hierarchy—the denial of equality; fatalism—the denial of free will; and physical geocentrism—the denial of heliocentrism) as well as the negative assertions of modernity (reductionist materialism—the denial of forms and purposes; exclusively quantitative temporality—the denial of qualitative time; and exclusively static and linear temporality—the denial of teleology and exponentiality). It may even be suggested that an integrative theory which denies the validity of archetypal cosmology, along with any other positive mode of thought, is an incomplete manifestation of that integrative impulse.

Furthermore, the fractal quality of process is a precondition for the archetypal cosmological perspective, as fractality is the quality that mediates the ingression of archetypes self-similarly across scale. The set of qualities that may correlate with a transit of Jupiter to the location of Uranus in an individual's natal chart is the same as the set of qualities that may correlate with a world transit of Jupiter and Uranus, when the two planets are in certain angular relationships in the sky, such as the expansive elevation and success (Jupiter) of the impulse toward innovation, discovery, and invention (Uranus). When an individual undergoes this transit, this is one of the inflections that the archetypal complex associated with these two planets can take and, similarly, events and experiences on the collective scale that manifest this archetypal potentiality become much more common when these planets are in a world-transit alignment. Indeed, people who are born during particular world transits often make their greatest contributions during successive periods when those same planets are in aspect, or when they are experiencing a personal transit of that complex.

For instance, Albert Einstein, the paradigmatic genius of the twentieth century, has a close opposition of Jupiter and Uranus in his natal chart. During much of his *annus mirabilis* of 1905 when he published four epochal papers that initiated profoundly new areas of research, including quantum theory and relativity, transiting Jupiter was squaring Einstein's natal Uranus. The jovial Jupiterian archetype, as king of the gods in the Greco-Roman pantheon, correlated with a crowning of Einstein's Promethean aspirations, granting his inspired creativity nearly unprecedented success and, ultimately, cultural elevation. Although this transit alone cannot account for Einstein's discoveries during that fateful year, as he (along with everyone else) experienced periodic Jupiter-Uranus transits over the course of his life, this synchronicity illustrates that the archetypal complexes associated with planetary transits seem to form the conditions for certain kinds of events to occur. They are temporal waves that require fortuitous positioning to be caught, and cultivated skill to be ridden gracefully. Such striking and statistically improbable correlations, at least improbable based on the assumption of random chance, can be consistently traced in the events of human history and in the activities of the individuals who mediate those events, a project undertaken in the pages of *Cosmos and Psyche* and the *Archai* journal.[87]

And of course, the concept of archetypes is a necessary precondition for an archetypal cosmology, as these potentialities for ingression are the entities which are shown by this method to correlate consistently with the movements of the planets. And conversely, the recognition of archetypes as a viable mode of thought also largely depends on their application in archetypal cosmology, for although the exploration of archetypal images in depth psychology has elucidated these formal potentialities in many profound ways, it is only with the method of archetypal cosmology that qualitative archetypes can be systematically correlated with the quantitative movements of materiality, in this case the largest and most regularly moving objects in our corner of the universe. These correlations provide a basis for empirical research that the archetypal interpretation of dreams or literature, though rich and highly productive areas of research, cannot offer.

It is one thing to note, for instance, that the father figure who appears in a particular dream is associated with the senex archetype, which is correlated with Saturn. However, it is another thing entirely to note that the night after Sigmund Freud's father's funeral, October 26, 1896, Freud had a vividly symbolic dream in which he was sitting in the barbershop that he visited daily, where he saw a sign that read: "You are requested to close your eyes." His interpretation of this dream is replete with Saturnian themes of the father, death, delay, mourning, judgment, duty, failure, and guilt. As Freud wrote in a letter to Wilhelm Fliess about a week later:

> On the day of the funeral I was kept waiting and therefore arrived a little late at the house of mourning. At that time my family was displeased with me because I had arranged for the funeral to be quiet and simple, which they later agreed was quite justified. They were also somewhat offended by my lateness. The sentence on the sign has a double meaning: one should do one's duty to the dead (an apology as though I had not done it and were in need of leniency), and the actual duty itself. The dream thus stems from the inclination to self-reproach that regularly sets in among survivors.[88]

It is striking to observe that on the day of the funeral and in the weeks encompassing these events, Saturn was closely opposite Freud's natal Sun, the archetype of the central self, the ego, and the personal identity. The death of Freud's father, the funeral, Freud's dream, and his interpretation of that dream were all events that participated in the Sun-Saturn archetypal complex constellated between the position of the Sun at the moment of Freud's birth and the position of Saturn during this period. These events brought Saturnian issues to a place of centrality for Freud, bearing on his sense of personal duty, the feeling of being judged by his family, the ultimate justification of his actions, and the guilt about his father's death, all occurring in coincidence with the precisely appropriate transit for those experiences. As Jung seems to have understood in his deep engagement with astrology during the last decades of his life, not only writing about astrology in *Synchronicity*, but regularly employing natal charts in his therapeutic sessions with clients, an archetypal cosmology can be described as the completion of the archetypes' reembrace by the modern mind, constituted in their integration with the materialist mode of thought represented by the quantitative science of astronomy.

The method of archetypal cosmology both depends on, and is a test case for the qualitative nature of time. That is, if one starts with the assumption of qualitative temporality and then searches for something material in our world by which to measure instances of synchronicity, one would immediately look to the largest and most regularly moving bodies available to our direct experience: the Sun, Moon, and planets. And in fact, this is what people have done for many thousands of years. If one accepts the validity of qualitative time, then there can be no reason to reject the synchronistic correlation of planetary motion with events on Earth other than inherited modern prejudice, as astrological correlations are simply a generalization of formal causation on an astronomical scale. Whereas the premodern approach to time did not differentiate adequately between temporality's qualitative and quantitative aspects, just as astrology and astronomy were considered the same art and science, modernity's shedding of qualitative time in favor of quantity, and thus its shedding of astrology in favor of astronomy, has produced the necessary differentiation in these two intimately connected polarities. However, the downside to this differentiation is that we now find that qualitative time and astrology are repressed, trivialized, and ridiculed by the preeminent cultures of our era. Although we may discern the historical necessity of this repression, it appears that the vanguard of thought must now redress this imbalance by bringing the critical rigor developed through the practice of science and rationalist philosophy to bear upon the repressed premises, producing a dialectical reembrace of the epistemological other by solitary mentality.

Until the publication of *Cosmos and Psyche* in 2006, this reintegration on a large scale of the astrological method for tracing time's qualities was simply not possible based on the discursive and rhetorical modes employed by earlier astrological texts. Although astrologers like Reinhold Ebertin, Dane Rudhyar, Robert Hand, Liz Greene, and Stephen Arroyo have made great contributions to the modern understanding of astrology, their work has primarily been directed toward the relatively marginal group of individuals already convinced of astrology's validity. While Tarnas owes a large debt to these astrological precursors, he was the first widely respected academic philosopher and cultural historian to present the astrological hypothesis in a manner that could conceivably be convincing to the skeptical majority in the form of archetypal cosmology. Much like *The Interpretation of Dreams* for psychoanalysis, it will most likely take some time for the radically novel perspective articulated in *Cosmos and Psyche* to begin to germinate in the academy and to enter the broader cultural awareness. However, as of this writing less than a decade after the publication of Tarnas' second major work, archetypal cosmology is already being studied with depth and rigor by brilliant, forward-thinking students and faculty at the California Institute of Integral Studies, Pacifica Graduate Institute, and a few other institutions, as well as in the pages of *Archai*.

Whitehead writes in *Science and the Modern World*: "Thoughts lie dormant for ages; and then, almost suddenly as it were, mankind finds that they have embodied themselves in institutions."[89] The emerging academic discipline of archetypal cosmology seems to exemplify this dictum, serving as the vanguard of a teleological trajectory toward the emergence of a more expansive mode of consciousness. This mode has traced a path from the origins of human thought, which appears to have emerged to a great extent in relation to the planets that would have been the most striking elements in the archaic, magic, and mythical skies, through the individuation of modern mentality, and on to the incipient reconciliation of the intellect with that which has been deeply repressed and rendered as other: the projected feminine shadow that is perhaps most completely embodied in the astrological perspective. If one accepts the premise that there is a trajectory toward novelty and consciousness endemic to process, then it seems that the most likely place to look for that factor with the capacity to carry the human mind beyond postmodern alienation, the logical conclusion of the Cartesian duality of mind and world, is in those perspectives that have been most vigorously expunged, including affective and intuitive epistemologies, formal and final causation, and astrology. The emergence of archetypal cosmology appears to be a telos for the ingression of historical novelty as well as a mode of thought that may mediate the further emergence of novelty.

That this emergence of novelty appears to be accelerating can be witnessed in the acceptance of archetypal cosmology into institutional academia, though still incipiently. Whereas it required a full century for the Copernican heliocentric hypothesis to be confirmed by Kepler and Galileo, and thus rendered a viable mode of thought on a collective scale, and it took eight years for Freud's *The Interpretation of Dreams* to sell the first printing of six-hundred copies, Tarnas' *Cosmos and Psyche*, less than a decade after its publication as of this writing, is already a widely popular book being employed as a text in a number of accredited graduate programs, and being read and studied by thousands of individuals around the world. The suggestion that archetypal cosmology may be the most likely successor to the depth psychology of Freud through the lineage of Jung (whom Freud declared the "crown prince" of psychoanalysis and then excommunicated), James Hillman and Stanislav Grof (the two psychologists whom many consider to be the most significant and creative successors to Jung), and Tarnas (who was a close student and colleague of both Grof and Hillman) appears to be an increasingly viable proposition. And this process of cultural advance, though still apparently in its nascence, seems to be accelerating in what may prove to be an exponential progression. Only time will tell if the broad adoption of archetypal cosmology will occur on the scale of decades or centuries, if at all, but it seems likely, based on the evidence traced in the preceding pages, that this perspective is uniquely situated to produce an integration of the seemingly incommensurable impulses at the heart of a schizophrenic modernity.

A decade ago, before the publication of *Cosmos and Psyche*, this supposition may have seemed absurd, and it still may seem so to some, but whereas there were no accredited academic institutions teaching the archetypal cosmological perspective just a few years ago, now there are several. This situation is reminiscent of the progress made by the Human Genome Project, which began in 1990 and was projected to be completed in 2005. Halfway through the fifteen years allotted for the project, only one percent of the genome had been sequenced, which skeptics took as evidence of the project's laughable impossibility. However, the sequencing turned out to be exponential so that, although in 1997 the progression appeared linear and, thus, hopeless, the project was actually completed ahead of schedule in 2003. This striking anecdote highlights the importance of remembering that fundamental transformation can occur with relative suddenness when all of the factors align to produce exponential growth. It appears possible, though not inevitable, that the cultural acceptance of archetypal cosmology may trace such a progression, for as an increasing number of individuals adopt this perspective, if each of those individuals was to introduce archetypal cosmology to two others, and then those individuals were to introduce this perspective to two more individuals in their turn, this discursive wave propagating through culture would in fact expand exponentially, like the doubling of grains of rice on a chessboard.

Finally, this apparently exponential growth of the archetypal cosmological perspective, should it continue, may prove to be a primary conceptual mode for bringing about the concretion of time. As suggested above, if the tracing of qualitative temporality can be visualized through the lower-dimensional analogy of weaving fabric to cover an invisible surface, an activity that would constitute the coming into actuality of this higher-dimensional landscape, then archetypal cosmology can be understood as a figurative loom upon which the temporal thread may be woven to produce the capacity for human perception of the fourth dimension as a complete integer. In this analogy, the archetypes could be visualized as different colors or textures of thread, which can be woven into ever-finer detail, into subtle shades of meaning represented by the interweaving of archetypal strands, and into immensely complex and multifaceted designs constructed from these elements, though it should be made clear that this qualitative patterning is not merely projected onto cosmic structure by the human mind, but is rather cocreatively elicited from potentiality. Although the current state of archetypal cosmological research generally correlates these archetypal threads with the movements of the planets, and distinct patterns are beginning to emerge from the relatively undifferentiated knotty jumble, it seems plausible to suggest that it is a primary project of the emerging world view collectively to construct the mathematically precise and aesthetically numinous apparatus for perceiving a fourth dimension of process partially through the method of archetypal cosmology.

However, despite the many correlations explicated in *Cosmos and Psyche*, in the *Archai* journal, and in works written by a growing number of archetypal cosmologists, it may still be difficult to fathom how tracing archetypal patterns in human history in relation to the movements of the planets could bring about the concretion of time. And it is certainly true that such a profound transformation will probably not be made manifest by the activities of a coterie of academics studying these correlations, as is currently the case. But one might envision a scenario in which increasing numbers of books are written, articles published, lectures and classes given, documentaries made, and conferences held, so that the emerging mode and its accompanying cosmology may begin to be accepted by a growing number of the more adventurous participants in the main streams of academic and intellectual discourse.

Though it may strain credulity based on current common sense derived from Cartesian and Newtonian premises, given the concepts traced in the preceding pages, it seems possible that archetypal cosmology could eventually become a discipline as central to the production of human knowledge as physics or psychology, just as science, once the province of a few marginal individuals clandestinely working out the heliocentric hypothesis and its implications, became a central endeavor of modern culture. One might expect that, if a radically new era is to emerge, a radically new cosmology analogous to the materialist cosmology's role in modernity must emerge coextensively. In this hypothetical scenario, as the emerging mode's validity may come to be asserted broadly by scholars, it would eventually permeate the culture at large, so that an aesthetically elegant and mathematically precise computational interface charting planetary transits and their corresponding archetypal complexes, a technology already in broad use, would be as basic an instrument of human life as are clocks and calendars in our contemporary cultural context.

This is a description of a possible world, however apparently distant from our current collective assumptions, in which the activities and interactions of billions of people would be set against the background not only of linear clock and calendar time, but also of the multivalent quality of each moment reflected in the planetary aspects. In this world, one would not only check the time and the weather on the way out the door to pursue one's daily activities, but one would also take a moment to glance at the current world transits and their relations to one's natal chart, the archetypal weather. This era would bring constant awareness to the archetypal impulses informing experience, and thus the immense creativity and ingenuity of humanity would be organized around producing novel inventions, concepts, works of art, institutions, and modes of relation, all implicitly focused on constructing a comprehensive map of the temporal dimension's contours. These billions of technologically extended hands and minds would together weave the threads of qualitative interconnection into a vast tapestry from which might emerge the perception of a more expansive degree of freedom, which appears to lie in wait just beyond the event horizon of human conception.

# APPENDIX
## ADDITIONAL EPIGRAPHS

### Chapter 1: "World Views Create Worlds":
### The Participatory Quality of Process

*The mentality of an epoch springs from the view of the world which is, in fact, dominant in the educated sections of the communities in question.*

Alfred North Whitehead, *Science and the Modern World*[90]

*Our way of perceiving the world depends entirely on the nature of our consciousness, for it establishes the boundaries and temporal limits of our world.*

Jean Gebser, *The Ever-Present Origin*[91]

*A world-creating quality attaches to human consciousness as such.*

C.G. Jung, *Mysterium Coniunctionis*[92]

*The reason why our sentient, percipient, and thinking ego is met nowhere within our scientific world picture can easily be indicated in seven words: because it is itself that world picture. It is identical with the whole and therefore cannot be contained in it as a part of it.*

Erwin Schrödinger, *Mind and Matter*[93]

*We do not see things as they are, we see them as we are.*

Anais Nin, *Seduction of the Minotaur*[94]

*When paradigms enter, as they must, into a debate about paradigm choice, their role is necessarily circular. Each group uses its own paradigm to argue in that paradigm's defense.*

Thomas Kuhn, *The Structure of Scientific Revolutions*[95]

*Each man, in whatever 'type' of culture he inhabits, must have a way of looking at the world—whatever that means to him—which is peculiar to his particular culture.*

Amiri Baraka, *Blues People*[96]

*When we look at the world through our theoretical insights, the factual knowledge that we obtain will evidently be shaped and formed by our theories. . . . It is in these world views that our general notions of the nature of reality and the relationship between our thought and reality are implicitly or explicitly formed.*

David Bohm, *Wholeness and the Implicate Order*[97]

*Any method of analysis constructs as much as discovers, imposes as much as reveals. Different methods, that is, bring forth different aspects or potential meanings of a given phenomenon. . . . It is not so much our experience of the world that changes, but rather our experience-and-the-world that undergo a mutually codetermined transformation. . . . The world does not have an intrinsic nature waiting to be discovered and represented by human cognition, but discloses itself in a variety of ways partially contingent on the dispositions, intentions, and modes of consciousness of the knower.*

Jorge N. Ferrer, *Revisioning Transpersonal Theory*[98]

*What I am trying to describe here is not a theory. Rather my target is our contemporary lived understanding; that is, the way we naively take things to be. We might say: the construal we just live in, without ever being aware of it as a construal, or—for most of us—without ever even formulating it. . . . I am trying to capture the level of understanding prior to philosophical puzzlement.*

Charles Taylor, *A Secular Age*[99]

*Each society perceives what it believes. Thus, each culturally imposed framework acts as a filter constraining our conception of the universe, while it enables our explorations. . . . We can never be taken out of the narrative of creation. We are always in some partial but essential way its cocreators. . . . We have never been anything other than collaborators with the universe. Always and again, we have been the cocreators of a time and a cosmos that exist together with us.*

Adam Frank, *About Time*[100]

## Chapter 2: "The Circle of the Given":
## Novelty and the Will to Believe

*Belief is one of the indispensable preliminary conditions of the realization of its object. There are then cases where faith creates its own verification.*

William James, *The Will to Believe*[101]

*If you have had your attention directed to the novelties in thought in your own lifetime, you will have observed that almost all really new ideas have a certain aspect of foolishness when they are first produced.*

Alfred North Whitehead, *Science and the Modern World*[102]

*In principle new points of view are not as a rule discovered in territory that is already known, but in out-of-the-way places that may even be avoided because of their bad name.*

C.G. Jung, *Synchronicity*[103]

*Acceptance and elucidation of the "new" always meets with strong opposition, since it requires us to overcome our traditional, our acquired and secure ways and possessions. This means pain, suffering, struggle, uncertainty, and similar concomitants which everyone seeks to avoid whenever possible.*

Jean Gebser, *The Ever-Present Origin*[104]

*Any new way of thinking has to come into being in the context of existing habits of thought. The realm of science is no exception. At any given time, the generally accepted models of reality, often called paradigms, embody assumptions that are more or less taken for granted and which easily become habitual.*

Rupert Sheldrake, *The Presence of the Past*[105]

*Skepticism is the chastity of the intellect, Santayana declared, and the metaphor is apt. The mind that seeks the deepest intellectual fulfillment does not give itself up to every passing idea. Yet what is sometimes forgotten is the larger purpose of such a virtue. For in the end, chastity is something one preserves not for its own sake, which would be barren, but rather so that one may be fully ready for the moment of surrender to the beloved, the suitor whose aim is true. Whether in knowledge or in love, the capacity to recognize and embrace that moment when it finally arrives, perhaps in quite unexpected circumstances, is essential to the virtue. Only with that discernment and inward opening can the full participatory engagement unfold that brings forth new realities and new knowledge.*

Richard Tarnas, *Cosmos and Psyche*[106]

*Many great conversions, or to put it differently, many of the great founding moves of a new spiritual direction in history, involve a transformation of the frame in which people thought, felt, and lived before. They bring into view something beyond that frame, which at the same time changes the meaning of all the elements of the frame. Things make sense in a wholly new way. . . . We have the analogue of a "paradigm change" in science, only one that affects the central issues of our lives.*

Charles Taylor, *A Secular Age*[107]

*Most people do not wish to accept that the order governing their lives is imaginary, but in fact every person is born into a pre-existing imagined order, and his or her desires are shaped from birth by its dominant myths. Our personal desires thereby become the imagined order's most important defences.*

Yuval Noah Harari, *Sapiens*[108]

## Chapter 3: "The Reconciling Third": An Integrative Method

*The unlike is joined together, and from the differences results the most beautiful harmony, and all things take place by strife.*

Heraclitus[109]

*Glorious is the power of the art of contradiction.*

Plato, *The Republic*[110]

*Contraries, after all, are extremes out of which changes arise.*

Aristotle, *The Metaphysics*[111]

*'True' and 'false' belong among those determinate notions which are held to be inert and wholly separate essences, one here and one there, each standing fixed and isolated from the other, with which it has nothing in common. Against this view it must be maintained that truth is not a minted coin that can be given and pocketed ready-made. Nor is there such a thing as false, any more than there is something evil.*

G.W.F. Hegel, *The Phenomenology of Spirit*[112]

*I am well aware that scarcely a single point is discussed in this volume on which facts cannot be adduced, often apparently leading to conclusions directly opposite to those at which I have arrived.*

Charles Darwin, *On the Origin of Species*[113]

*Whether the various spheres or systems are ever to fuse integrally into one absolute conception, as most philosophers assume that they must, and how, if so, that conception may best be reached, are questions that only the future can answer. What is certain now is the fact of lines of disparate conception, each corresponding to some part of the world's truth, each verified in some degree, each leaving out some part of real experience.*

William James, *The Varieties of Religious Experience*[114]

*Above all we should have a philosophy to which one could not oppose others, for it would have left nothing outside of itself that other doctrines could pick up; it would have taken everything. . . . To the multiplicity of systems contending with one another, armed with different concepts, would succeed the unity of a doctrine capable of reconciling all thinkers in the same perception,—a perception which moreover would grow ever larger, thanks to the combined effort of philosophers in a common direction.*

Henri Bergson, *The Creative Mind*[115]

*Contradiction is part of nature's general method; it is a sign that she is working towards a greater harmony. The reconciliation is achieved by an evolutionary progress.*

Sri Aurobindo, *The Future Evolution of Man*[116]

*In its turn every philosophy will suffer a deposition. But the bundle of philosophic systems expresses a variety of general truths about the universe, awaiting coordination and assignment of their various spheres of validity. Such progress in coordination is provided by the advance of philosophy; and in this sense philosophy has advanced from Plato onward.*

Alfred North Whitehead, *Process and Reality*[117]

*All of our structures of awareness that form and support our present consciousness structure will have to be integrated into a new and more intensive form, which would in fact unlock a new reality.*

Jean Gebser, *The Ever-Present Origin*[118]

*In the history of human thinking the most fruitful developments frequently take place at those points where two different lines of thought meet.*

Werner Heisenberg, *Physics and Philosophy*[119]

*When I speak of integration I do not mean some kind of fantastic syncretism of science and religion. They have different purposes, different limitations, different modes of action. But they are both part, and I would argue a necessary part, of every culture and every person. They need to exist in some vital and healthy whole in which each is integral. This means not simply tacit agreement to ignore each other but open interchange between them with all the possibilities of mutual growth and transformation that that entails.*

Robert Bellah, *Beyond Belief*[120]

*What is difficult, of course, is to see both images, both truths, simultaneously: to suppress nothing, to remain open to the paradox, to maintain the tension of opposites. Wisdom, like compassion, often seems to require of us that we hold multiple realities in our consciousness at once.*

Richard Tarnas, *Cosmos and Psyche*[121]

*Some dilemmas have to be understood in a kind of two-dimensional space. The horizontal space gives you the dimension in which you have to find the point of resolution, the fair "award," between two parties. The vertical space opens the possibility that by rising higher, you'll accede to a new horizontal space where the resolution will be less painful/damaging for both parties. . . . The vertical dimension I've been talking about here is one of reconciliation. . . . It is in moves of this kind that we need to seek the third element in our program. . . . Their power lies not in suppressing the madness of violent categorization, but in transfiguring it in the name of a new kind of common world.*

Charles Taylor, *A Secular Age*[122]

## Chapter 4: "Jumps of All Sorts": The Discontinuity of Process

*Just as the first breath drawn by a child after its long, quiet nourishment breaks the gradualness of merely quantitative growth— there is a qualitative leap, and the child is born—so likewise the Spirit in its formation matures slowly and quietly into its new shape, dissolving bit by bit the structure of its previous world, whose tottering state is only hinted at by isolated symptoms. The frivolity and boredom which unsettle the established order, the vague foreboding of something unknown, these are the heralds of approaching change. The gradual crumbling that left unaltered the face of the whole is cut short by a sunburst which, in one flash, illuminates the features of the new world. . . . But this new world is no more a complete actuality than is a new-born child.*

G.W.F. Hegel, *The Phenomenology of Spirit*[123]

158

*The transitions are abrupt, absolute, truly shot out of a pistol; for while many possibilities are called, the few that are chosen are chosen in their sudden completeness.*

William James, *The Will to Believe*[124]

*Species pass through alternate periods of stability and transformation. When the period of "mutability" occurs, unexpected forms spring forth in a great number of different directions.*

Henri Bergson, *Creative Evolution*[125]

*A true process always occurs in quanta, that is, in leaps; or, expressed in quasi-biological and not physical terms, in mutations. It occurs spontaneously, indeterminately, and, consequently, discontinuously.*

Jean Gebser, *The Ever-Present Origin*[126]

*The modern discovery of discontinuity (e.g. the orderedness of energy quanta, of radium decay, etc.) has put an end to the sovereign rule of causality.*

C.G. Jung, *Synchronicity*[127]

*As singular boundaries between two realms of existence, phase transitions tend to be highly nonlinear in their mathematics. The smooth and predictable behavior of matter in any one phase tends to be little help in understanding the transitions.*

James Gleick, *Chaos*[128]

## Chapter 5: "A Series of Stages": Development through Emergent Phases

*The single individual must also pass through the formative stages of universal Spirit so far as their content is concerned, but as shapes which Spirit has already left behind, as stages on a way that has been made level with toil. Thus, as far as factual information is concerned, we find that what in former ages engaged the attention of men of mature mind, has been reduced to the level of facts, exercises, and even games for children; and, in the child's progress through school, we shall recognize the history of the cultural development of the world traced, as it were, in a silhouette.*

G.W.F. Hegel, *The Phenomenology of Spirit*[129]

*Like the universe as a whole, like each conscious being taken separately, the organism which lives is a thing that endures. Its past, in its entirety, is prolonged into its present, and abides there, actual and acting. How otherwise could we understand that it passes through distinct and well-marked phases, that it changes its age—in short, that it has a history?*

Henri Bergson, *Creative Evolution*[130]

*Each phase of generalization exhibits its own peculiar simplicities which stand out just at that stage, and at no other stage. There are simplicities connected with the motion of a bar of steel which are obscured if we refuse to abstract from the individual molecules; and there are certain simplicities concerning the behavior of men which are obscured if we refuse to abstract from the individual peculiarities of particular specimens. . . . The doctrine of emergent evolution . . . is the doctrine of real unities being more than a mere collective disjunction of component elements.*

Alfred North Whitehead, *Process and Reality*[131]

*We wish to present as a working hypothesis the four, respectively five, structures we have designated as the archaic, magic, mythical, mental, and integral. We must first of all remain cognizant that these structures are not merely past, but are in fact still present in more or less latent and acute form in each one of us.*

Jean Gebser, *The Ever-Present Origin*[132]

*We need not pay too much attention to those historians who cautiously refuse to detect any process in history, because it is difficult to divide into periods, or because the periods are difficult to date precisely. The same objections apply to the process of growth from child to man.*

Owen Barfield, *Saving the Appearances*[133]

*The organismic or holistic philosophy . . . recognizes the existence of hierarchically organized systems which, at each level of complexity, possess properties which cannot be fully understood in terms of the properties exhibited by their parts in isolation from each other; at each level the whole is more than the sum of its parts.*

Rupert Sheldrake, *A New Science of Life*[134]

*Human history has been characterized by a series of broadly overlapping epochs, each of which represented a particular style of understanding and experiencing reality. . . . A more technically accurate description of the whole picture is that of a large hypercomplex chaotic attractor whose global pattern represents a structure of consciousness, and nested within it, as part of itself, appear the fluctuating chaotic patterns (or sub-attractors) that represent states of consciousness.*

Allan Combs, "Open Reply to Ken Wilber"[135]

*While this modern understanding of the mind certainly opens itself to Cartesian type theories in a way that the earlier "enchanted" understanding does not, it isn't itself such a theory. Put another way, the modern idea of mind makes something like the "mind-body problem" conceivable, indeed, in a way inescapable, where on the earlier understanding it didn't really make sense. . . . A fundamental shift has occurred in naïve understanding in the move to disenchantment.*

Charles Taylor, *A Secular Age*[136]

*From the creation of politically charged city-based empires five thousand years ago to the establishment of mercantile, factory-based empires two centuries ago, human culture has reinvented itself again and again. The digital world we so quickly assembled in the last four decades has been yet another turning of the creative wheel. At every stage, the invention of a new time has been central to the cultural transformation.*

Adam Frank, *About Time*[137]

## Chapter 6: "An Extraordinary Threshold":
## The Emergence of a New World View

*Suppose these other forms of consciousness brought together and amalgamated with intellect: would not the result be a consciousness as wide as life? . . . Such a science would be a mechanics of transformation of which our mechanics of translation would become a particular case, a simplification, a projection on the plane of pure quantity. . . . But such an integration can be no more than dreamed of.*

Henri Bergson, *Creative Evolution*[138]

*New epochs emerge with comparative suddenness.*

Alfred North Whitehead, *Science and the Modern World*[139]

*Anyone today who considers the emergence of a new era of mankind as a certainty and expresses the conviction that our rescue from collapse and chaos could come about by virtue of a new attitude and a new formation of man's consciousness, will surely elicit less credence than those who have heralded the decline of the West. . . . Such a reaction, the reaction of mentality headed for a fall, is only too typical of man in transition. . . . The present book is, in fact, the account of the nascence of a new world and a new consciousness.*

Jean Gebser, *The Ever-Present Origin*[140]

*We may be seeing the beginnings of a reintegration of our culture, a new possibility of the unity of consciousness. If so, it will not be on the basis of any new orthodoxy, either religious or scientific. Such a new integration will be based on the rejection of all univocal understandings of reality, of all identifications of one conception of reality with reality itself. It will recognize the multiplicity of the human spirit, and the necessity to translate constantly between different scientific and imaginative vocabularies. It will recognize the human proclivity to fall comfortably into some single literal interpretation of the world and therefore the necessity to be continuously open to rebirth in a new heaven and a new earth.*

Robert Bellah, *Beyond Belief*[141]

*I believe that this divine marriage of Individuality and Essential Ground, of the Masculine and Feminine, of* samsara *and* nirvana *is the dawn that humanity's dark night is driving toward. This is the dawn that, if successfully navigated, will unite humankind and elevate us into a form that has never before walked this Earth: a humanity healed of the scars of history, its ancient partitions reabsorbed; a people with new capacities born in the chaos of near-extinction. Only when we have made this pivot, when our long labor has birthed this future Child, only then will we fully understand what we have accomplished. And when this moment finally comes, I deeply believe that, like all mothers before us, we will count our pain a small price.*

Christopher M. Bache, *Dark Night, Early Dawn*[142]

*Let's call this the Age of Authenticity. It appears that something has happened in the last half-century, perhaps even less, which has profoundly altered the conditions of belief in our societies. . . . I believe, along with many others, that our North Atlantic civilization has been undergoing a cultural revolution in recent decades. The 60s provide perhaps the hinge moment, at least symbolically.*

Charles Taylor, *A Secular Age*[143]

## Chapter 7: "Symmetry across Scale": The Fractal Quality of Process

*In each of us there are the same principles and habits which there are in the State.*

Plato, *The Republic*[144]

*A remarkable parallel, which I think has never been noticed, obtains between the facts of social evolution on the one hand, and of zoological evolution as expounded by Mr. Darwin on the other.*

William James, *The Will to Believe*[145]

163

*What is true of the production of a new species is also true of the production of a new individual, and, more generally, of any moment of any living form.*

Henri Bergson, *Creative Evolution*[146]

*My theory involves the entire abandonment of the notion that simple location is the primary way in which things are involved in space-time. In a certain sense, everything is everywhere at all times. For every location involves an aspect of itself in every other location. Thus every spatio-temporal standpoint mirrors the world. . . . Each actual entity is itself only describable as an organic process. It repeats in microcosm what the universe is in macrocosm.*

Alfred North Whitehead, *Science and the Modern World*[147]

*The parallels between the developmental stages of mankind and those of the individual, in the context of the various structures of consciousness, have also been documented.*

Jean Gebser, *The Ever-Present Origin*[148]

*The shapes described here tend to be* scaling, *implying that the degree of their irregularity and/or fragmentation is identical at all scales.*

Benoit Mandelbrot, *The Fractal Geometry of Nature*[149]

*A key question concerning the information content of biological systems is how it is possible for the genome, which contains comparatively little information, to produce a system such as a human, which is vastly more complex than the genetic information that describes it. One way of understanding this is to view the designs of biology as "probabilistic fractals."*

Ray Kurzweil, *The Singularity is Near*[150]

*Self-organizing systems including cells, tissues, organs, organisms, societies and minds are made up of nested hierarchies or holarchies of holons or morphic units. At each level the whole is more than the sum of the parts, and these parts themselves are wholes made up of parts.*

Rupert Sheldrake, *Science Set Free*[151]

## Chapter 8: "A Potentiality for Actual Entities": Forms, Archetypes, and Eternal Objects

*Whenever a number of individuals have a common name, we assume them to have also a corresponding idea or form.*

Plato, *The Republic*[152]

*Anything that is accounted for in terms of its potentiality has also, and by the same token, a potentiality for opposites.*

Aristotle, *The Metaphysics*[153]

*The archetype is the introspectively recognizable form of a priori psychic orderedness.*

C.G. Jung, *Synchronicity*[154]

*The concept of the archetype may be regarded as an incipient manifestation of the aperspectival world, for despite its psychological determination, it is ultimately apsychic. Only the forms of appearance of the archetypes are psychic phenomena, which in their allegory and imagery evidence an irrational character. The archetypes themselves and the "archetypical structures" are "eternally present"; this means that they are time-free. They are such that although "lacking a material existence" they perform the psyche. This means that they are not only immaterial, as the psychic is in and of itself, but amaterial; they underlie and perform the psyche achronically and ameterially.*

Jean Gebser, *The Ever-Present Origin*[155]

*Jung and Whitehead both reassert something like the Platonic view of the importance of formal causes in the nature of things. Jung does this, of course, by making archetypes central. The technical term for formal causes in Whitehead's thought is "eternal objects."*

David Ray Griffin, *The Archetypal Process*[156]

*For our present purposes, we can define an archetype as a universal principle or force that affects—impels, structures, permeates— the human psyche and the world of human experience on many levels. One can think of them in mythic terms as gods and goddesses (or what Blake called "The Immortals"), in Platonic terms as transcendent first principles and numinous Ideas, or in Aristotelian terms as immanent universals and dynamic indwelling forms. One can approach them in a Kantian mode as a priori categories of perception and cognition, in Schopenhauerian terms as the universal essences of life embodied in great works of art, or in the Nietzschean manner as primordial principles symbolizing basic cultural tendencies and modes of being. In the twentieth-century context, one can conceive of them in Husserlian terms as essential structures of human experience, in Wittgensteinian terms as linguistic family resemblances linking disparate but overlapping particulars, in Whiteheadian terms as eternal objects and pure potentialities whose ingression informs the unfolding process of reality, or in Kuhnian terms as underlying paradigmatic structures that shape scientific understanding and research. Finally, with depth psychology, one can approach them in the Freudian mode as primordial instincts impelling and structuring biological and psychological processes, or in the Jungian manner as fundamental formal principles of the human psyche, universal expressions of a collective unconscious and, ultimately, of the* unus mundus.

Richard Tarnas, *Cosmos and Psyche*[157]

*Say someone falls in love. And this has an impact, good or ill, on his life. An "internal" event, we think. . . . But now let's say that we see this whole side of life as under the aegis of a goddess, Aphrodite. That means that its going well is its being smiled on by Aphrodite. This means not only that she is keeping the external dangers at bay; like a human patron, she is in this aspect causally responsible for the conditions being propitious. It also means that the blooming of the right internal motivation is a gift from her. In other words, my being in the highest motivational condition is not just a fact about my inner realm of desires;*

*it is my being the recipient of the gift of the goddess. The highest
condition can't just be placed unambiguously within; it is placed in that
interspace, where the gift is received.*

Charles Taylor, *A Secular Age*[158]

## Chapter 9: "A Falling Together in Time": Qualitative Temporality and Formal Causation

*To every thing there is a season, and a time to every purpose under
the heaven.*

*Ecclesiastes 3:1*[159]

*Both kinds of causes should be acknowledged by us.*

Plato, *Timaeus*[160]

*What is time? Who can readily and briefly explain this? Who can
even in thought comprehend it, so as to utter a word about it? But what
in discourse do we mention more familiarly and knowingly, than time?
And, we understand, when we speak of it; we understand also, when we
hear it spoken of by another. What then is time? If no one asks me, I
know: if I wish to explain it to one that asketh, I know not. . . . Let us see
then, thou soul of man, whether present time can be long: for to thee it is
given to feel and to measure length of time.*

Saint Augustine, *Confessions*[161]

*The length of this path has to be endured, because, for one thing,
each moment is necessary; and further, each moment has to be lingered
over, because each is itself a complete individual shape.*

G.W.F. Hegel, *The Phenomenology of Spirit*[162]

*Concentrated on that which repeats, solely preoccupied in welding
the same to the same, intellect turns away from the vision of time. It
dislikes what is fluid, and solidifies everything it touches. We do not think
real time. But we live it, because life transcends intellect.*

Henri Bergson, *Creative Evolution*[163]

*Passage from phase to phase is not in physical time. . . . Physical time expresses some features of the growth, but not the growth of the features. . . . The actual entity is the enjoyment of a certain quantum of physical time. But the genetic process is not the temporal succession: such a view is exactly what is denied by the epochal theory of time. Each phase in the genetic process presupposes the entire quantum, and so does each feeling in each phase.*

Alfred North Whitehead, *Process and Reality*[164]

*Certain "processes" . . . seem to take place "outside" spatial and temporal understanding and conceptualization, thus preventing us from making a spatial-temporal cause-and-effect relationship.*

Jean Gebser, *The Ever-Present Origin*[165]

*Emotion is time. Each moment is structured in a rhythm. The time we make with our minds is arbitrary and rigid.*

James Hillman, personal letter[166]

*The hypothesis of formative causation proposes that morphogenetic fields play a causal role in the development and maintenance of the forms of systems at all levels of complexity. . . . Morphogenetic fields can be regarded as analogous to the known fields of physics in that they are capable of ordering physical changes, even though they themselves cannot be observed directly.*

Rupert Sheldrake, *A New Science of Life*[167]

*Jung used the terms synchronicity for such meaningful coincidences. His investigation of coincidences that occurred in his own life and in the lives of others led Jung to conclude that they are related to unconscious psychological processes. He did not, however, stop with the psychological side of synchronicity. He worked with his friend Wolfgang Pauli, the great quantum physicist who explicated the Pauli exclusion principle, to develop the notion that the laws of physics themselves should be rewritten to include acausal as well as causal accounts of the world of physical events.*

Allan Combs and Mark Holland, *Synchronicity*[168]

*Most of us in the course of life have observed coincidences in which two or more independent events having no apparent causal connection nevertheless seem to form a meaningful pattern. On occasion, this patterning can strike one as so extraordinary that it is difficult to believe the coincidence has been produced by chance alone. The events give the distinct impression of having been precisely arranged, invisibly orchestrated.*

Richard Tarnas, *Cosmos and Psyche*[169]

## Chapter 10: "The Teleological Introduction of Novelty": Final Causation

*The final cause tends to be the greatest good and end of the rest.*

Aristotle, *The Metaphysics*[170]

*When we wish to see an oak with its massive trunk and spreading branches and foliage, we are not content to be shown an acorn instead. So too, Science, the crown of a world of Spirit, is not complete in its beginnings. The onset of the new spirit is the product of a widespread upheaval in various forms of culture, the prize at the end of a complicated, tortuous path and of just as variegated and strenuous an effort. It is the whole which, having traversed its content in time and space, has returned into itself, and is the resultant simple Notion of the whole. But the actuality of this simple whole consists in those various shapes and forms which have become its moments, and which will now develop and take shape afresh, this time in their new element, in their newly acquired meaning.*

G.W.F. Hegel, *The Phenomenology of Spirit*[171]

*Everything makes strongly for the view that our world is incompletely unified teleologically and is still trying to get its unification better organized.*

William James, *Pragmatism*[172]

*Finalism is not, like mechanism, a doctrine with fixed rigid outlines. It admits of as many inflections as we like. The mechanistic philosophy is to be taken or left; it must be left if the least grain of dust, by straying from the path foreseen by mechanics should show the slightest trace of spontaneity. The doctrine of final causes, on the contrary, will never be definitively refuted. If one form of it be put aside, it will take another. Its principle, which is essentially psychological, is very flexible. It is so extensible, and thereby so comprehensive, that one accepts something of it as soon as one rejects pure mechanism.*

Henri Bergson, *Creative Evolution*[173]

*The awkward expression 'negative entropy' . . . is itself a measure of order. Thus the device by which an organism maintains itself stationary at a fairly high level of orderliness ( = fairly low level of entropy) really consists in continually sucking orderliness from its environment. . . . Whether we find it astonishing or whether we find it quite plausible that a small but highly organized group of atoms be capable of acting in this manner, the situation is unprecedented, it is unknown anywhere else except in living matter. . . . We must be prepared to find a new type of physical law prevailing in it. . . . It is, in my opinion, nothing else than the principle of quantum theory over again.*

Erwin Schrödinger, *What Is Life?*[174]

*The stuff of the universe goes on becoming concentrated into ever more organized forms of matter.*

Pierre Teilhard de Chardin, *The Phenomenon of Man*[175]

*The visible patterns in turbulent flow—self-entangled stream lines, spiral vortices, whorls that rise before the eye and vanish again—must reflect patterns explained by laws not yet discovered. . . . The dissipation of energy in a turbulent flow must still lead to a kind of contraction of the phase space, a pull toward an attractor.*

James Glick, *Chaos*[176]

*These two basic elements of synchronicities—meaning and purpose—represent straightforward expressions of what Aristotle called formal and final causes, respectively. Compared with the simpler (or simplistic) modern view of causality, which is entirely linear-mechanistic in nature, Aristotle's more nuanced and capacious formulation defined "cause" as that which is a necessary, though not in itself sufficient, condition for the existence of something. Such conditions included formal and final (teleological) factors, in addition to the material and efficient factors stressed by mainstream modern science.*

Richard Tarnas, *Cosmos and Psyche*[177]

*Purposes exist in a virtual realm, rather than a physical reality. They connect organisms to ends or goals that have not yet happened; they are* attractors, *in the language of dynamics, a branch of modern mathematics. Purposes or attractors cannot be weighed; they are not material. Yet they influence material bodies and have physical effects. . . . Purposes or motives are causes, but they work by pulling toward a virtual future rather than pushing from an actual past. . . . The mechanistic revolution in seventeenth-century science abolished ends, purposes, goals, and final causes. Everything was to be explained mechanically, by matter being pushed from the past, as in billiard-ball physics, or by forces acting in the present, as in gravitation. This four-hundred-year-old doctrine is still an article of faith in the creed of science, but it does not fit the facts. Therefore scientists keep reinventing ends or goals in disguised forms.*

Rupert Sheldrake, *Science Set Free*[178]

## Chapter 11: "An Exponentially Accelerating Process" The Increasing Ingression of Novelty

*The scope of the practical control of nature newly put into our hands by scientific ways of thinking vastly exceeds the scope of the old control grounded on common sense. Its rate of increase accelerates so that no one can trace the limit.*

William James, *Pragmatism*[179]

*The pace of change has not remained the same. It has accelerated and is accelerating.*

Owen Barfield, *Saving the Appearances*[180]

*The upward curve indicates faster than exponential growth, an accelerating rate of innovation. . . . The rate shows no sign of abatement. If anything, it hints that further contractions in timescale are in store.*

Hans Moravec, *Robot*[181]

*A compression of time characterizes the life of the century now closing.*

James Gleick, *Faster*[182]

*Our brains are not well equipped to understand sustained exponential growth. . . . Steady exponential improvement has brought us into the second half of the chessboard—into a time when what's come before is no longer a particularly reliable guide to what will happen next. . . . Sometimes a difference in degree . . . becomes a difference in kind.*

Erik Brynjolfsson and Andrew McAfee, *The Second Machine Age*[183]

## Chapter 12: "The Concretion of Time"
## Progressive Degrees of Spatio-Temporal Freedom

*When the father creator saw the creature which he had made moving and living, the created image of the eternal gods, he rejoiced, and in his joy determined to make the copy still more like the original; and as this was eternal, he sought to make the universe eternal, so far as might be. Now the nature of the ideal being was everlasting, but to bestow this attribute in its fulness upon a creature was impossible. Wherefore he resolved to have a moving image of eternity, and when he set in order the heaven, he made this image eternal but moving according to number, while eternity itself rests in unity; and this image we call time.*

Plato, *Timaeus*[184]

*Who shall hold the heart of man, that it may stand still, and see how eternity ever still-standing, neither past nor to come, uttereth the times past and to come? Can my hand do this, or the hand of my mouth by speech bring about a thing so great?*

Saint Augustine, *Confessions*[185]

*Man is something that shall be overcome. . . . All beings so far have created something beyond themselves. . . . Man is a rope, tied between beast and overman—a rope over an abyss. . . . What is great in man is that he is a bridge and not an end.*

Friedrich Nietzsche, *Thus Spoke Zarathustra*[186]

*Intellect, such at least as we find it in ourselves, has been fashioned by evolution during the course of progress; it is cut out of something larger, or, rather, it is only the projection, necessarily of a plane, of a reality that possesses both relief and depth. It is this more comprehensive reality that true finalism ought to reconstruct, or, rather, if possible, embrace in one view. . . . Thanks to philosophy, all things acquire depth,—more than depth, something like a fourth dimension which permits anterior perceptions to remain bound up with present perceptions, and the immediate future itself to become partly outlined in the present. . . . It would be a living and consequently still moving eternity where our own duration would find itself like the vibrations in light, and which would be the concretion of all duration as materiality is its dispersion.*

Henri Bergson, *Creative Evolution* and *The Creative Mind*[187]

*Sensible reality is too concrete to be entirely manageable—look at the narrow range of it which is all that any animal, living in it exclusively as he does, is able to compass. To get from one point in it to another we have to plough or wade through the whole intolerable interval. . . . But with our faculty of abstraction and fixing concepts we are there in a second, almost as if we controlled a fourth dimension, skipping the intermediaries as by a divine winged power, and getting at the exact point we require without entanglement with any context.*

William James, *A Pluralistic Universe*[188]

*Time needs to be explicated primordially as the horizon for the understanding of Being, and in terms of temporality as the Being of Dasein, which understands Being. This task as a whole requires that the conception of time thus obtained shall be distinguished from the way in which it is ordinarily understood. This ordinary way of understanding has become explicit in an interpretation precipitated in the traditional concept of time. . . . The central problematic of all ontology is rooted in the phenomenon of time. . . . Though one allows 'non-reversibility' as a distinct predicate of time, one does so on the understanding that one would much rather reverse time's direction, that is, that one would very much like to repeat and retrieve time and have it completely available in the present moment as something present-at-hand.*

Martin Heidegger, *Being and Time* and *The Concept of Time*[189]

*It is difficult to draw the line distinguishing characteristics so general that we cannot conceive any alternatives, from characteristics so special that we imagine them to belong merely to our cosmic epoch. Such an epoch may be, relatively to our powers, of immeasurable extent, temporally and spatially. But in reference to the ultimate nature of things, it is a limited nexus. Beyond that nexus, entities with new relationships, unrealized in our experiences and unforeseen by our imaginations, will make their appearance, introducing into the universe new types of order. . . . Space might as well have three hundred and thirty-three dimensions, instead of the modest three dimensions of our present epoch. . . . Nature is never complete. It is always passing beyond itself. This is the creative advance of nature. Here we come to the problem of time. . . . In the temporal world, it is the empirical fact that process entails loss: the past is present under an abstraction. But there is no reason, of any ultimate metaphysical generality, why this should be the whole story.*

Alfred North Whitehead, *Process and Reality*[190]

*Every world line of matter occurring in the solution is an open line of infinite length, which never approaches any of its preceding points again; but there also exist closed time-like lines. . . . It is theoretically possible in these worlds to travel into the past, or otherwise influence the past.*

Kurt Gödel, *Collected Works: Volume II*[191]

*Perhaps it is something more than an accident that in this period,
which, with its revolutionary discoveries in the natural sciences and
above all physics, is in process of transition from three-dimensional to
four-dimensional thinking, the most modern trend in depth psychology,
that of Jung, should have selected the archetype of the four as its central
structural concept. Just as it became necessary for modern physics to
introduce time, a fourth dimension, which strikes us as fundamentally
different from the three familiar spatial dimensions, if it was to gain a
comprehensive view of the physical world, so a comprehensive view of
the psyche called for consideration of the fourth.*

Jolande Jacobi, *The Psychology of C.G. Jung*[192]

*This final vision, which is generally interpreted as referring to the
relationship of Christ to his Church, has the meaning of a "uniting
symbol" and is therefore a representation of perfection and wholeness:
hence the quaternity. . . . Empirically it can be established, with a
sufficient degree of probability, that there is in the unconscious an
archetype of wholeness which manifests itself spontaneously in dreams,
etc., and a tendency, independent of the conscious will, to relate other
archetypes to this centre. Consequently, it does not seem improbable that
the archetype of wholeness occupies as such a central position which
approximates it to the God-image.*

C.G. Jung, *Answer to Job*[193]

*People like us, who believe in physics, know that the distinction
between past, present and future is only a stubbornly persistent illusion. .
. . Time and space are modes by which we think, and not conditions in
which we live.*

Albert Einstein, personal letter[194] and *Albert Einstein*[195]

*We shall have to describe and interpret the vital revolution in
human consciousness brought about by the quite modern discovery of
duration. Here we need only ask ourselves how our views about matter
are enlarged by the introduction of this new dimension. . . .
Consciousness, in order to be integrated into a world-system,
necessitates consideration of the existence of a new aspect or dimension
in the stuff of the universe.*

Pierre Teilhard de Chardin, *The Phenomenon of Man*[196]

*The intellectual life of man, his culture and history and religion and science, is different from anything else we know of in the universe. That is fact. It is as if all life evolved to a certain point, and then in ourselves turned at a right angle and simply exploded in a different direction.*

Julian Jaynes, *The Origin of Consciousness in the Breakdown of the Bicameral Mind*[197]

*A classical observer using a classical clock tends to measure time intervals with his own definition of time, which is a physical quantity of topological dimension 1. . . . A fractal dust is characterized by an infinite number of points, and also by an infinitesimal "length." Then it is suggested that the hereabove equation should be interpreted as demonstrating that time in nonrelativistic quantum mechanics may behave in some situations as a fractal dust of fractal dimension ½.*

Laurent Nottale, *Fractal Space-Time and Microphysics*[198]

*One of the very large creodes that we can see at work in nature and society is what I call the conquest of dimensionality. Biology is a strategy for moving into and occupying ever more dimensions. . . . Biology begins as a point-like chemical replicating system attached to a primordial clay in the proverbial warm pond somewhere at the dawn of time. And as life develops it folds itself, it becomes a three-dimensional object. It replicates itself in time, and that means it claims the temporal dimension. After two or three billion years of that it has evolved itself to the point where with strong muscles it can move through space, with superb visual organs, it can coordinate its exterior environment. And finally, through the advent of language it can tell its story, it can move information around not present, and as soon as you begin to code that information into stone, or magnetic medium . . . in a sense time has stopped, you are moving outward now. And this very large creode seems to inform not only biology but the human enterprise as well.*

Terence McKenna, *Appreciating Imagination*[199]

*Human time changes from one era to the next, and there is nothing
God-given or physics-given about the form of time each person is born
into. When we teach our children how to read a clock, we are setting
them into a specific framework of imagined time. . . . We are so deep in
this cultural time, we can barely see it for what it is: an invention. . . . By
recognizing that we have invented, and are reinventing, time, we give
ourselves the opportunity to change it yet again.*

Adam Frank, *About Time*[200]

*My own personal opinion is that time is a human construct.*

Tom O'Brian, Chief of the National Institute of Standards and
Technology's Quantum Physics and Time and Frequency Divisions[201]

*If Einstein's theory of Relativity and Brownian motion were both
right, there would be no essential distinction between the past and the
future in the same way that none was then known to exist between left
and right. Einstein's theory of relativity did not account for time flowing
in one direction, while his theory of Brownian motion was eventually
used to prove that reversibility was a fundamental property of atoms.*

Jimena Canales, *The Physicist and the Philosopher*[202]

*Scholars can hardly broach the metaphysics of change and
causality without discussing time travel and its paradoxes. Time travel
forces its way into philosophy and infects modern physics. . . . Have we
spent the last century developing a lurid pipe dream? Have we lost touch
with the simple truth about time? Or is it the other way around: perhaps
the blinders have come off and we are finally evolving, as a species, an
ability to understand the past and the future for what they are. . . . How
strange, then, to realize that time travel, the concept, is barely a century
old. . . . We have achieved a temporal sentience that our ancestors
lacked.*

James Gleick, *Time Travel: A History*[203]

*Like the movement of time outside of a black hole, space inside a black hole becomes a linear dimension inexorably flowing forward toward the central Singularity. Similarly, like movement through space outside of a black hole, movement through time inside a black hole is both forward and backward, so that the past and future can be seen simultaneously*

Timothy Desmond, *Psyche and Singularity*[204]

## Epilogue: "A Third Copernican Revolution": Archetypal Cosmology

*God invented and gave us sight to the end that we might behold the courses of intelligence in the heaven, and apply them to the courses of our own intelligence.*

Plato, *Timaeus*[205]

*Everything breathes together.*

Plotinus, *Enneads*[206]

*In order to advance with the moving reality, you must place yourself within it. Install yourself within change, and you will grasp at once both change itself and the successive states in which* it might *at any instant be mobilized. . . . By following the new conception to the end, we should come to see in time a progressive growth of the absolute, and in the evolution of things a continual invention of forms ever new.*

Henri Bergson, *Creative Evolution*[207]

*Each age has its dominant preoccupation; and, during the three centuries in question, the cosmology derived from science has been asserting itself at the expense of older points of view with their origins elsewhere. Men can be provincial in time, as well as in place. We may ask ourselves whether the scientific mentality of the modern world in the immediate past is not a successful example of such provincial limitation. . . . Thoughts lie dormant for ages; and then, almost suddenly as it were, mankind finds that they have embodied themselves in institutions.*

Alfred North Whitehead, *Science and the Modern World*[208]

*The conflict between the opposites can strain our psyche to the breaking point, if we take them seriously, or if they take us seriously. . . . If all goes well, the solution, seemingly of its own accord, appears out of nature. Then and only then is it convincing. . . . Our psyche is set up in accord with the structure of the universe, and what happens in the macrocosm likewise happens in the infinitesimal and most subjective reaches of the psyche. . . . In this way the imagination liberates itself from the concretism of the object and attempts to sketch the image of the invisible as something which stands behind the phenomenon.*

C.G. Jung, *Memories, Dreams, Reflections*[209]

*The time has come to realise that an interpretation of the universe— even a positivist one—remains unsatisfying unless it covers the interior as well as the exterior of things; a mind as well as matter. The true physics is that which will, one day, achieve the inclusion of man in his wholeness in a coherent picture of the world.*

Pierre Teilhard de Chardin, *The Phenomenon of Man*[210]

*Each moment of consciousness has a certain* explicit *content, which is a foreground, and an* implicit *content, which is a corresponding background. We now propose that not only is immediate experience best understood in terms of the implicate order, but that thought also is basically to be comprehended in this order. . . . It follows, then, that the explicate and manifest order of consciousness is not ultimately distinct from that of matter in general. Fundamentally these are essentially different aspects of the one overall order.*

David Bohm, *Wholeness and the Implicate Order*[211]

*Human knowledge constantly evolves and changes, sometimes in quite unexpected ways. What is unequivocally rejected in one age may be dramatically reclaimed in another, as happened when the ancient heliocentric hypothesis of Aristarchus, long ignored by scientific authorities as valueless and absurd, was resurrected and vindicated by Copernicus, Kepler, and Galileo. Widespread or even universal conviction at any given moment has never been a reliable indication of the truth or falsity of an idea.*

Richard Tarnas, *Cosmos and Psyche*[212]

*Challenging the most fundamental assumptions of materialistic science, transpersonal experiences suggest that human consciousness is continuous with the inner nature of the universe, which from this perspective appears to be a unified web of events in consciousness permeated by interiority.*

Stanislav Grof, *Archai: the Journal of Archetypal Cosmology*[213]

# NOTES

[1] Richard Tarnas, *Cosmos and Psyche: Intimations of a New World View* (New York: Plume, 2006) 15.

[2] Alfred North Whitehead, *Science and the Modern World* (New York: The Free Press, 1967) 2. Because the concepts synthesized in these pages more often than not distill the arguments of entire books, I will generally refer the reader to specific page numbers in these texts only when a quote is marshaled or a specific fact is cited. The epigraphs at the beginning of each chapter and in the Appendix suggest the provenance of the ideas synthesized in their respective chapters.

[3] William James, *Pragmatism* (New York: Dover Publications, 1995) 1.

[4] Although this text touches on most of these areas as examples of the more general concepts, my first book, *How Does It Feel?: Elvis Presley, The Beatles, Bob Dylan, and the Philosophy of Rock and Roll*, explores in depth how some of these ideas can illuminate popular music.

[5] For thinkers prior to Bergson (and some after), duration often means simply the passage of time. I will be using the term in Bergson's sense.

[6] There are other trajectories of novelty that have evolved independently of humanity, which may or may not trace exponential curves, but these developmental lines are beyond the scope of this study.

[7] *Pragmatism* 20.

[8] Although it seems clear that the pervasive fractal correspondence of developmental processes across scale obtains, there is still much work that needs to be done in delineating precisely where the lines between the individual stages should be drawn. The three- and five-stage schemas are only two ways of dividing these developmental processes, and there are other, finer-grained schemas that are useful for illuminating certain features of reality. Furthermore, one issue that should be addressed in future research is whether the division of species in the five-stage schema should be parsed in correspondence with the exponential temporal progression from nonlife (more than ten billion years ago) through the emergence of prokaryotic organisms (billions of years ago), animals (hundreds of millions of years ago), hominids (millions of years ago), and anatomically modern humans (hundreds of thousands of years ago) or, alternatively, whether biology divided into five distinct stages should be correlated with the dimensional perception and freedom of movement of the organisms, from nonlife (zero dimensions), perhaps through prokaryotes (one dimension), lichen or mold (two dimensions), animals (three dimensions), and humans (four dimensions). In fact, this latter progression requires a great deal more research to determine precisely where the lines should be drawn in determining the perceptual capacities of these organisms in relation to dimensionality. Similarly, there is some controversy concerning the issue of whether the development of the individual organism from conception to birth

should be considered a different order of magnitude than the development of the individual from infancy to adulthood, or whether these two developmental phases should be taken together, as I have tended to do here. It might be suggested that both approaches are valid ways of understanding these developmental processes. It might even be suggested that the perinatal process as elucidated by Stanislav Grof could be fractally correlated with these other magnitudes of development. Nevertheless, it should be reiterated that the theoretical intuitions of many of the theorists referred to in these pages, as well as a great deal of the scientific and phenomenological data that they examine, support the fractal self-similarity of developmental processes in resonance with exponentiality and dimensional ingression.

[9] Mircea Eliade, *Shamanism: Archaic Techniques of Ecstasy* (Princeton, NJ: Princeton University Press, 2004).

[10] Cf. Owen Barfield, *Saving the Appearances A Study in Idolatry* (Middletown, CT: Wesleyan University Press, 1988).

[11] Charles Taylor, *A Secular Age* (Cambridge, MA: Harvard University Press, 2009) 508, 732.

[12] *Science and the Modern World* 47.

[13] Benoit Mandelbrot, "How Fractals Can Explain What's Wrong With Wall Street," *Scientific American*, February 1999.

[14] The preceding two paragraphs are adapted from my essay, "Archetype and Eternal Object: Jung, Whitehead, and the Return of Formal Causation," published in *Archai: The Journal of Archetypal Cosmology*, Issue 3, *Beyond a Disenchanted Cosmology*, edited by Keiron Le Grice, Bill Streett, and myself for Archai Press, 2011, 51-71.

[15] C.G. Jung, *Synchronicity: An Acausal Connecting Principle* (Princeton, NJ: Princeton University Press, 1973) 22-23.

[16] Whitehead writes in *Process and Reality*: "Modern physical science, with its dependence on the exact notions of mathematics, began with the foundation of Greek Geometry" (302).

[17] Most ancient mythical and religious traditions exhibit an early form of compatibilism in which individuals have free will, but the gods also have foreknowledge of fate, or they control the events on Earth as they unfold, so while the idea of free will seems to have existed in germ, it was almost always superseded by divinely ordained fate until the nascent emergence of mentality in the Axial Age.

[18] Although Immanuel Kant recognizes the efficacy of teleology in his *Critique of Judgment* (1790), he explicitly favors efficient causation over final causation.

[19] Although some of the other terms are more conventional, I prefer the term "syntropy," introduced by Nobel Prize-winning physiologist Albert Szent-Gyorgyi and mathematician Luigi Fantappie, as "negative entropy," shortened to "negentropy," is essentially a double negative naming a positive phenomenon, which Schrödinger aptly describes as an "awkward expression." Entropy is a

quantitative measure of lack of order, so syntropy seems the best term for a quantitative increase in order, definable as the conservation of information.
[20] This figure will almost certainly be outdated by the time the present book is published.
[21] The majority of arguments leveled against Kurzweil generally seem to take two forms. First, his critics often mention Kurzweil's intention to resurrect his deceased father once technology becomes sufficiently advanced. While certainly a quirky ambition, this critique is the clearest kind of *argumentum ad hominem*, and thus fallacious. Just because Kurzweil holds some unconventional ambitions does not invalidate his discoveries. If we judged new theories based on the theorist's personal eccentricities, many transformative revolutions would not have occurred, including Newtonian physics, as Isaac Newton was a truly bizarre and pugnacious individual. Second, and perhaps more plausibly, some critics have claimed that Kurzweil's predictions are overly optimistic, that such an exponential trajectory cannot possibly continue. And it is definitely possible that some unknown factor, whether ecological catastrophe or collective human choice, will inhibit the current trajectory. However, it seems to me that such critics must bear the burden of proof, as it appears more likely that processing power will continue to follow the smooth exponential curve that it has traced for billions of years than that it will deviate from this trend, if such an exceptionally consistent movement on such a vast scale can be described as such.
[22] Born and Einstein xxii.
[23] Cf. Niels Bohr, *Albert Einstein: Philosopher-Scientist* (Cambridge University Press, 1949).
[24] Laurent Nottale, *Fractal Space-Time and Microphysics: Towards a Theory of Scale Relativity* (River Edge, NJ: World Scientific Publishing, 1993) 104 and Kerri Welch *A Fractal Topology of Time* (San Francisco, CA: Doctoral Dissertation for California Institute of Integral Studies, 2010) 122-23. It should be noted that Nottale himself, as a physicist, does not speculate about whether or not this fractal dimensionality of time at the quantum scale holds significance for the experience of temporality in human consciousness, though scale relativity's emphasis of the fractal self-similarity of structures and processes across scale seems to suggest this correspondence of microcosm and macrocosm.
[25] *Pragmatism* 1.
[26] *Cosmos and Psyche* 16.
[27] As Terence McKenna noted, the city is an early, but incredibly durable form of "virtual reality," as here the natural world is almost completely covered by concrete and steel.
[28] Max Weber, *The Protestant Ethic and the 'Spirit' of Capitalism and Other Writings* (New York: Penguin Books, 2002) 104.
[29] G.W.F. Hegel, *Hegel's Phenomenology of Spirit*, Ed. J.N. Findlay (New York: Oxford University Press, 1977) 18-19.

30 William Shakespeare, *Hamlet* (New York: Signet Classics, 1998) 50.
31 Cf. Adrian Bardon, *A Brief History of the Philosophy of Time* (New York: Oxford University Press, 2013) and J. M. E. McTaggart, "The Unreality of Time," *Mind* 17: 457-73, 1908.
32 Ingram Bywater Heraclitus Patrick, *The Fragments of the Work of Heraclitus of Ephesus on Nature* (New York: Forgotten Books, 2012) fragment 116.
33 Henri Bergson, *Creative Evolution* (New York: Barnes & Noble Books, 2005) 158-9.
34 This is a phrase employed by Terence McKenna on numerous occasions in various lectures.
35 The irony of Bruno's martyrdom for science at the hands of the Church, of course, is that early Christians similarly suffered at the hands of the previous world view, exemplified by the Romans, for their radically novel ethical and spiritual innovation. However, this similarity demonstrates that the revolution inevitably becomes the new orthodoxy.
36 Not only are institutions like the California Institute of Integral Studies, Pacifica Graduate Institute, and Naropa University, all founded in the wake of the massive revolutionary upheavals of the nineteen-sixties and -seventies, leading the way in this fundamental transformation of our cultural premises, but many in the main streams of academia are beginning to bring the emerging modes of thought generally privileged at these forward-thinking schools increasingly into the central nodes of the networks of discursive power, particularly in relation to earlier thinkers like Hegel, James, Jung, Bergson, and Whitehead. Indeed, the present book would not have been possible without having earned my doctorate at the City University of New York's Graduate Center, a public institution located at the heart of New York City (cattycorner to the Empire State Building), while simultaneously giving a great deal of attention to the activities of the institutions mentioned above, which are clustered in the western United States, and which still carry some of the pioneering spirit of their inception.
37 As is so often the case with those who make transformative discoveries, Mandelbrot was initially an outsider in the academic community, a "maverick" as he calls himself in the subtitle of his autobiography, *The Fractalist: Memoir of a Scientific Maverick.*
38 Sigmund Freud and C.G. Jung, *The Freud/Jung Letters* (Princeton, NJ: Princeton University Press, 1994) 155.
39 John Stuart Mill, *Essays on Ethics, Religion and Society* (Toronto: University of Toronto Press, 1985) 120.
40 *Cosmos and Psyche* 266.
41 This quotation is an ancient paraphrase of several passages in Plato's *Apology.*
42 UNESCO Institute for Statistics.
43 Erich Auerbach, *Mimesis: The Representation of Reality in Western Literature* (Princeton, NJ: Princeton University Press, 2003) 3-23.

[44] Cf. Terence McKenna, *The Archaic Revival* (New York: HarperCollins, 1992).

[45] Pierre Teilhard de Chardin, *The Phenomenon of Man* (New York: Harper Perennial Modern Thought, 2008) 78.

[46] Erwin, Schrödinger, *What Is Life? with Mind and Matter and Autobiographical Sketches* (Cambridge, UK: Cambridge University Press, 1967) 48-50.

[47] Nottale 104.

[48] *Pragmatism* 72.

[49] Robert N. Bellah, *Beyond Belief: Essays on Religion in a Post-Traditionalist World* (Berkley, CA: University of California Press, 1970) 24.

[50] Jean Gebser, *The Ever-Present Origin* (Athens, OH: Ohio University Press, 1985) 197.

[51] Alfred North Whitehead, *Process and Reality: Corrected Edition*, Ed. David Ray Griffin and Donald W. Sherburne (New York: The Free Press, 1985) 5.

[52] Taylor 3.

[53] Cf. Chip Walter, *Last Ape Standing: The Seven-Million-Year Story of How and Why We Survived* (London: Walker Books, 2013).

[54] Cf. Arthur O. Lovejoy, *The Great Chain of Being: A Study of the History of an Idea* (Cambridge, MA: Harvard University Press, 1936).

[55] "You may feel, as so many do, that your life could be plotted on a scale where the years from age 10 to age 20 seem as long (as event-full) as the years from age 20 to age 40 or from 40 to 80. Exponential growth at its most damning." James Gleick, *Faster: The Acceleration of Just About Everything* (New York: Vintage, 2000) 340.

[56] Cf. William James, *A Pluralistic Universe* (Lincoln, NE: University of Nebraska Press, 1996).

[57] Hegel 6-7.

[58] *Cosmos and Psyche* xiii.

[59] Paul Ricoeur, *Freud and Philosophy: An Essay on Interpretation* (New Haven, CT: Yale University Press, 1977).

[60] *Ayurveda*, http://www.hindupedia.com/en/Sthapatyaveda.

[61] James Gleick, *Chaos: Making a New Science* (New York: Penguin Books, 2008) 103, 299, 311.

[62] "How Fractals Can Explain What's Wrong with Wall Street."

[63] Edward N. Lorenz, "Noisy Periodicity and Reverse Bifurcation," *Annals of the New York Academy of Sciences*, Volume 357, December 26, 1980, 282-91.

[64] *Process and Reality*, 44.

[65] James Hillman, *Re-Visioning Psychology* (New York: William Morrow Paperbacks, 1997) xix.

[66] *Synchronicity*, 8, 19, 25.

[67] Taylor 55, 714.

[68] Alfred North Whitehead, *Adventures of Ideas* (New York: The Free Press, 1967) 207.

[69] Thomas Nagel, *Mind and Cosmos: Why the Materialist Neo-Darwinian Conception of Nature Is Almost Certainly False* (New York: Oxford University Press, 2012) 7.

[70] James Gleick, *Time Travel: A History* (New York: Pantheon, 2016) 211.

[71] Terence McKenna, Interview on *Coast to Coast AM*, May 22, 1997, http://miqel.com/entheogens/terrence_mckenna_interview_1.html.

[72] Ray Kurzweil, *The Singularity is Near: When Humans Transcend Biology* (New York: Penguin Books, 2006) 42-43, 47.

[73] Cf. Ramez Naam, *The Infinite Resource: The Power of Ideas on a Finite Planet* (Lebanon, NH: University Press of New England, 2013).

[74] Gebser 16, 22.

[75] David Bohm, *Wholeness and the Implicate Order* (New York: Routledge Classics, 2002) 268.

[76] Friedrich Nietzsche, *Thus Spoke Zarathustra: A Book for All and None.* Cambridge (UK: Cambridge University Press, 2006) 3, 5.

[77] C.G. Jung and Joseph Campbell, ed., *The Portable Jung* (New York: Penguin Books, 1973) 648.

[78] Kurzweil 11.

[79] Sean Kelly, *Coming Home: The Birth and Transformation of the Planetary Era* (Aurora, CO: Lindisfarne Books, 2010) 166-7.

[80] Keiron Le Grice, *The Archetypal Cosmos* (Edinburgh, UK: Floris Books, 2011) 21.

[81] Richard Tarnas, "World Transits: 2000-2020," *Archai: The Journal of Archetypal Cosmology*, Issue 2, 2010.

[82] *Cosmos and Psyche* 407.

[83] The discovery of Eris prompted the demotion of Pluto to the status of "dwarf planet," though this reclassification does not seem to affect or reflect Pluto's archetypal potency. Ceres, discovered in 1801, Haumea, discovered in 2004, and Makemake, discovered in 2005, are also designated as dwarf planets, though they are all significantly smaller than Pluto, while Eris is approximately 27% more massive. The relative lack of attention paid to Ceres, the first planet named after a female goddess besides Venus, is perhaps concomitant with that era's repression of the feminine when not serving as the object of masculine desire (one inflection of the Venus archetype). The discovery of Haumea, named after the Hawaiian goddess of childbirth, and the discovery of Makemake, named after the Rapa Nui creator god associated with fertility, within a year of Eris' discovery, seem to suggest the emergence of a generative archetypal multiplicity perhaps characteristic of the emerging mode. See Keiron Le Grice, *Discovering Eris* for more on the Eris archetype.

[84] Daniel Levinson, *The Seasons of a Man's Life* (New York: Ballantine Books, 1979) 58.

[85] Philosopher of science Paul Feyerabend has written an excellent critique of "Objections to Astrology," the letter published in *The Humanist*, called "The Strange Case of Astrology." Patrick Grim, ed., *Philosophy of Science and the Occult* (Albany, NY: State University of New York Press, 1982) 14-23.

[86] Richard Tarnas, "The Ideal and the Real," *Archai: The Journal of Archetypal Cosmology*, Issue 1, 2009 and "The Ideal and the Real (Part Two)," *Archai: The Journal of Archetypal Cosmology*, Issue 2, 2010.

[87] Einstein also had transiting Uranus in a 120° trine aspect to his natal Uranus during this year. A "soft" or "confluent" aspect, trines seem to be the most significant form of correlation besides the three primary hard aspects, which I have emphasized for the sake of simplicity. Similar to Saturn-Saturn transits during which senex themes are emphasized, Uranus-Uranus transits seem to correlate with the emphasis of Promethean themes in the experience of the person undergoing the transit.

[88] Masson 202.

[89] *Science and the Modern World* viii.

[90] *Science and the Modern World* vii.

[91] Gebser 205.

[92] C.G. Jung, *Mysterium Coniunctionis* (Princeton, NJ: Princeton University Press, 1977) 110.

[93] Erwin Schrödinger, *What Is Life? with Mind and Matter and Autobiographical Sketches* (Cambridge, UK: Cambridge University Press, 1967) 128.

[94] Anais Nin, *Seduction of the Minotaur* (Chicago, IL: The Swallow Press, 1972) 124.

[95] Thomas S. Kuhn, *The Structure of Scientific Revolutions* (Chicago, IL: The University of Chicago Press, 1996) 94.

[96] Amiri Baraka, *Blues People: Negro Music in White America* (New York: Harper Perennial, 1999) 3.

[97] Bohm 6-7, 10.

[98] Jorge N. Ferrer, *Revisioning Transpersonal Theory: A Participatory Vision of Human Spirituality* (Albany, NY: State University of New York Press, 2001) 98, 118, 130.

[99] Taylor 30.

[100] Adam Frank, *About Time: Cosmology and Culture at the Twilight of the Big Bang* (New York: The Free Press, 2012) 333.

[101] William James, *The Will To Believe and Other Essays in Popular Philosophy, and Human Immortality* (Lawrence, KS: Digireads.com, 2010) 52.

[102] *Science and the Modern World* 47.

[103] *Synchronicity* 97.

[104] Gebser 36.

[105] Rupert Sheldrake, *The Presence of the Past: Morphic Resonance and the Habits of Nature* (Rochester, VT: Park Street Press, 1988) xx.

[106] *Cosmos and Psyche* xiii.

[107] Taylor 730-31.

[108] Harari, Yuval Noah, *Sapiens: A Brief History of Humankind* (New York: Harper, 2015) 114.

[109] *Heraclitus*, fragment 46.

[110] Plato, *The Republic* (New York: Dover Publications, 2000) 120.

[111] Aristotle, *The Metaphysics* (New York: Penguin Classics, 1999) 298.

[112] Hegel 22.

[113] Charles Darwin, *On the Origin of Species* (Cambridge, MA: Harvard University Press, 1964) 2.

[114] William James, *The Varieties of Religious Experience: A Study in Human Nature* (New York: Vintage Books, 1990) 117.

[115] Henri Bergson, *The Creative Mind: An Introduction to Metaphysics* (New York: Dover Publications, 2007) 111.

[116] Sri Aurobindo, *The Future Evolution of Man: The Divine Life Upon Earth* (Detroit, MI: Lotus Press, 1971) 2.

[117] *Process and Reality* 7.

[118] Gebser 4.

[119] Werner Heisenberg, *Physics and Philosophy: The Revolution in Modern Science* (New York: Harper Perennial Modern Classics, 2007) 187.

[120] Bellah 244.

[121] *Cosmos and Psyche* 13-14.

[122] Taylor 706, 710.

[123] Hegel 6-7.

[124] *The Will to Believe* 119.

[125] *Creative Evolution* 52.

[126] Gebser 37.

[127] *Synchronicity* 101.

[128] *Chaos* 160.

[129] Hegel 16-17.

[130] *Creative Evolution* 13

[131] *Process and Reality* 16, 229.

[132] Gebser 42.

[133] Barfield 92.

[134] Rupert Sheldrake, *A New Science of Life: The Hypothesis of Morphic Resonance* (Rochester, VT: Park Street Press, 1981) 12.

[135] Allan Combs, "Open Reply to Ken Wilber: A response to his commentary on *The Radiance of Being*" (www.integralworld.net/combs2.html, 1999).

[136] Taylor 30.

[137] Frank 317

[138] *Creative Evolution* xxii, 27.

[139] *Science and the Modern World* 1.

[140] Gebser 1.

[141] Bellah 246.
[142] Christopher M. Bache, *Dark Night, Early Dawn: Steps to a Deep Ecology of Mind* (Albany, NY: State University of New York Press, 2000) 278.
[143] Taylor 473.
[144] *The Republic 270.*
[145] *The Will to Believe* 97.
[146] *Creative Evolution* 23.
[147] *Science and the Modern World* 91 and *Process and Reality* 216.
[148] Gebser 58.
[149] Benoit B. Mandelbrot, *The Fractal Geometry of Nature* (London: W.H. Freeman and Company, 1982) 1.
[150] Kurzweil 46.
[151] Rupert Sheldrake, *Science Set Free: 10 Paths to New Discovery* (New York: Crown Publishing Group, 2013) 99-100.
[152] *The Republic* 421.
[153] Aristotle 278.
[154] *Synchronicity* 100.
[155] Gebser 401-2.
[156] David Ray Griffin, ed., *The Archetypal Process: Self and Divine in Whitehead, Jung, and Hillman* (Evanston, IL: Northwestern University Press, 1990) 11.
[157] *Cosmos and Psyche* 84.
[158] Taylor 36.
[159] The Holy Bible, King James Version (New York: American Bible Society, 1999) Ecclesiastes 3:1.
[160] Plato, *Timaeus* (London, UK: Pearson, 1959) 114.
[161] Augustine, *The Confessions of St. Augustine.* Trans. E. B. Pusey (New York: P. F. Collier and Son, 1909) Book XI.
[162] Hegel 17.
[163] *Creative Evolution* 37-38.
[164] *Process and Reality* 283.
[165] Gebser 39.
[166] Dick Russell, *The Life and Ideas of James Hillman: Volume 1: The Making of a Psychologist* (New York: Helios Press, 2013) 462.
[167] *A New Science of Life* 71-72.
[168] Allan Combs and Mark Holland, *Synchronicity: Through the Eyes of Science, Myth and the Trickster* (Cambridge, MA: Da Capo Press, 2000) xii.
[169] *Cosmos and Psyche* 50.
[170] Aristotle, Book 5, 1013b.
[171] Hegel 7.
[172] *Pragmatism* 54.
[173] *Creative Evolution* 33.
[174] Schrödinger 73, 79-81.

[175] Teilhard 49.

[176] *Chaos* 138.

[177] *Cosmos and Psyche* 499n5.

[178] *Science Set Free* 130-31.

[179] *Pragmatism* 72.

[180] Barfield 146.

[181] Hans Moravec, *Robot: Mere Machine to Transcendent Mind* (New York: Oxford University Press, 2000) 61, 53.

[182] *Faster* 5.

[183] Erik Brynjolfsson and Andrew McAfee, *The Second Machine Age: Work, Progress, and Prosperity in a Time of Brilliant Technologies* (New York: W. W. Norton & Company, 2014) 44, 54.

[184] *Timaeus* 107.

[185] Augustine, Book XI.

[186] Nietzsche 3-5.

[187] *Creative Evolution* 42-43 and *The Creative Mind* 131, 158.

[188] *A Pluralistic Universe* 82.

[189] Martin Heidegger, *Being and Time* (New York: Harper and Row Publishers, 1962) H. 18 and Martin Heidegger, *The Concept of Time* (New York: Bloomsbury Academic, 2011) 68.

[190] *Process and Reality* 288-289, 340.

[191] Kurt Gödel, *Kurt Gödel: Collected Works: Volume II: Publications 1938-1974* (New York: Oxford University Press, 1990) 191.

[192] Jolande Jacobi, *The Psychology of C.G. Jung* (New Haven, CT: Yale University Press, 1973) 48.

[193] *The Portable Jung* 623, 648.

[194] *Time Travel: A History* 84.

[195] Aylesa Forsee, *Albert Einstein: Theoretical Physicist* (New York: MacMillan, 1963) 81.

[196] Teilhard 47, 55.

[197] Julian Jaynes, *The Origin of Consciousness in the Breakdown of the Bicameral Mind* (Boston, MA: Mariner Books, 2000) 9.

[198] Nottale 104.

[199] Terence McKenna, "Appreciating Imagination," Transcription of lecture given at Esalen Institute, 1997. http://www.scribd.com/doc/76264877/Appreciating-Imagination---Esalen---T-McKenna---1997 17.

[200] Frank 319.

[201] npr.org, Tom O'Brian quoted in "New Clock May End Time As We Know It," November 3, 2014, http://www.npr.org/2014/11/03/361069820/new-clock-may-end-time-as-we-know-it

[202] Jimena Canales, *The Physicist and the Philosopher* (Princeton, NJ: Princeton University Press, 2015) 280-81.

[203] *Time Travel: A History* 23, 36.

[204] Timothy Desmond, *Psyche and Singularity: Jungian Psychology and Holographic String Theory* (Nashville, TN: Persistent Press, 2017).

[205] *Timaeus* 114.

[206] Plotinus, *The Enneads* (New York: Neeland Media, 2009) II, 3, 7.

[207] *Creative Evolution* 253-4, 284.

[208] *Science and the Modern World* vii-viii.

[209] C.G. Jung, *Memories, Dreams, Reflections* (New York: Vintage, 2011) 335.

[210] Teilhard 35-6.

[211] Bohm 259, 264.

[212] *Cosmos and Psyche* 64.

[213] Stanislav Grof, "The Birth of a New Discipline," *Archai: The Journal of Archetypal Cosmology*, Summer 2009 53.

# BIBLIOGRAPHY

Aristotle. *The Metaphysics*. New York: Penguin Classics, 1999.

Auerbach, Erich. *Mimesis: The Representation of Reality in Western Literature*. Princeton, NJ: Princeton University Press, 2003.

Augustine. *The Confessions of St. Augustine*. Trans. E. B. Pusey. New York: P. F. Collier and Son, 1909.

Aurobindo, Sri. *The Future Evolution of Man: The Divine Life Upon Earth*. Detroit, MI: Lotus Press, 1971.

*Ayurveda*, http://www.hindupedia.com/en/Sthapatyaveda.

Bache, Christopher M. *Dark Night, Early Dawn: Steps to a Deep Ecology of Mind*. Albany, NY: State University of New York Press, 2000.

Baraka, Amiri. *Blues People: Negro Music in White America*. New York: Harper Perennial, 1999.

Bardon, Adrian. *A Brief History of the Philosophy of Time*. New York: Oxford University Press, 2013.

Barfield, Owen. *Saving the Appearances: A Study in Idolatry*. Middletown, CT: Wesleyan University Press, 1988.

Bellah, Robert N. *Beyond Belief: Essays on Religion in a Post-Traditionalist World*. Berkley, CA: University of California Press, 1970.

Bergson, Henri. *Creative Evolution*. New York: Barnes & Noble Books, 2005.

Bergson, Henri. *The Creative Mind: An Introduction to Metaphysics*. New York: Dover Publications, 2007.

Bohm, David. *Wholeness and the Implicate Order*. New York: Routledge Classics, 2002.

Bohr, Niels. *Albert Einstein: Philosopher-Scientist*, Cambridge University Press, 1949.

Born, Max and Albert Einstein. *The Born–Einstein Letters*. London, UK: Macmillan, 1971.

Brynjolfsson, Erik and Andrew McAfee. *The Second Machine Age: Work, Progress, and Prosperity in a Time of Brilliant Technologies*. New York: W. W. Norton & Company, 2014.

Canales, Jimena. *The Physicist and the Philosopher*. Princeton, NJ: Princeton University Press, 2015.

Combs, Allan and Mark Holland. *Synchronicity: Through the Eyes of Science, Myth and the Trickster*. Cambridge, MA: Da Capo Press, 2000.

Combs, Allan. "Open Reply to Ken Wilber: A response to his commentary on *The Radiance of Being*." www.integralworld.net/combs2.html, 1999.

Darwin, Charles. *On the Origin of Species*. Cambridge, MA: Harvard University Press, 1964.

Desmond, Timothy. *Psyche and Singularity: Jungian Psychology and*

*Holographic String Theory*. Nashville, TN: Persistent Press, 2017.

Eliade, Mircea. *Shamanism: Archaic Techniques of Ecstasy*. Princeton, NJ: Princeton University Press, 1964.

Ferrer, Jorge N. *Revisioning Transpersonal Theory: A Participatory Vision of Human Spirituality*. Albany, NY: State University of New York Press, 2001.

Forsee, Aylesa. *Albert Einstein: Theoretical Physicist*. New York: MacMillan, 1963.

Frank, Adam. *About Time: Cosmology and Culture at the Twilight of the Big Bang*. New York: The Free Press, 2012.

Freud, Sigmund and C.G. Jung. *The Freud/Jung Letters*. Princeton, NJ: Princeton University Press, 1994.

Gebser, Jean. *The Ever-Present Origin*. Athens, OH: Ohio University Press, 1985.

Gleick, James. *Chaos: Making a New Science*. New York: Penguin Books, 2008.

Gleick, James. *Faster: The Acceleration of Just About Everything*. New York: Vintage, 2000.

Gleick, James. *Time Travel: A History*. New York: Pantheon, 2016.

Gödel, Kurt. *Kurt Gödel: Collected Works: Volume II: Publications 1938-1974*. New York: Oxford University Press, 1990.

Gould, Stephen Jay. *The Structure of Evolutionary Theory*. Cambridge, MA: Harvard University Press, 2002.

Griffin, David Ray, ed. *The Archetypal Process: Self and Divine in Whitehead, Jung, and Hillman*. Evanston, IL: Northwestern University Press, 1990.

Grim, Patrick, ed. *Philosophy of Science and the Occult*. Albany, NY: State University of New York Press, 1982.

Grof, Stanislav. "The Birth of a New Discipline." *Archai: The Journal of Archetypal Cosmology*, Summer 2009.

Harari, Yuval Noah. *Sapiens: A Brief History of Humankind*. New York: Harper, 2015.

Hegel, G.W.F. *Hegel's Phenomenology of Spirit*. Ed. J.N. Findlay. New York: Oxford University Press, 1977.

Heidegger, Martin. *Being and Time*. New York: Harper and Row Publishers, 1962.

Heidegger, Martin. *The Concept of Time*. New York: Bloomsbury Academic, 2011.

Heisenberg, Werner. *Physics and Philosophy: The Revolution in Modern Science*. New York: Harper Perennial Modern Classics, 2007.

Hillman, James. *Re-Visioning Psychology*. New York: William Morrow Paperbacks, 1997.

The Holy Bible, King James Version. New York: American Bible Society, 1999.

Jacobi, Jolande. *The Psychology of C.G. Jung*. New Haven, CT: Yale University Press, 1973.

James, William. *A Pluralistic Universe*. Lincoln, NE: University of Nebraska Press, 1996.

James, William. *Pragmatism*. New York: Dover Publications, 1995.

James, William. *The Varieties of Religious Experience: A Study in Human Nature*. New York: Vintage Books, 1990.

James, William. *The Will To Believe and Other Essays in Popular Philosophy, and Human Immortality*. Lawrence, KS: Digireads.com, 2010.

Jaynes, Julian. *The Origin of Consciousness in the Breakdown of the Bicameral Mind*. Boston, MA: Mariner Books, 2000.

Jung, C.G. *Memories, Dreams, Reflections*. New York: Vintage, 2011.

Jung, C.G. *Mysterium Coniunctionis*. Princeton, NJ: Princeton University Press, 1977.

Jung, C.G., and Joseph Campbell, ed. *The Portable Jung*. New York: Penguin Books, 1973.

Jung, C.G. *Synchronicity: An Acausal Connecting Principle*. Princeton, NJ: Princeton University Press, 1973.

Kant, Immanuel. *Critique of Judgment*. Indianapolis, IN: Hackett Publishing Co., 2011.

Kelly, Sean. *Coming Home: The Birth and Transformation of the Planetary Era*. Aurora, CO: Lindisfarne Books, 2010.

Kuhn, Thomas S. *The Structure of Scientific Revolutions*. Chicago, IL: The University of Chicago Press, 1996.

Kurzweil, Ray. *The Singularity is Near: When Humans Transcend Biology*. New York: Penguin Books, 2006.

Le Grice, Keiron. *The Archetypal Cosmos*. Edinburgh, UK: Floris Books, 2011.

Le Grice, Keiron. *Discovering Eris*. Edinburgh, UK: Floris Books, 2012.

Levinson, Daniel. *The Seasons of a Man's Life*. New York: Ballantine Books, 1979.

Lorenz, Edward N. "Noisy Periodicity and Reverse Bifurcation." *Annals of the New York Academy of Sciences*, Volume 357, pages 282-91, December 26, 1980.

Lovejoy, Arthur O. *The Great Chain of Being: A Study of the History of an Idea*. Cambridge, MA: Harvard University Press, 1936.

Mandelbrot, Benoit B. *The Fractal Geometry of Nature*. London: W.H. Freeman and Company, 1982.

Mandelbrot, Benoit B. "How Fractals Can Explain What's Wrong With

Wall Street." *Scientific American*, February 1999.

Masson, J.M., Ed. *The Complete Letters of Sigmund Freud to Wilhelm Fliess, 1887-1904*. Cambridge, MA: Harvard University Press, 1985.

McKenna, Terence. "Appreciating Imagination." Transcription of lecture given at Esalen Institute, 1997. http://www.scribd.com/doc/76264877/Appreciating-Imagination---Esalen---T-McKenna---1997

McKenna, Terence. *The Archaic Revival*. New York: HarperCollins, 1992.

McKenna, Terence. Interview on *Coast to Coast AM*, 1997-05-22, http://miqel.com/entheogens/terrence_mckenna_interview_1.html

McTaggart, J. M. E. "The Unreality of Time." *Mind* 17: 457-73, 1908.

Mill, John Stuart. *Essays on Ethics, Religion and Society*. Toronto: University of Toronto Press, 1985.

Moravec, Hans. *Robot: Mere Machine to Transcendent Mind*. New York: Oxford University Press, 2000.

Naam, Ramez. *The Infinite Resource: The Power of Ideas on a Finite Planet*. Lebanon, NH: University Press of New England, 2013.

Nagel, Thomas. *Mind and Cosmos: Why the Materialist Neo-Darwinian Conception of Nature Is Almost Certainly False*. New York: Oxford University Press, 2012.

Nietzsche, Friedrich. *Thus Spoke Zarathustra: A Book for All and None*. Cambridge, UK: Cambridge University Press, 2006.

Nin, Anais. *Seduction of the Minotaur*. Chicago, IL: The Swallow Press, 1972.

Nottale, Laurent. *Fractal Space-Time and Microphysics: Towards a Theory of Scale Relativity*. River Edge, NJ: World Scientific Publishing, 1993.

*npr.org* . Tom O'Brian quoted in "New Clock May End Time As We Know It." November 3, 2014. http://www.npr.org/2014/11/03/361069820/new-clock-may-end-time-as-we-know-it

Patrick, Ingram Bywater Heraclitus. *The Fragments of the Work of Heraclitus of Ephesus on Nature*. New York: Forgotten Books, 2012.

Plato. *The Republic*. New York: Dover Publications, 2000.

Plato. *Timaeus*. London, UK: Pearson, 1959.

Plotinus. *The Enneads*. New York: Neeland Media, 2009.

Ricoeur, Paul. *Freud and Philosophy: An Essay on Interpretation*. New Haven, CT: Yale University Press, 1977.

Russell, Dick. *The Life and Ideas of James Hillman: Volume 1: The Making of a Psychologist*. New York: Helios Press, 2013.

Schrödinger, Erwin. *What Is Life? with Mind and Matter and Autobiographical Sketches*. Cambridge, UK: Cambridge University Press, 1967.

Shakespeare, William. *Hamlet*. New York: Signet Classics, 1998.

Sheldrake, Rupert. *A New Science of Life: The Hypothesis of Morphic Resonance*. Rochester, VT: Park Street Press, 1981.

Sheldrake, Rupert. *The Presence of the Past: Morphic Resonance and the Habits of Nature*. Rochester, VT: Park Street Press, 1988.

Sheldrake, Rupert. *Science Set Free: 10 Paths to New Discovery*. New York: Crown Publishing Group, 2013.

Tarnas, Richard. *Cosmos and Psyche: Intimations of a New World View*. New York: Plume, 2006.

Tarnas, Richard. "The Ideal and the Real." *Archai: The Journal of Archetypal Cosmology*. Issue 1, 2009.

Tarnas, Richard. "The Ideal and the Real (Part Two)." *Archai: The Journal of Archetypal Cosmology*. Issue 2, 2010.

Tarnas, Richard. *The Passion of the Western Mind: Understanding the Ideas that Have Shaped Our World View*. New York: Ballantine Books, 1991.

Tarnas, Richard. "World Transits: 2000-2020." *Archai: The Journal of Archetypal Cosmology*. Issue 2, 2010.

Taylor, Charles. *A Secular Age*. Cambridge, MA: Harvard University Press, 2009.

Teilhard de Chardin, Pierre. *The Phenomenon of Man*. New York: Harper Perennial Modern Thought, 2008.

UNESCO Institute for Statistics (UIS). *World Illiteracy Rate 1970–2000 (prognosis for 2005–2015), age 15 years and over*.

Chip Walter. *Last Ape Standing: The Seven-Million-Year Story of How and Why We Survived*. London: Walker Books, 2013.

Weber, Max. *The Protestant Ethic and the 'Spirit' of Capitalism and Other Writings*. New York: Penguin Books, 2002.

Welch, Kerri. *A Fractal Topology of Time*. San Francisco, CA: Doctoral Dissertation for California Institute of Integral Studies, 2010.

Whitehead, Alfred North. *Adventures of Ideas*. New York: The Free Press, 1967.

Whitehead, Alfred North. *Modes of Thought*. New York: The Free Press, 1968.

Whitehead, Alfred North. *Process and Reality: Corrected Edition*. Ed. David Ray Griffin and Donald W. Sherburne. New York: The Free Press, 1985.

Whitehead, Alfred North. *Science and the Modern World*. New York: The Free Press, 1967.

# ACKNOWLEDGMENTS

Many thanks to the numerous people who have played a role in the development of this book, and especially to those who read various versions of the manuscript, in part or in whole: Renn Butler, Aaron Cheak, Leslie Allan Combs, Thomas Conner, Tod Desmond, Nancy Ellegate, Sean Kelly, Keiron Le Grice, Kyle Leimetter, Jeremy Liebman, Dick Mann, Ginny Maxwell, James Moran, Carol Orsborn, Daniel Pinchbeck, Tim Read, Joan Richardson, Matt Segall, Rupert Sheldrake, Becca Tarnas, Rick Tarnas, William Irwin Thompson, Stephanie von Behr, and Kerri Welch.

Thanks to Christian Kurt Ebert for permission to use his painting *Untitled Symbiosis* on the cover of the book.

Thanks to *Archai: The Journal of Archetypal Cosmology* (of which I am an editor) for permission to reproduce, in somewhat altered form, part of my essay "Archetype and Eternal Object: Jung, Whitehead, and the Return of Formal Causation."

And thank you to my friends and colleagues, my sister, Jody Orsborn, my sons, Mason and Dylan Maxwell, my in-laws, Don and Susan Edwards, and my wife, Ginny Maxwell, the love of my life, who now knows considerably more about philosophy than she ever thought possible. This book is dedicated to my mother, Carol Orsborn, and my father, Dan Orsborn, who have always enthusiastically encouraged my wild ideas and generously supported me in their realization.

# INDEX